The Human Aspects of Project Management

Human Resource Skills for the Project Manager

Volume Two

The Human Aspects of Project Management

Volume One:
Organizing Projects for Success

Volume Two:
Human Resource Skills for the
Project Manager

Volume Three:
Managing the Project Team

The Human Aspects of Project Management

Human Resource Skills for the Project Manager

Volume Two

Vijay K. Verma, P. Eng., M.B.A.

Project Management Institute
4 Campus Boulevard
Newtown Square, PA 19073
610-356-4600

Library of Congress Cataloging-in-Publication Data

Verma, Vijay K., (1949–   )
   The human aspects of project management / Vijay K. Verma.
      p.   cm.
   Includes bibliographical references and index
   Contents: v. 2. Human Resource Skills for the Project Manager
   ISBN: 1-880410-41-9 (pbk. : alk. paper)
   1. Industrial project management. 2. Matrix organization.
3. Work groups. I. Title.
   HD69.P75V47   1995
   658.4'04--dc20   95-40579
                                                            CIP

ISBN 13: 9781880410417

PMI® books are available at special quantity discounts to use
as premiums and sales promotions, or for use in corporate
training programs as well as other educational programs. For
more information, please write to the Bookstore
Administrator, PMI Publishing Department, Four Campus
Boulevard, Newtown Square, PA 19073-3299 USA. Or
contact your local bookstore.

The paper used in this book complies with the Permanent
Paper Standard issued by the National Information Standards
Organization (Z39.48—1984).

10   9   8   7   6

Table of Contents

Dedication

For my late parents and Taya Ji for their inspiration; for Shiksha, my wife and my best friend; and for our children, Serena, Naveen, and Angelee, who taught me the practical side of dealing with people.

Listen effectively to learn and succeed!

Foreword to *The Human Aspects of Project Management* Series

Today's ever-changing business environment requires new approaches to project management, which has become an important tool for dealing with time-to-market, resource limitations, downsizing, and global competition. As markets and project organizations become more dynamic, administrative and technical skills alone are no longer sufficient to deal with the complexities of modern project undertakings. Project managers who want to compete on a world-class level must understand the human side of their organizations and business processes. They must be social architects who can work across levels and functions of the organization, continuously improving the business process and fostering an ambiance conducive to innovation, risk-taking, self-directed teamwork, commitment, quality and self-improvement.

The Human Aspects of Project Management series offers project managers and their teams the conceptual and practical guidelines for leading people effectively and confidently towards challenging project objectives. The series goes beyond the traditional, linear approach to project management, which assumes that project budgets and schedules can always be clearly defined and can form the cornerstone for tracking and controlling a project. By focusing on the human side, Verma offers a fresh approach to modern project management. He shows how to unleash higher levels of creativity, productivity, quality and commitment from the project team by considering the human aspects.

With these books, the seasoned management practitioner or scholar who understands the conventional tools and techniques of project management but wants to go beyond the basic framework can gain a better understanding of the factors that drive project performance. *The Human Aspects of Project Management* provides a conceptual construct for managing modern projects. It offers concrete suggestions for dealing with diverse project teams, issues of delegation, empowerment, accountability, control, commitment, organizational linkages, alliances, and the intricacies of matrix management. Perhaps most important, the concepts set forth in this series will allow project leaders to build a true project team, which includes alliances with the business organization, support groups, and project sponsors. Such a project team establishes the foundation for an effective and productive project management system that can solve complex problems and produce quality results.

— *Hans J. Thamhain, Ph.D.*
Bentley College

Why This Series of Books?

Managing projects requires unique skills and techniques, different from those needed to manage ongoing operations. As project management moves into the 21st century, project managers face the challenges of operating in a project environment characterized by high levels of uncertainty, cross-cultural teams, and global competition for competent human resources. These challenges can be met by developing a clear understanding of human factors in project management and by effective use of the human resource management skills that are required to inspire project stakeholders to work together in order to meet project objectives.

Extensive literature and many software packages are available for the traditional aspects of project management: planning, scheduling, and reporting; cost control and risk analysis; and management of scope and quality. Yet most project managers agree that the real management challenges lie not in technical problems but in the behavioral and organizational aspects of projects.

We sometimes forget that, despite the recent information and technology revolution in project management, people are at the center of projects. People determine the success or failure of a project. They define project goals. They plan, organize, direct, coordinate, and monitor project activities. They meet project goals and objectives by using interpersonal and organizational skills such as communication, delegation, decision making and negotiation. In project environments, people can be viewed as problems and constraints—or as solutions and opportunities.

Human resource management is therefore a vital component of project management. Many books on general management, personnel management, and organizational behavior contain concepts and techniques that support project management. But understanding the myriad complex human factors that determine project success requires research and experience specific to the project environment. The Project Management Institute has played a leadership role in this area by developing practical and thought-provoking literature and the *Project Management Body of Knowledge*, which includes human resource management as one of the eight knowledge areas. This series gathers together these and many other resources on the human aspects of management. It focuses on making the most of human resources on projects. The emphasis is on people and how they can be organized to increase their overall effectiveness as individuals, as project teams, and as members of organizations.

Throughout my working life, I have always been fascinated by the degree to which human factors influence the success of project management. The ideas presented in this series developed from years of study and research; from my practical experience at TRIUMF; and from discussions with friends, colleagues, other project management professionals, consultancy clients, and those who have attended my classes and seminars.

8

These ideas are not likely to become the last word in human factors in project management, but I hope they will incite an increased awareness, just as the efforts of researchers and project management practitioners who have successfully implemented creative leadership motivated me to think further about effective project human resources management. Project management will be more successful, and my efforts in writing this series well rewarded, if project management educators and practitioners are inspired to devote more energy to this important area.

One final note: As you read, you may occasionally come across a concept or an idea that you feel you already know. That may be true indeed. As Somerset Maugham said, "Basic truths are too important to be new."

About This Book

Volume 2: Human Resource Skills for the Project Manager

Many books cover the technical aspects of project management but few include an in-depth discussion of the human aspects of project management. In addition, the numerous books on general management, industrial psychology and behavioral science generally lack relevance to and emphasis on the project environment. And there are hardly any books focusing exclusively on the human aspects of project management, even though such focus is critical to making the most of human resources on projects and programs. This book is intended to fill this long-standing need by providing a comprehensive, unified and practical combination of project management skills (with emphasis on human relations and interpersonal skills), general management principles, and relevant theoretical and practical background information on organizational behavior.

Because of severe economic and manpower constraints and consequent "flatter" organizations, *management by projects* is becoming recognized as one of the most effective ways of managing an organization. One of the toughest challenges in managing a project is to manage the people involved. *People* are the backbone of any organization and its most important resource. They define project goals, plan, organize, direct, coordinate and control project activities by using their technical and human skills.

A project manager's performance is dependent upon the performance of the project team and associated stakeholders. Normally, project managers have substantial responsibility but very little authority, especially over functional managers, client representatives and local officials. However, they are dependent upon the cooperation of these parties and—above all—of their team members. They must be able to effectively integrate all project resources and functions by using interpersonal skills.

In most cases, project management problems are of a behavioral nature. Therefore the project manager must understand the dynamics of human behavior and how it influences relationships, perceptions and productivity. A better understanding of people, of what turns people *on* and *off*, combined with effective communication and interpersonal skills, will help project managers to influence and motivate project stakeholders and hence to optimize their performance.

Project managers must acquire six important types of interpersonal skills: effective communication, motivation, negotiation, conflict management, stress management, and leadership. To compete globally, they must emphasize the human factors in project management and create an environment that provides effective leadership and facilitates open and effective communication; an environment in which everyone involved feels committed to produce their best while having fun as well.

Personal satisfaction and the quality of worklife are becoming key factors for many employees. Most organizations now realize that people want more than just a paycheck. They want challenging work that they can be proud of, a sense of accomplishment, and a sense of achievement. A project manager strong in interpersonal skills knows how to create an environment where people feel valued and motivated to contribute to their maximum potential; where problems are considered challenges and errors are considered learning experiences.

This book focuses on human relations and interpersonal skills required in project management, with the aim of inspiring the achievement of high performance among all project stakeholders. It is organized around the six major types of skills (listed above) that project managers must learn and practice in order to manage projects effectively in the 21st century. Topics have been organized in such a way that readers can easily find their particular areas of interest. No previous knowledge of organizational behavior is required, but a keen interest in project management will be useful to thoroughly understand and apply the concepts presented. Each chapter deals with important aspects of human skills in a project environment and outlines practical guidelines to help apply those skills successfully. The concepts and ideas are illustrated by figures and the main points are highlighted by bullets.

Who should read this book? Management by projects is now regarded as a competitive way to manage organizations. Because it emphasizes the importance of human skills in meeting project objectives and deals with interpersonal skills that can optimize the performance of project participants, this book should help anyone, from project management academics and practitioners to a novice in the field. It will help project management professionals learn the human skills needed to interface with major stakeholders and achieve synergy. It will help top management, project managers, project team members, major project stakeholders, and all other project participants (functional managers, support personnel, etc.) increase their effectiveness in managing people and meeting project objectives. Project management educators and academics can use this book to develop a short course, seminar, or training workshop.

The ideas presented here apply to projects in any industry, such as conventional construction, utilities, transportation, defense, manufacturing, petrochemical, service industries, systems development, computer and communications, pharmaceutical, education, research and development, high-tech, financial, hospitality, and the arts.

Learning objectives. After reading this book and relevant reference materials, the readers will have an understanding of:
• Interpersonal communication; types, channels, and links in project communication

- Communicating to achieve high performance through openness and trust; four communication styles and their relationships to the project life cycle
- Effective listening (with emphasis on verbal and nonverbal behaviors) and the role of perception in gaining understanding among project participants
- Basic motivational process, theories and models of motivation and guidelines for motivating project participants
- Sources of project conflicts, various conflict management styles and choosing an appropriate conflict management approach
- Practical guidelines for preparing for, facing and resolving conflict
- Impact of culture on negotiations, communication and leadership
- Negotiating strategies to achieve win-win results
- Sources of stress; effects of stress on health, personality and performance; and guidelines for managing stress
- Project leadership; project leader versus manager; and leadership and project life cycle
- Power versus influence, leadership and control; categories of power; and how to increase power base and use it effectively.
- Managing politics at upper management level and at the project level.

Through this book, I would like to share with the readers my ideas and experiences about managing projects characterized by dignity, purpose, vision and competitive advantage. I hope you will enjoy reading this book and use it for years to come as a reference for managing projects *successfully* through managing project human resources *effectively*.

Minds are like parachutes: they function best when open.

— Anonymous

Acknowledgments

Writing this book has been a labor of love. Like many challenges in life, writing requires diligence, perseverance, patience, and discipline—characteristics that don't come easily to many of us, and I am no exception. However, I am very fortunate to have people who encouraged me to stay on track and finish this book, despite many rewrites.

This book would not have been possible without the help of my friend, colleague, and mentor, R. Max Wideman, who stood by me throughout this project. If I acknowledge all Max's ideas and discussions, his name will be all over this book. Max helped me a great deal in developing my views, reviewing my manuscript, and discussing the topics covered. I cannot repay Max for the extraordinary amount of time he devoted to this project.

Another whose help was invaluable is Raso Samarasekera, who entered my handwritten manuscript into the computer. She went through several revisions cheerfully, with special attention to detail and quality. In addition, my colleague Mark Keyzer helped me by preparing figures and tables.

I am also thankful to Francis M. Webster, Jr.,Walter Wawruck, and Robert Youker, who reviewed my manuscript and gave me many thought-provoking comments. I am very grateful to Jim Pennypacker, Editor-in-Chief, PMI Communications, who encouraged me to stay with this project and played a significant role in expediting it. Another person who deserves special thinks is Jeannette Cabanis, my editor, whose patience, editorial guidance, and hard work were invaluable. I wish also to acknowledge the support of Michelle Triggs, the book designer, and other staff members of PMI Communications who helped me to close this project in a very professional manner.

I also wish to thank members of the PMI West Coast B.C. Chapter and my colleagues at TRIUMF with whom I shared my ideas and who gave me help and moral support in this endeavor. I especially wish to acknowledge the senior management members of TRIUMF—Dr. Erich Vogt, Dr. Alan Astbury, and Dr. Ewart Blackmore for their continuous support. Thanks are also owed to the participants in my classes and seminars for their excellent ideas and discussions.

On a personal level, I would like to thank my late parents and Taya Ji; my brothers, Rajinder and Sudesh Verma and their spouses, Seema and Rita Verma; my sisters, Prem and Sangeeta and their spouses, Sat Parkaash and Surrinder Tony; my in-laws; and my special friends, Raksha and K.L. Toky. Although they are thousands of miles away, they have always inspired me in this endeavor.

Finally, special thanks to my daughters Serena and Angelee and my son Naveen, who supported me, suggested ideas about the basics of understanding people, and gave me an opportunity to complete this book while wondering what Daddy was doing at night in his study. Most of all, I am indebted to my wife, Shiksha Verma, for her love, understanding, and support. All that I am today, I owe to her love, friendship, and devotion. She does not truly know the extent to which she has helped me in completing this project. Shiksha, my appreciation for your support and love cannot be expressed in words, but thanks many times.

Vijay K. Verma
February 1995

13

Outline

Communication provides the wings for you to fly to success.
— Anonymous

Communication:
A Key to Project Success

THE COMMON MANAGEMENT skill of effective communication is crucial to project success because project management involves formal and informal communication at different levels in the organization. Such communication includes all the activities and behavior by which information or ideas are transferred between the project manager and individuals working on the project. The project manager must give directions, hold meetings, and relay information and ideas to and from the project team members, superiors, clients, contractors, functional managers, other project managers and outside personnel.

It is not the intent to provide here an in-depth discussion of the communication process, environment, applications, and tools. Here only the goals of interpersonal communication, importance of verbal and nonverbal communication, and barriers to successful interpersonal communication will be discussed, along with some practical guidelines for effective communication.

Major types and channels of communication are also outlined along with some practical ideas about communicating to achieve high performance through openness, developing trust and effective counseling. The importance of listening, barriers to effective listening, and guidelines for effective listening are discussed, along with four management styles and their relationships to the project life cycle. ∎

Interpersonal Communication

It's not what you say, it's how you say it.

— *Anonymous*

Communication is a two-way effort, involving the transmission of information and understanding from one person or group to another through the use of common symbols. These common symbols can be verbal or nonverbal, written, graphic, or multimedia. The information represented by the symbols—expressed as thoughts, ideas, facts or figures—is useful only if it conveys meaning or knowledge to the receiver. Therefore, both sender and receiver should seek an exact mutual understanding when communicating.[1]

By using communication skills, project managers help to plan, direct, control, and coordinate their operations throughout the project life cycle. Most of the communication activities of project managers involve interpersonal communication and project communications, sharing information with project team members and other stakeholders (as distinct from machine-to-machine communication for automated tasks). Peter Drucker emphasizes the importance of communication for managers, and points out that communicating ability is essential for success.[2] He states that one's effectiveness is determined by one's ability to reach others through the spoken or written word, and this ability is perhaps the most important of all the skills an individual should possess.

In project management, the importance of communication is emphasized by Sievert, who says that a high percentage of the frictions, frustrations and inefficiencies in working relationships are traceable to poor communication. In almost every case, the misinterpretation of a design drawing, a misunderstood change order, a missed delivery date, or a failure to execute instructions are the results of a breakdown in communication.[3] Even engineers and technical personnel typically spend 50–75 percent of their time in communicating verbally—although most discount the importance of this aspect of their work.[4,5]

Goals of interpersonal communications

All communication should be aimed at producing one or more of these responses:[1]

- Understanding the exact meaning and intent of others
- Being understood by others
- Gaining acceptance for yourself and/or your ideas
- Producing action or change.

All of these goals indicate that, to ensure that messages are received and understood clearly, two-way communication is necessary. When communicating in a project environment, both the sender and receiver have a duty to seek common understanding—to be understood and to understand. In

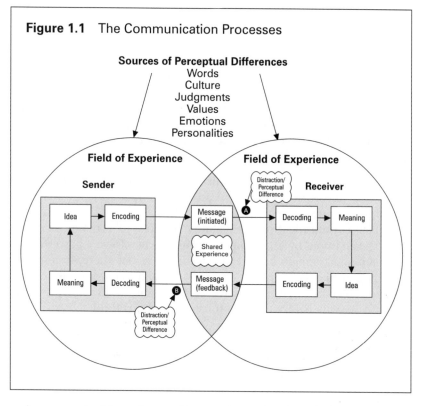

Figure 1.1 The Communication Processes

order to reach this understanding, each person must know the other's meaning and intent. This requires feedback.

One or both parties may need to ask questions to determine exactly what the other person means. The sender may get feedback to a message by asking the receiver in a non-threatening manner (such as *what* he or she understood, rather than *whether* he or she understood) and ask the receiver to respond to it in a way that will reveal whether or not a common understanding has been reached.

How interpersonal communication works
Interpersonal communication is the process of sharing information with other individuals. It has three basic elements (see Figure 1.1):
1. The sender/encoder of information
2. The signal or the message
3. The receiver/decoder.

Wilbur Schramm's classic work[6] explains the role of these three elements. The sender determines what information he or she intends to share, encodes this information in the form of a message, and then transmits the message as a signal to the receiver. The destination decodes the transmitted message to determine its meaning and then responds accordingly. If the message decoded is the same as the sender intended, communication is successful.

To increase the probability that successful communication will take place, a message must be encoded in such a way that the sender's experience as to how the signal should be decoded is equivalent to the receiver's experience of the way it should be decoded. In this situation, the probability is higher that the receiver will interpret the signal as intended by the sender. These overlapping fields of experience ensure successful communication.

Methods of communication
Project managers must have the ability to think logically and communicate effectively. Interpersonal communication takes three forms: verbal, non-verbal, and written (or graphic).

Verbal communication. Our ability to talk—to communicate both ideas and emotions by using common spoken symbols—is a powerful type of communication.[7] In project management, as elsewhere, it is used to transmit information, explanations, and instructions on short notice or in situations that are highly interactive. Negotiations, for example, are often initiated verbally before they are finalized, and it is through verbal communication that negotiating parties develop a mutual understanding of the problem and of each other's positions. In verbal communication, choice of words and clarity of expression are important to transmit the appropriate meaning and achieve the desired impact. Verbal communication is effective in a project environment because it permits:[7]
• Timely exchange of information
• Rapid feedback
• Immediate synthesis of message
• Timely closure.

However, there are some disadvantages to verbal communication, especially in complex projects where technical jargon makes it difficult to be understood by outsiders and nontechnical personnel. Project managers must recognize the limitations of verbal communication when communicating with the public, external stakeholders, marketing personnel and top management, and use appropriate language or alternate types of communication.

An effective verbal/oral presentation or communication usually contains three stages or parts, each having a definite purpose:
• The introduction (Tell 'em what you're going to tell 'em)
• The explanation (Tell 'em)
• The summary (Tell 'em what you told 'em).

This writing plan is sometimes referred to as the "ABC" format: Abstract (introduction), Body (explanation) and Conclusion (summary). Each stage can be broken down into various activities that must be accomplished

Table 1.1   Planning Your Presentation

Step 1: **Tell 'em what you're going to tell 'em**
   (Introduction or Abstract)
   Get the audience's attention.
   Arouse their interest.
   Introduce yourself, your idea, and your purpose.

Step 2: **Tell 'em**
   (Explanation or Body)
   Develop your idea logically: use examples.
   Tell your audience how the idea relates to them.
   Use language your audience can understand.
   Stay on track; be brief.
   Use visual aids.
   Invite questions and comments (feedback).

Step 3: **Tell 'em what you told 'em**
   (Summary or Conclusion)
   Restate your idea; remind the audience how it benefits or affects them.
   Call for questions; also ask questions to verify that the audience has understood you.
   Make a call for action: be specific.

in order to properly achieve effective communication. Table 1.1 shows a guide to planning a verbal/oral presentation.

Nonverbal communication. This refers to encoding a message without using words. It includes gestures, vocal tones, facial expressions, and body language. Generally, a receiver's interpretation of a message is based not only on the words in the message, but also on the nonverbal behaviors of the sender. In an interpersonal communication situation in projects, nonverbal factors generally have more influence on the total impact of a message than verbal factors. This dynamic is expressed in a formula developed by Albert Meharabian:

Total Message Impact = Words (7%) + Vocal tones (38%) + Facial expressions (55%)[8]

Besides vocal tones and facial expressions, gestures,[9] gender,[10] and dress[11] can also influence the impact of a verbal message. To achieve successful interpersonal communication, project managers should use nonverbal ingredients to complement verbal message ingredients whenever possible.[12] Project managers may combine vocal and nonverbal factors but must be careful that the two do not present contradictory messages. For example, in a project meeting, if the project manager's words imply approval but the nonverbal factors express disapproval, the resulting ambiguity of the message will frustrate team members. Of course, the best way to avoid such ambiguity is to "Walk your talk": to mean what you say and say what you mean.

Written communication. In a project environment, written communication includes reports, plans (strategic and tactical), proposals, standards, policies, procedures, letters, memoranda, legal documents, and other forms of information to be transmitted. All project participants write something to convey a meaning/information to their readers. *The main aim of business writing is that it should be understood clearly when read quickly.* To meet this goal, the message should be well-planned, simple, clear and direct.

The field of writing is so large that it is not possible to cover it in depth here. Project managers and team members should review the ample materials available and get some training in written communication. However, the major steps (as shown in Figure 1.2) are summarized below.[13]

Establish the basic purpose of the message. This means defining the general or specific purpose of the message. The general purpose may be to direct, inform, inquire or persuade, while the specific purpose may require more thought, data, and/or analysis. In the case of a major report, proposal or plan, project managers should work closely with their project team members to develop a consensus on the basic purpose of the message.

Collect and organize material. This includes collecting and analyzing the facts and assumptions that have a bearing on the purpose of the message. Organize the material into topics and subtopics and then develop a logical sequence or grouping.

Prepare draft. The effort required in this step depends upon the complexity of the message. Be prepared to go through several drafts for complex, major documents and reports. Check for spelling, grammar, punctuation, format, abbreviations and the use of the right words and phrases. Use active voice rather than passive voice. After the draft is finished, evaluate it. The following questions should be addressed to improve the quality:[13]

- Is it objective and logical?
- Are facts and assumptions valid and justifiable?
- Did you say what you intended to say?
- Is there information overload (or lack of)?
- Does the main text flow smoothly in a clear, direct and logical manner?
- Are all the words used essential to the purpose of the message?
- Have you used language that will appeal to your audience?

Check the overall structure. If the message is a report, make sure that it follows the conventional structure, which contains:

- Executive summary (main ideas and conclusions)
- Introduction (synopsis, background, or main issues)
- Main text and observations
- Summary, conclusions or recommendations.

20

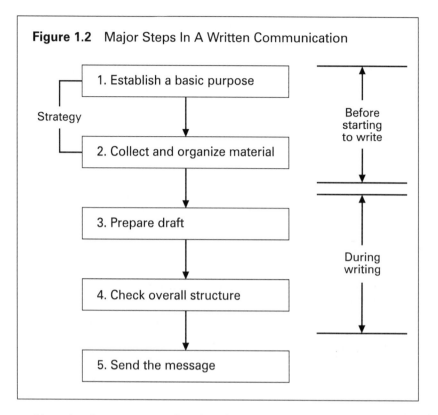

Figure 1.2 Major Steps In A Written Communication

Strategy

1. Establish a basic purpose

2. Collect and organize material

Before starting to write

3. Prepare draft

4. Check overall structure

During writing

5. Send the message

Also, the three stages outlined earlier (introduction, explanation and summary) should be used in any verbal or written method to communicate a message or idea to a project team.

Send the message. Use the appropriate medium to send the message. Both oral and written methods of communication are useful, but their degree of effectiveness varies according to the situation. An oral message followed by a written one is usually most effective because it clarifies and reinforces the message. Table 1.2 shows the effectiveness of oral and/or written communication in various situations.

By following the above steps diligently, project participants will increase the chances that the receiver will get the message clearly.

Improving your written messages. Writing bid proposals, progress reports, training manuals, etc., is an important part of project management. The following guidelines should help improve any type of written message.[14]

Determine when to put your messages in writing. Written communication is effective in the following cases:

• When conveying complex information or data
• When communicating information requiring future action from team members

Table 1.2 How and When to Use Oral and Written Messages

Purpose of Communication	Communication Method		
	Oral	*Written*	*Oral + Written*
	Level of Effectiveness		
General overview (an overview, background, etc.)	Medium	Medium	High
Immediate action required	Medium	Low	High
Future action required	Low	High	Medium
Directive, order, or policy change	Low	Medium	High
Progress report to supervisor	Low	Medium	High
Awareness campaign	Low	Low	High
Commendation for quality work	Low	Low	High
Reprimand a team member	High	Low	Medium
Settle a dispute	High	Low	Medium

- When it is the receiver's preferred communication style
- When communicating information regarding company policies or change in company policies
- When conveying a message that could be misunderstood (either accidentally or intentionally).

Make your messages easy to read. The message should follow the structure outlined earlier and highlight the most important information. Avoid jargon or obscure technical terms and use short words rather than longer ones. Present the subject with clarity and in a logical, progressive sequence. To increase the forcefulness, intelligibility and readability of your message, follow the "3–4–5" principle:[13]

- Divide the message into 3, 4 or 5 major topics; each major topic may contain 3, 4 or 5 subtopics with appropriate headings.
- Each subtopic should be limited to 3, 4 or 5 paragraphs.
- Each paragraph should contain only 3, 4 or 5 sentences.
- Each sentence should contain no more than 35 words.

Additional tips.

- Ask yourself, "would I say what I have written?" (And, perhaps more importantly, would you take the time to *read* it?)
- Write with a "you" attitude, not a "me" attitude; that is, remember to make the message easy for your reader to understand. Use specific examples to bring your points to life.
- Write your conclusions first, and refine all information to bring your conclusions into focus.
- Design your document for quick reply by providing a space at the bottom or on the back for a response from the receiver.

Using communication to increase your personal power

Effective communication is the key to success for the individual as well as for the project. Project managers and other project participants can increase their personal power or influence by developing a "power" vocabulary when writing executive summaries, covering letters, bid proposals, special project reports, marketing strategies, and making presentations. It can be achieved by using the following guidelines:[14]

- *Front-load your message.* Put up front what matters to your audience. Use the receiver's name. ("John, you will want to know that ...")
- *Use concise language and stick to the point.* Use words that are crisp and unambiguous. Resist the urge to embroider sentences and use active voice rather than passive voice because passive voice is powerless.
- *Use powerful visual language* to paint a picture of what you want to communicate; use anecdotes or stories to illustrate your message.
- *Watch out for "is" and "but".* Use "and" instead of "but" if possible. "But" negates what you said before and weakens what is to follow. "Is" and other forms of the verb "to be" provide a red flag that you are using passive construction.
- *Use persuasive language.* Marketing experts say that some of the most persuasive words in the English language are: you, we, new, save, results, free, guarantee, money, easy, and proven.
- *Own the message and show confidence.* Tell what you *can* do rather than what you *can't* do.
- *Avoid jargon and acronyms* because they can be specific to a particular industry and could be confusing to others not involved in that project/sector.

Producing good written communication requires a knowledge of the language, grammar and elements of style and can play a significant role in project success, since effective communication is vital for successful project management. Therefore, to increase their power and effectiveness in communicating with clients, management, team members, functional managers and other project stakeholders, project managers should develop a power vocabulary and learn to organize and explain their ideas in words.

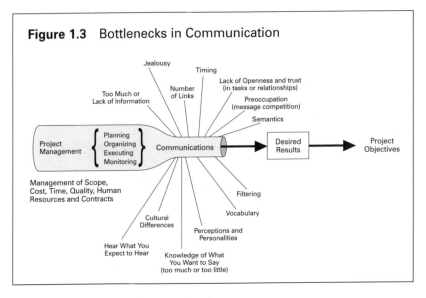

Figure 1.3 Bottlenecks in Communication

Barriers to successful communication

> *... there isn't anyone who does not appreciate kindness and compassion. We must build closer relationships of mutual trust, understanding, respect, and help, irrespective of differences of culture, philosophy, religion or faith.*
> — *The Dalai Lama*

If any of the ingredients or elements of the communication process are defective in any way, clarity of meaning and understanding will be reduced. Several macro-barriers and micro-barriers to communication can arise that will lead to bottlenecks and unsuccessful communication (as shown in Figure 1.3).

Communication macro-barriers. These are elements of the communication environment that hinder successful communication in a general sense. Communication macro-barriers, and suggestions for removing them, include:[15]

Amount of information. The efficiency of team communications can be increased by providing sufficient information but limiting the amount of information transmitted to project team members, minimizing information overload. Follow the principle of KISS (keep it simple and short).

Lack of subject knowledge. Since mutual understanding is based on a shared field of experience, a lack of such shared experience can inhibit communication. Acquire a thorough knowledge of your subject matter, and ascertain what your audience's knowledge level of the subject might be.

Cultural differences. Do not overlook cultural differences, especially in international projects and joint ventures. Meanings and interpretations may vary in different cultures, which can influence the communication process. Encourage project team members to learn each other's cultures

24

and to understand other languages. Remember that gender and regional or ethnic differences among team members of the same nationality can also create cultural barriers.

Organizational climate. Minimize the difficulties associated with status and ego in the organization. Create an atmosphere of openness and trust by talking with, rather than down to, people.

Number of links. Reduce the number of transmission links. The more links there are in the chain, the more opportunities there are for distortion to creep into the message.

Communication micro-barriers. These barriers obstruct successful communication in a specific situation. These barriers relate to the communicated message itself, to the sender and/or to the receiver. Communication micro-barriers include:[16]

Perceptions. Both the sender and the receiver may have their own perceptions about each other's knowledge and skills.

- *Sender's view of the receiver.* Senders communicate differently depending on how they perceive the receiver's level of knowledge and ability to understand the message. Senders should not imply any negative attitudes towards the receiver through communication behavior.
- *The receiver's view of the sender.* Personal feelings (based on sender's expertise) towards the sender may influence how carefully the receiver listens to the sender. If negative, these feelings may cause the receiver to ignore the message, resulting in the loss of valuable information. If overly positive, these feelings may inhibit the receiver's judgment.

Such perceptions influence the interpretation of a message and differing interpretations result in unsuccessful communication. To overcome perceptual differences, make messages specific and unambiguous.

Message competition. Communicate only when you have the total attention of the recipient, otherwise your message will be competing with whatever the other party is preoccupied with at that time, either mentally or physically. Try to minimize noise or other factors contributing to message interference.

Project jargon and terminology. Define the project terminology used in messages. Project team members (collectively) should try to use words in the way the receivers use them.

Many of these micro-barriers derive from the macro-barriers. For instance, perceptions can derive from cultural differences, and jargon from subject knowledge. Project managers must understand both macro- and micro-barriers thoroughly in order to maximize communication success. They must create an environment that minimizes the impact of these barriers to communication so that project objectives can be effectively accomplished.

Communication in a Project Environment

Because of the unique features of projects and the way project teams are organized in a matrix fashion, effective communication is vital for project success. Overlapping responsibilities, frequent changes in scope and constraints, complex integration and interface requirements, decentralized decision-making processes and a potential for conflict all pose communication challenges. Often, a significant number of project problems are caused by poor and/or ineffective communications. Because of all these difficulties, communication is the biggest single factor influencing the quality, effectiveness, satisfaction and productivity of a project team.[17]

Thus, one of the most critical roles of the project manager is that of *communicator*. The project manager must try to create an environment that is conducive to open communication and the development of trust among project participants. This section deals with the general types of project communication (e.g., interpersonal, formal, informal and management information systems); project meetings, including the purpose and frequency of meetings and guidelines for managing them effectively; different communication channels; and using communication to increase your personal power.

Types of project communications

In a project environment, communication refers to the exchange or sharing of messages and information to convey meaning and knowledge between and among the project manager, internal stakeholders, and external stakeholders. The intent and the content of these messages are designed to meet various purposes, including:

- Dissemination of records, status reports and other information (including statistics and research) about the project
- Information-sharing about decisions in order to gain acceptance and hence commitment to those decisions
- Management of project interfaces and systems integration.

A project manager uses communication more than any other element in the project management process to ensure that team members are working cohesively on project problems and opportunities. As discussed earlier, communications can be verbal, nonverbal or written. Communications in a project environment can be of several types, all of which must be managed effectively to accomplish project success. The main types of project communication are discussed below.

Interpersonal communication includes listening, self-presentation, problem solving, decision making, negotiating and conflict management. The good interpersonal communicator develops these necessary skills for interacting with the project team and with the client on a daily basis.

Communication with public and community includes all the public relations efforts necessary to encourage community involvement, enhance public understanding of the project, break down resistance, gain acceptance, and generally play the role of spokesperson for the project organization. Such communication may involve public speaking, making presentations, dealing with media representatives, and producing written publicity or PR materials.

Formal communication is carried out through the traditional responsibility/relationship channels described by the organization chart. It deals with organizational design, strategic plans, project planning systems, standards, policies, procedures, proposals, letters and other forms of information. It is most effectively done in a written form.

Informal communication, by contrast, is carried out through informal groups in which relationships are dependent upon common ties, such as interests, hobbies, social status, friendship, kinship. People join informal groups to satisfy their psychological and social needs and through the desire to accomplish personal and project objectives.

Why should a project manager be concerned about informal communications? How can the project manager be effective in an informal project climate? The informal communication of information is inevitable in a project environment. Such informal channels should be managed effectively because of their ability to influence overall communications in a project and hence project team performance. A project manager must identify the strengths and limitations of informal communications and explore strategies to increase overall project effectiveness through informal communications. They must:[18]

- Establish a project culture in which informal communication helps create an atmosphere that encourages openness in communication.
- Identify informal leaders and listen to them to get feedback or overall impressions on various issues and decisions. Informal leaders can help test new ideas, technical approaches, strategies, and administrative actions, the acceptance of which is crucial to project success. However, project managers should be careful so that they are not seen as "playing favorites."

Project managers should recognize that the attitudes and behavior of people in informal organizations influence the cultural ambiance of the project. Therefore they should try to establish a good rapport with informal organizations and align the goals of informal groups with those of the project and the organization as a whole.[19]

Communication and project management information system. In a project environment, an effective management information system is vital to monitor project progress, exercise project control, and facilitate good communication. Management information systems planning affects communication by addressing questions such as:

- How will data and information be gathered, organized, processed, updated and communicated among project stakeholders? By frequent meetings? written memos? reports?

- What communication medium will be most effective: hard copy? phone? electronic mail?
- What reporting and control procedures will be implemented? Project management reports should be attention-directing, problem-solving and scorekeeping. Such a system may produce exception reports and risk analyses. The review process should be designed to achieve a reasonable balance between frequency of reviews/reports and their potential benefits.

Since controls can be quite expensive, these should be designed and implemented carefully by making them *economic, efficient,* and *effective.* Unfortunately, the following problems lessen the effectiveness of the project management information system in controlling and optimizing financial and other resources in a project:[20]

- Easily measured goals receive greater attention. Resources are allocated to new projects and developments rather than to preventive maintenance, updating of drawing, etc., until problems become serious.
- Short-run goals may be overemphasized. Sometimes the training of personnel receives lower priority than getting the job done immediately.

Managing project meetings effectively

There are often too many meetings. The trouble is, how do you export meetings?
— Robert Half

Meetings have become a way of life in project management, providing a means to exchange and share messages, ideas and information. Project managers and team members therefore spend an appreciable amount of time in project meetings. The effectiveness of these meetings tells a good deal about the emphasis a project manager places on communication. However, it is not certain how cost-effective meetings are as a way of managing communications in a project environment. Meetings require a great deal of time and effort and therefore should only be called when necessary. Unfortunately, many meetings are unproductive, poorly conceived and badly run. Therefore, it is important to understand when and how many meetings are necessary, and how to run project meetings effectively.

Purpose of project meetings. Project managers may require many meetings of various types, each type needed to meet a different project objective and therefore handled in a different way. These meetings include: Start up (or kick off) meetings, planning meetings, status/review meetings, problem-solving meetings, public meetings, presentation meetings, negotiation and conflict resolution meetings.

Through meetings, project managers:[21]
- Define the project and the major team players.
- Provide an opportunity to revise, update and add to the project team's knowledge base, including facts, assumptions, perceptions, experience, judgments, and other information pertinent to the project.

Such opportunities increase the cohesiveness and knowledge of the team, producing more accurate cost, schedule and performance status reports.

- Assist team members in identifying where and how their individual efforts fit into the big picture and in understanding how their individual successes can increase the team's success.
- Help team members increase their commitment to the project. When team members participate in making decisions during meetings, they are more likely to accept and feel committed to these decisions. Often, people oppose decisions, not because of the decision content itself, but because they were not consulted about it. Also, team decisions are harder to challenge than decisions made by individuals.
- Provide a collective opportunity to discuss the overall project and decide on actions and individual work assignments.
- Provide the feeling that a project team exists and really does work as a team.
- Provide visibility for project leaders' roles in managing the project.
- Provide an opportunity to team members to demonstrate their creativity in solving project problems in an ad hoc setting. The process and objectives of such ad hoc meetings may depend upon the situation.

Project managers must define meeting goals which are specific, measurable, realistic, achievable, results-oriented, and timely. They must clarify the roles of all project team members and should even rotate these roles so that everyone gets opportunity and experience.

Frequency of reviews/meetings. In complex projects, a high number of activities and resources must be planned and coordinated. Because of the large number of interactions, overlapping goals, and the need for a significant amount of resources, the review process must be well designed.

A reasonable balance should be kept between the *frequency* of reviews and meetings and their potential *benefits*. The number of meetings and frequency of reviews is related to the project life cycle and resembles a "bathtub curve," as shown in Figure 1.4.[20] During the conceptual and feasibility stage, it is desirable to have more planning meetings to achieve an agreement in principle on the final goals and methods to achieve them. At this stage, customer needs are fleshed out. However, once the concepts are finalized and project team members are working on the detailed design, fabrication or assembly of the components, the number of meetings and reviews may reduce. Frequency of reviews may increase again towards the end when loose ends have to be coordinated. Such reviews are helpful in avoiding the use of significant time and resources during the last 10 percent of the job, when close coordination and integration is often necessary.

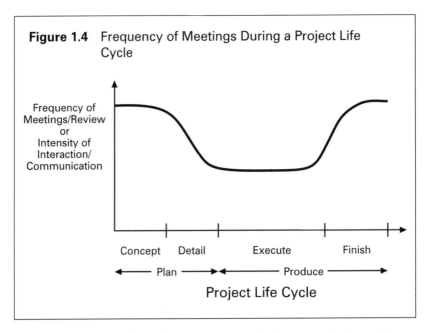

Figure 1.4   Frequency of Meetings During a Project Life Cycle

Frequency of Meetings/Review or Intensity of Interaction/ Communication

Concept   Detail   Execute   Finish

← Plan → ← Produce →

Project Life Cycle

Reducing the number of meetings: a practical process. Before calling a meeting, the project manager should address the following questions:[22]

- What is the main issue (problem or opportunity) requiring the meeting?
- What are the facts or assumptions causing the problem or suggesting the opportunity?
- What are the potential alternatives and their costs versus benefits?
- What specific recommendations can be proposed to the meeting participants to deal with the problems or opportunities at hand?
- What are the likely consequences of not holding the meeting?

Answering these questions may reveal that the meeting is not absolutely essential.

How to manage project meetings. Managing a meeting is an important management function that includes planning, organizing, directing and controlling. A well-managed project meeting is an efficient way to share information, clarify directions and ambiguities, coordinate project team efforts, and obtain immediate feedback on project issues. It brings a collective approach to project issues and opportunities. The chairperson of the meeting creates the proper team environment by planning, hosting and leading the meeting. He or she must clarify the expectations for the meeting. The chairperson must guide, stimulate, clarify, control, summarize, enhance and evaluate the meeting's outcome in terms of attaining project goals and objectives. Meetings are likely to be ineffective if the chairperson does most of the talking. The chairperson's influence depends upon how positively the participants perceive his or her commitment to objectives of the meeting and his or her skill and efficiency in helping participants to meet those objectives.

Meetings can become unproductive and a total waste of time, especially if the project manager makes some of these common mistakes:

- Holding too many or too few meetings
- Neglecting to distribute an agenda in advance
- Neglecting to invite people with decision-making authority
- Failing to consult with people responsible for making presentations
- Spending too much time on trivial items
- Neglecting to assign action items to specific personnel.[23]

The outcome of a project meeting depends upon various factors, including the type of structure (rigid or free), degree of formality, intensity of pre-planning, and level of authority displayed by the chair. Project managers must be aware of these factors and use them appropriately to manage meetings effectively.

Guidelines for managing meetings effectively. Well-planned and well-managed project meetings can be productive. Effective meeting management takes place *before, during* and *after* the meeting, as discussed below.[24]

Before the meeting. Follow the question-and-answer process outlined above to determine if the meeting is really necessary. Then:

- Determine the purpose of the meeting; hold progress or status review meetings separately from problem-solving meetings.
- Set the ground rules for the discussion.
- Determine who really needs to be present and invite only those people.
- Notify participants well in advance of the meeting's purpose, location, and time.
- Distribute an agenda in advance.
- Make notes and rehearse your presentation.
- Start and end the meeting on time.

During the meeting. In order to keep meetings as brief as possible, yet productive:

- Specify a time limit and stick to it.
- Begin by identifying the specific objectives of the meeting.
- Gather input from the participants (listen more than talk).
- Keep things moving; discourage participants from getting off the subject.
- Use visual aids to get your point across, and encourage other participants to do the same.
- Periodically summarize the results of the discussion in terms of consensus achieved or disagreements still in progress.
- When further work is required, assign action items to team members.

After the meeting. Most of the real work, of course, takes place outside of meetings. Therefore, follow up on the individual action items assigned and distribute concise minutes and use them at the next meeting to measure results.

It is essential to keep minutes of meetings, especially for project planning, organizing and evaluating meetings. These minutes should be precise and clearly specify the following facts:[22]

- Time, place and instructions for the next meeting
- Time and place of the meeting and a list of attendees with their project role (The issue of who should attend project meetings changes according to allocated work packages)
- Agenda items discussed
- Decisions reached or held for further studies
- Action items and persons responsible for follow-up and reporting back to the team at next meeting.

On average, a project manager spends approximately eight years of his or her lifetime in meetings.[14] Therefore, in a project environment, where schedules are normally tight, it is important to develop specific ways to make team meetings more focused and productive. This can be done by ensuring that both leaders and participants play their roles properly. Following are some commonsense ideas that can be used to make team meetings more productive:[14]

The leaders role is to set expectations, stay focused and on track, and increase participation. Participation increases acceptance and hence commitment, or "buy-in."

The participant's role is to be prepared, look confident and interested, and speak up without monopolizing the discussion.

The role of humor is both to raise and to indicate the level of morale. If morale is low, humor will go underground and project participants will become cynical snipers. Humor should be healthy; that is, not sarcastic or directed at any particular team member. Avoid humor based on ethnic or gender bias at all times. The type of jokes published by *Reader's Digest* provide a guideline.

MANAGERS AND FUNCTIONAL MANAGERS ALIKE dislike meetings—especially if they are called by someone else. Undoubtedly, well-run project meetings provide an effective focus to manage the project successfully; but sometimes, project managers can resolve important issues and problems by working individually with the team members by telephone, personal discussion, or a brief ad hoc meeting.

Project managers must remember that good project meetings don't end with communication at the meeting itself. Project managers must then get team members to follow through on their promises by increasing their level of commitment to the outcome. Such commitment is encouraged by using the techniques shown in Figure 1.5 to create a *GREAT* meeting; that is, one that makes team members more effective and productive.

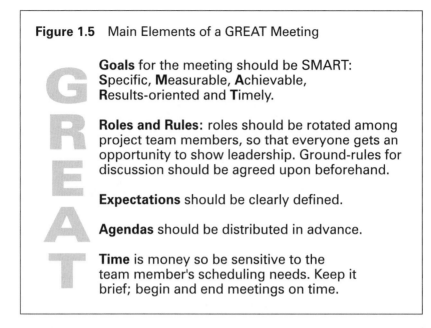

Figure 1.5   Main Elements of a GREAT Meeting

Goals for the meeting should be SMART: **S**pecific, **M**easurable, **A**chievable, **R**esults-oriented and **T**imely.

Roles and Rules: roles should be rotated among project team members, so that everyone gets an opportunity to show leadership. Ground-rules for discussion should be agreed upon beforehand.

Expectations should be clearly defined.

Agendas should be distributed in advance.

Time is money so be sensitive to the team member's scheduling needs. Keep it brief; begin and end meetings on time.

Communication channels and links

Along with the significant informal communication that takes place in a project environment, the project manager must recognize and understand the project's formal communication channels. The traditional project organization chart depicts the relationship between people and jobs and shows the formal channels of communication between them (see Figure 1.6).

Three basic channels of communication in a project environment exist.

Upward communication (vertically or diagonally with managers and officers) primarily contains information that higher management (project director or sponsor) needs to evaluate the overall performance of the projects for which they are responsible, or to refine organizational strategy. Project managers may use the "by exception" format for project status reports, production reports, shipping reports and customer concerns. This feedback helps top management assess priorities and make organizational modifications to effectively meet project goals and objectives and be more successful in the future.

Downward communication (vertically or diagonally) provides direction and control for project team members and other employees. It contains job-related information focusing on:

- What actions are required (scope and definition)
- To what standard (quality)
- When the activities should be performed (schedule)
- How the activities should be done (implementation)
- How the progress will be measured (evaluation and feedback).

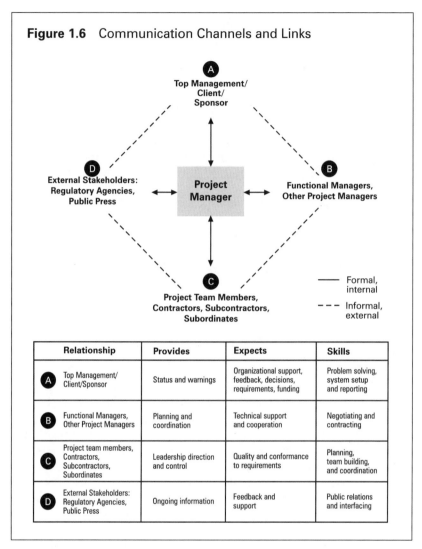

Figure 1.6 Communication Channels and Links

	Relationship	Provides	Expects	Skills
A	Top Management/ Client/Sponsor	Status and warnings	Organizational support, feedback, decisions, requirements, funding	Problem solving, system setup and reporting
B	Functional Managers, Other Project Managers	Planning and coordination	Technical support and cooperation	Negotiating and contracting
C	Project team members, Contractors, Subcontractors, Subordinates	Leadership direction and control	Quality and conformance to requirements	Planning, team building, and coordination
D	External Stakeholders: Regulatory Agencies, Public Press	Ongoing information	Feedback and support	Public relations and interfacing

Source: R. Max Wideman. 1994. Personal communication.

Downward communication may include statements of organizational philosophy, policies, project objectives, schedules, budgets and constraints, position descriptions and other written information relating to the importance, rationale and interrelationships and interactions of various departments projects, and jobs in an organization.

Lateral communication (horizontally) flows between the project manager and his or her peers: functional managers, line/staff personnel, other project managers, contractors, subcontractors, clients, service/support

Human Resource Skills for the Project Manager

personnel and other project stakeholders. It involves negotiating resources, schedules, and budgets and coordinating activities with contractors, regulatory agencies and clients, as well as developing plans for future operating periods.

Lateral communication is vital to the success of a project and is also the most important factor for survival and growth in a highly competitive and turbulent environment where management by projects is likely to be the most effective style of managing organizations. It requires diplomacy and experience. If managed properly, it creates a harmonious, cooperative environment based on trust and respect for one another. When poorly managed, however, it may lead to conflict, unconstructive finger-pointing and failure to meet project objectives.

IN A PROJECT ENVIRONMENT, project managers communicate with the client, project sponsor or project director (for requirements, guidance and funding); with the top management (for organizational support); functional managers (for resources); and project team members, contractors, subcontractors, etc. (for project management). They should expedite the communication process to reduce ambiguity and the probability of making wrong assumptions and interpretations that can lead to conflict, delays and other unpleasant results. Figure 1.6 shows the typical communication links of a project manager along with the function of each link.

Communicating to Achieve High Performance
The performance of a project manager depends upon how well he or she can get the work done by the project team as they work together in planning, implementation, coordination, interfacing, integration, and control. Self-awareness is one of the key factors in this process. It implies being aware of your own communication strengths and weaknesses.

The project manager achieves project objectives by using effective communication to inspire high team performance. Openness in communication, the development of trust to achieve accuracy in communication, and continuous support and counseling are key requirements for achieving high team performance. These attributes also create an environment in which it is possible to develop self-awareness, because team members feel comfortable sharing opinions and preferences and constructively critiquing each other's communication behaviors.[25]

The "closed communication" environment
In a project environment where communication is closed, people are not able to communicate effectively.[25] They censor themselves, only saying the things that project leaders would like to hear and only in the way they prefer to hear it. They don't express ideas that might contribute to the team's success. Some people who play this communication game appear quiet but they may in fact:

- Press for hidden agendas
- Vent frustrations in unproductive ways
- Sabotage the project, the project leader or the project team
- Drop out and not contribute to team's output
- Influence other team members negatively.

Thus, closed communication in a project environment is ineffective because it restricts synergy within the project team. On the other hand, openness allows communication about project goals, tasks, and interactions and creates a team spirit that binds the people together and enhances the team's productivity. Project leaders must set the standards for openness and then create an environment where openness among the project team members grows.

Here are a few techniques that can be practiced to create openness in the project environment. While this list does not include everything that project participants can do, these practices will begin to build an open communications environment.[25]

Encourage openness by repeating and summarizing the main points of any message you receive in order to confirm your understanding and clarify the meaning and intentions of the message.

Never close communication by discouraging new ideas or prohibiting constructive criticism.

Create partnership by respecting the opinions and ideas of others. Show your sincere commitment to support each other and work together as a team to resolve project problems.

Create a permissive environment that encourages openness and creativity by having a tolerance for failure.

How openness enhances communication

In an environment where competition is minimal, functional departments may be able to operate independently or in isolation, and a leader may have most of the right answers. Even with closed communication, a leader operating in such a functional structure may be able to produce good results and profits. However, in today's complex, competitive world, it is becoming necessary to pool knowledge and resources to achieve high performance. The success of project leaders or managers is largely dependent on the level of openness in communications that they create in their project teams. Openness ensures that the right questions are asked, that answers are direct and honest, that the right solutions are generated and the right decisions are made.[25] This section deals with task openness, relationship openness and how to create an open communication environment.

Dimensions of open communication. In addition to just learning the skills of speaking, listening or writing, a good communicator examines the behavioral issues that impact open communication in the interactions among project team members. Project managers must look for those behaviors that send silent messages that scream louder than even the loudest words. These silent messages actually make all the difference between closed and open communication.[25]

The two main dimensions of openness are described below.[25]

Task openness refers to communication related to tasks. A task communication between the project manager and his or her boss can be closed either by words that are said that cut off further communication, or by words that are *not* said, such as;

- Displaying lack of interest while listening
- Not asking any questions to ensure clear understanding
- Not asking an opinion on how to solve a problem
- Not offering any additional support that could be useful.

Since communication is a two-way process, a closed communication environment can be caused not only by higher management but by behaviors displayed by the project manager. For instance, a director of project management may not listen to project managers who are unable to:

- Define the problem and identify key issues
- Present the problem logically and seek a solution
- Present fact-based arguments
- Present information in the same way they would like to receive it.

Both parties, therefore, can have direct and indirect impact on task openness. To achieve such openness, both communicators must create a partnership in which each tries to understand the other. Both should make sure what they want from the communication, and both should take responsibility for reaching a complete resolution of key issues that are brought to the table.[25]

Relationship openness refers to the openness in the relationship between two communicating parties. Relationship communication between the project manager and project team members can be closed for any of the following reasons:

- The project manager may not have effective listening skills, failing to show interest, support or commitment to resolve problems or not removing distractions.
- The environment and setting may display inequality of power, creating barriers to communication.
- The project manager may talk down to the team members instead of talking with them.
- The communicators may be on different wavelengths in terms of the priority of the situation being discussed.

Many project managers lack the skills for building relationships at work. Some may even feel that this "soft" side of communication is unnecessary and unprofessional in a technical environment. However, in order to achieve high team performance, communication must go beyond emphasizing the task only. Highly successful teams recognize the need to develop good, warm working relationships. They tend to create a partnership and establish the rapport, trust and understanding that encourages them to listen to each other, rely on each other and help each other succeed. Openness creates the partnership, and the partnership leads to even more openness, further increasing team performance.

PROJECT PARTICIPANTS SEND both task and relationship messages through their communication. These messages, if ineffective and negative, create many interpersonal and task problems. Project leaders set the tone for open or closed communication. They can create openness by setting examples with every word and action rather than by sending memos or just talking about it. They must reinforce the behaviors that support open communication and discourage those behaviors that lead to closed communication in the project team.

Trust and accuracy in communications

Trust and respect are the pillars of success.

— Anonymous

Sometimes project disasters happen because of a lack of facts and information. Why don't project teams supply all of the facts? Are they lying or are they simply unable to convey pertinent information?

This distinction between "lying" and "failing to present all the facts" has tremendous implications for project managers and functional managers who want to create an open communication environment.[26] Several studies have indicated that the degree of trust between project specialists and the various levels of management is highly related to the degree of openness, accuracy and clarity in project communication.[27,28] In addition to trust, the level of security and autonomy and the overall organizational climate also have a tremendous effect on the accuracy or distortion of project communications. The literature supports two principal assumptions:[29]

1. The accuracy of upward communication is directly proportional to the authority delegated to accomplish project tasks. When project teams are empowered to make decisions and authority is widely distributed across the project team members, there is likely to be less distortion in communication.
2. A supportive organizational climate leads to higher trust.[30]

Thus, trust is one of the pillars of effective project management.

Counseling and support

Sometimes team members have problems that they cannot solve by themselves. In such circumstances, project managers should provide support, positive reinforcement and counseling (as needed) to make project team members feel comfortable and valued. It is important to identify whom to counsel and how to counsel, which are described below.

Project managers are, of course, not professional counselors. They should not attempt to involve themselves in personal problems of a serious nature, but should refer team members to professional career counselors or therapists.

Counseling, as it applies to the project workplace, can be defined as the process of assisting an individual in coming to terms with the personal issues related to career plans, work requirements, quality of work, or personal conflicts that impacts work performance. The counseling relationship is characterized by mutual respect and trust. Ideally, it should be free of any suggestion of "superior-subordinate" status. Counseling is *not* solving others' problems for them, or even giving advice. It *is* providing a safe environment where concerns can be aired and solutions sought in an atmosphere of teamwork and equality.

In a project environment, team members may go to their project manager for input on personal or work-related issues, to try out their ideas, or to "blow off steam." Three concerns that project team members may have about their project managers are:[31]

1. Does the project manager really know the team members, their ambitions and their family and individual needs?
2. Is the project manager willing to listen to the problems of project team members, and make a sincere and honest attempt to help the team member find a way to solve the problem?
3. Can the project manager be trusted to keep everything between them confidential?

How to counsel. A few practical tips to achieve effective counseling in a project are:

- Keep communication channels *open and honest* in all directions (up, down and laterally).
- Avoid arguments and displays of temper with project stakeholders.
- If wrong, be ready to apologize. Be quick to forgive a colleague even if he or she was unreasonable. Remember that you, as a project manager, will always need their help and cooperation.
- Be objective and focus on problems and issues and not on people and personalities. Project managers do not have to call all peers "friends" but they *should not* call any of them "enemies" either.
- Enrich the returns to project participants by sharing success with others. And, by sharing their sorrows, capture their respect.

Whom to counsel. A project manager must understand that the main purpose of counseling is to cement and improve good working relationships and to help team members achieve their personal goals as far as is possible. However, as a word of caution, it is one thing to be asked for your opinion and another to give it without being asked. Personal advice should be avoided as much as possible unless an informal relationship exists between the parties involved. Project managers should avoid any

Communication: A Key to Project Success

counseling unless it is specifically solicited. And, they must always remember that confidentiality is of the utmost importance in counseling.

In a project environment, counseling, like communication, can take place in several directions:

Counseling peers. The key to counseling peers is maintaining a "we care" attitude because this attitude leads to a better understanding of the other person's feelings and state of mind, which develops mutual trust and appreciation.

Counseling by top management. The project manager may sometimes need encouragement, positive reinforcement and moral support from top management regarding problems with clients, contractors and functional managers.

Counseling team members. Subordinates or team members may at times need the project manager to listen to their ideas, problems and difficulties—to provide them with "emotional first aid." A project manager may bring a certain objectivity and neutrality on the issues that team members are unable to muster on their own.

Project managers should follow four principles when handling counseling sessions with subordinates or project team members:

1. Involve project team members so that they are committed to the solution.
2. Do not *tell* your team member what to do or even how to do it, but rather *help them develop* solutions themselves. Raise relevant questions and help them find an effective solution in a timely manner rather than leading them by the hand.
3. Make sure everyone understands the meaning of what is being discussed and said.
4. Listen more than talk.
5. Refer more serious concerns to professional counselors.

IN MOST PROJECT AND BUSINESS ENVIRONMENTS, a supportive, relationship-oriented climate helps build trust, which leads to more complete, accurate and less distorted communication. Positive support, positive reinforcement and counseling must be provided to project team members so that they will feel valued and motivated to achieve high team performance. These elements build trust and create an environment that fosters human synergy.

Listening

Nature has given us one tongue but two ears, so that we may hear twice as much as we speak.

— Epictetus

Effective listening is an important component of communication and a skill that many project managers lack. But project managers can develop this skill by studying active listening practices and applying them in a

40

conscious program of self-development. Most of us spend about half our waking hours listening; yet research studies show that we retain only 25 percent of what we listen to, because listening is the one skill we are never really taught in a formal manner.[32] Yet anyone can learn to listen actively, by involving themselves mentally, physically, and emotionally in the act of listening.

Importance of effective listening

Because effective listening not only improves communication but also helps develop mutual rapport, trust and respect among project participants, it is one of the most important skills that project managers must acquire and practice. Listening is one of the most powerful ways to stroke team members, project stakeholders or top management. A good listener communicates positive feelings to others about their ideas and themselves because only ideas that are listened to can be understood and considered for implementation. To reinforce this, even "Mother Nature" has given us a hint about the importance of listening by giving us two ears to listen and only one mouth to talk.

Many of us find it easier to listen to superiors (because we have to) than to subordinates (because we feel we don't really have to and we often do so only to be polite). Many people also find it more comfortable to talk "down" to subordinates than to talk "up" to superiors.[33] Nevertheless, project communication (including listening) must be carried on with functional managers, other project managers, customers/clients, contractors, support staff personnel, and other stakeholders. Building and maintaining alliances with these stakeholders can only be accomplished by effective listening and by opening up communication channels so that messages can flow in both directions. Davis has emphasized the role of communication and its relationship to management style in encouraging frankness and integrity in the management of a project.[34] In other words, interpersonal communication—especially effective listening—is essential for successful project management.

Verbal and nonverbal listening behaviors

Beware of the man whose belly does not shake when he laughs.
— *Chinese Proverb*

Project managers must be aware of verbal and nonverbal listening behaviors, including body language, of both themselves and of project team members.[35]

Verbal listening behaviors include:
- Asking questions to clarify and gather more information. Questions should be probing and constructive.
- Paraphrasing what the speaker has said to clarify terminology. Simply paraphrase the information in words that are meaningful to you to confirm that what you understood was what the speaker meant.

- Summarizing at intervals what the speaker said, to confirm what you have understood.
- Asking the speaker for examples.
- Ascertaining the speaker's feelings and acknowledging them: "You seem angry" or "I get the feeling you are disappointed."
- Directing the speaker to the most appropriate listener. Sometimes a speaker may want to get something off his or her chest. If it is relevant to your relationship with the speaker or the project, deal with it yourself; otherwise suggest who might be best able to help.

Nonverbal listening behaviors are those "actions that speak louder than words." They can reinforce your message or undermine it. They include:

- Making eye contact with the speaker, which indicates honesty and openness and creates the personal bond necessary for good communication
- Being expressive; an alert, interested expression motivates the speaker to be open
- Moving closer to the speaker, which establishes a more friendly and constructive communication
- Listening for the intention behind the speaker's communication. Sometimes the real message is not just what is said but also *how* it is said.

The total impact of a message is strongly influenced by nonverbal factors, including body language. Body language signals and their interpretations differ from culture to culture, but a few of the more common body language signals and their interpretations are shown in Table 1.3.[14,36]

Because body language may convey a message different from what is being said in words, to communicate effectively it is extremely important to be aware of what your body says that your mouth does not.

Body language that creates rapport. Since body language accounts for 55 percent of communication, it is an important factor in creating rapport and understanding among project participants.[8] Some ideas that might be helpful in using body language effectively are:[14]

Facial expressions. When you smile while talking, it puts your listener at ease, and you are likely to get a smile back in response. As you read the body language of others, remember that *real* smiles make the corners of the eye crinkle. Eye contact is important because it establishes a communication bond. However, it's important to make eye contact with an awareness of cultural difference. Nodding the head while listening indicates agreement and understanding.

Touching. Touch can be an important communication tool—or an unwanted intrusion. When touching, be aware of cultural differences that may cause your intentions to be misunderstood. For example, some gestures that seem innocuous to North Americans may not be appreciated in

Table 1.3   Body Language Signals

Body Language	Interpretation
Pointing	Aggressiveness
Sighing	Impatience, boredom, or grief
Scratching head or face	Uncertainty or risk
Concealing mouth with hands	Uncertainty about words—or dishonesty
Bending forward	Interest
Leaning back with hands behind head	Superiority or confidence
Clenched fists or crossed arms	Defensive attitude
Rubbing hands	Expectation

other cultures. When dealing with culturally diverse stakeholders, educate yourself about such matters to avoid offense. In addition, there is a "cultural" difference between the genders that must be respected. In most cases, it is wise to avoid touching a person of the opposite sex, except for the universally acceptable warm handshake. Otherwise, a light touch on the back of the hand, forearm or shoulder/upper back generally is acceptable and shows warmth and closeness.

Use of space. An individual's "personal space"—an area of up to 20 inches on all sides—functions like an emotional safety zone, and should not be invaded. Maintain an appropriate "communication zone" distance of between 20 and 40 inches. Getting too close may intimidate some people, while staying too far away may show a lack of interest in listening. It is difficult to communicate effectively when more than 40 inches away.

People who are especially tall should be aware of the effect of their height on others. Towering over shorter people or people who are seated can intimidate a listener, or seem to indicate status differences. When communicating, it's best to sit side by side or facing each other without any desk or table in between. This positioning promotes a sense of equality and willingness to collaborate. In addition, leaning forward expresses your interest in the communication.

Use of time. Don't keep people waiting. Such behavior shows that you don't care about their schedule or priorities, which could have a very negative effect on your working relationship.

Body language plays a significant role in the communication process, especially in listening. Effective listening involves listening to the message in terms of not only *what* is said but *how* it is said. Just as people try to "read between the lines," project managers must be willing to "listen between the words." Listen and watch for the intent of what the speaker is trying to communicate. Even in a seemingly trivial exchange, a team member may be expressing frustration in getting part of the job completed, which may indicate a global problem.

Barriers to effective listening

The mismatch between our speed of talking (100–400 words per minute) and our speed of thinking (approx. 600 words per minute) makes effective listening tough. In addition, there are numerous barriers to effective listening such as differing perceptions, personality differences, lack of trust or mutual understanding, fear of conflict, and inappropriate environment.

Some of the personal and environmental barriers that stand in the way of effective listening and influence the effectiveness of overall communication include:[33]

Poor listeners. In the absence of good listeners, people do not talk freely, which inhibits effective communication. And only one bad listener is required to impair the flow of communication in the human chain. Poor listeners communicate their lack of attention via body language, discouraging future attempts to communicate. Or they miss the main idea and end up paying more attention to details instead.

Resistance to the message. People don't like to listen to something that is contrary to their preconceived ideas. When they should be listening, they concentrate instead on preparing their response or defense. Listening may uncover some unexpected problems regarding project status in terms of schedule or cost overruns, so if top management is inclined not to listen to bad news, team members may not present all of the facts, censoring themselves to the detriment of the project.

Our emotions act as aural filters, allowing us to ignore what we don't want to hear. Some situations in which people have difficulty listening include:[26]
- Dealing with a conflict situation
- Feeling anxious, angry or fearful
- Being reprimanded
- Being criticized
- Dealing with emotional colleagues or customers.

Physical distractions such as telephone calls or people coming in and out of the office inhibit good listening. Also, environments that create feelings of inequality in status discourage effective listening.

PROJECT MANAGERS MUST BE AWARE of these barriers to effective listening that might be caused by interpersonal conflict, distractions, management response to new ideas or the overall project climate. They should try to minimize these barriers by nurturing better understanding and good working relationships necessary to effective communication among project participants.

The role of perceptions. To most people, perceptions are important simply because they are their own—feelings and beliefs about themselves, others and the world that are based on their cultural backgrounds, past experiences, judgments, values, emotional reactions and personalities.[14] These perceptions play a very significant role in communication. For example, different people get different meanings from the same message because of differences in their perceptions. Powerful as they are, however, perceptions can be influenced by proper communication (written, verbal or nonverbal). Figure 1.1 shows how some of the common sources of perceptual differences impact the communication process, and how the effect of perceptual differences is reduced when individuals share common ideas and experiences.

Perceptual differences influence the behavior of people, which in turn can affect success in communication. For example, when perceptual differences occur, people tend to:[14]

- Jump to conclusions
- Confuse facts with opinions
- Make frozen evaluations (those that cannot be easily changed).

Overcoming differences in perceptions. Mistaken perceptions (regardless of the reason) often lead to communication problems and poor relationships among project participants. Many people make judgments based on their own perceptions, especially when the atmosphere is tense and there is already misunderstanding and lack of trust. However, it is possible to overcome perceptual differences by handling situations appropriately. Here are some ideas that can be used to overcome differences in perception as a listener or a speaker:[14]

As a listener, check your perceptions continually, by stating your observations about body language and your interpretation of it and asking for verification or clarification: "I noticed you covered your mouth with your hands; does that mean you are uncertain about the words I used in that proposal? Am I reading you accurately?"

As a speaker you should strive to be specific, state the facts, and stay neutral. Avoid labeling and use non-judgmental, non-punishing language. One technique for remaining neutral while injecting a positive tone into communication is known as the "I message." When using the "I message," a speaker refrains from naming, criticizing, blaming, or even referring to the person they are talking to. They confine their remarks to communicating their personal feelings, opinions, and observations. For example,

Table 1.4 What Makes A Good Listener?

The Poor Listener...	The Good Listener...
Always interrupts	Does not interrupt
Is impatient	Waits until the end, then asks questions
Makes hasty judgments	Asks for clarification
Shows disinterest (poor posture, wandering eyes)	Pays close attention
Doesn't try to understand	Verifies understanding by repeating what was said
Doesn't respond	Gives feedback: smiles, nods, or frowns
Mentally prepares an argument to "win"	Avoids arguing and its negative effects on relationship
Reacts to person, loses temper	Responds to idea, not to person
Fidgets with pen, paper clips	Gets rid of distractions
Goes off the subject	Concentrates on both the words and the feelings behind them; stays on track.

instead of saying, "You didn't turn in your report on time," which the listener might interpret as critical, the speaker might say, "I don't seem to have that report yet. Is it ready?"

Repeat instructions to confirm that exact meaning of what you meant or wanted to communicate has been understood.

When information-gathering, ask, "Did you personally observe?" and "When?" This forces people to say only what they have observed and are sure of. It takes out personal biases and opinions that may distort the message.

Mistaken perceptions (if not corrected immediately) can become ingrained and significantly impact subsequent understanding and interrelationships among project participants. Project managers should analyze and evaluate perceptual differences and try to overcome them. The key to overcoming differences in perceptions is to work on increasing mutual understanding by developing an area of common ground and shared experiences. This area is illustrated by the overlap between the two circles in Figure 1.1. To develop this area, one can ascertain possible common interests or influences.

Effective listening is a give-and-take process. It creates a better environment for influencing, negotiating, conflict resolution, problem solving,

Human Resource Skills for the Project Manager

and decision making. Barriers to effective communication can be caused by closed communication in the task, the relationship, or the environment dimensions of communication. Therefore it is important that project managers recognize these barriers to effective listening and the role perceptions play in listening and take steps to overcome these barriers to effective communication.

Guidelines for active listening

Active listeners are active receivers and are often very effective communicators. (However, sometimes a good listener may be a poor speaker or vice versa due to shyness or other personal habits.) They are equally aware, in addition to the verbal component of communication, of the influence of vocal tones, facial expressions and other nonverbal components including body language, eye contact, gestures and mannerisms, empathy, dress, surroundings, symbols, interpersonal space. They empathize with the speaker, ask questions to clarify the message, and give frequent feedback so that the sender can evaluate the accuracy of his or her message. The characteristics of poor and good listeners are summarized in Table 1.4.[37]

Effective listening, in a nutshell, requires paying attention to the task, relationship and environment dimensions of communication (see Figure 1.7). It requires one to be genuinely concerned for the individual as a person, be neutral on all subjects, and take an objective approach. It requires patience, which means that you never make decisions for the other party but help them to verbalize their own decisions. Developing mutual trust and respect makes both parties feel comfortable in talking and listening. Project participants must identify and overcome the barriers to effective listening that exist within their own organization. The following practical guidelines for effective listening will help build trust and good relationships and hence enhance team performance. These guidelines emphasize patience, empathy, and creating a permissive and appropriate environment.

Stop talking! Decision makers who do not listen have less information upon which to base decisions—and you cannot listen while you are talking. Remember Epitectus and use your two ears to listen twice as much as you talk. As Polonius said in Shakespeare's *Hamlet,* "Give every man thine ear, but few thy voice."

Show the speaker that you are ready to listen. Put the speaker at ease by creating a "permissive" communication-friendly environment. Some elements of such an environment are:[38]

Silence. A space in the conversation, even if uncomfortable, should be tolerated. It encourages others to talk by signaling that you are ready to listen, and are waiting patiently to hear what they have to say.

Few distractions. Shut the door, put the phone on hold, and refrain from impatient mannerisms such as doodling, tapping pencils, shuffling

Figure 1.7 Active Listening In A Nutshell

A   **Attention** (reduce distractions)

C   **Concern** (for the person, the process, and project objectives

T   Appropriate **timing** (choose a time when neither party is preoccupied)

I   **Involvement** (mental and emotional)

V   **Vocal tones** (represent 38 percent of message)

E   **Eye contact** (shows that you are paying attention)

L   **Look** (observe body language)

I   **Interest** (take interest in other person as a human being)

S   **Summarize** (play back to confirm and verify real meaning of the message)

T   **Territory** (manage the space appropriately; lean forward to reduce distance)

E   **Empathy** (listen "between the words" to understand feelings)

N   **Nod** (to show that you understand)

papers, opening mail. These communicate lack of time and/or respect for the speaker.

A receptive attitude. Make an effort to empathize with the speaker's point of view. Listen for the total meaning, not just for points of opposition. Use one ear to listen for the meaning of the words, and the other to "hear" the feelings behind them. Allow plenty of time for the communication to take place—if it runs over, end it in a manner sensitive to the speaker's feelings, not by interrupting, walking away or repeatedly checking your watch.

Ask questions to encourage further communication and the development of a point. This proves to the speaker that you are paying attention.

And, above all, hold your temper. An angry person takes things the wrong way. Suspend judgment while listening in order to avoid putting the speaker on the defensive. Don't argue—even if you win, you lose by impairing the relationship.

48

LISTENING IS AN IMPORTANT PART of project communication. Through active listening, project managers are able to identify problem areas, prepare better negotiation and conflict management strategies, make decisions, and resolve problems among clients, project team members, and other stakeholders. Active listeners are also effective listeners because they really become involved in the communication process. Active listening develops a better appreciation of what the other person is thinking and feeling because giving and asking for feedback clarifies meaning. Failure to listen effectively not only creates problems but also affects business relationships.

Communication Styles and the Project Life Cycle

A project manager uses communication more than any other skill set to manage the project throughout its life cycle and ensure that team members are working cohesively and resolving problems. Included in this communication skill set are various communication styles which are a combination of two dimensions:[14]

1. The thinking and decision-making approach, which varies from logical (sequential) to intuitive (random), and
2. The action style, which varies from concrete (hands-on) to abstract (research-based).

When these two dimensions are combined they produce four major communication styles (see Figure 1.8), all of which have their application to project needs at various times in the life cycle. These styles are:[14,39]

Concrete-sequential. This "Mr./Ms. Fix-it" likes to focus on ideas and tasks, thinks systematically and predictably, and wants to complete tasks and minimize change.

Abstract-sequential. This person is an organizer who relies on logical analysis and systematic planning to solve problems. Abstract-sequential communicators are people- and task-oriented, which makes them effective team builders. They prefer to have all information before making a decision and they know how to control information and resources.

Concrete-random. This explorer/entrepreneur type relies on people and technology, finds practical use for theories and models, makes decisions after thorough analysis and evaluation, and excels at facilitating planning sessions, discussions and changes.

Abstract-random. This intuitive free-thinker has "the vision thing." He or she views experiences from different perspectives, sees the big picture and the long-term view, and makes a good brainstormer because he or she can listen actively and enjoy the process of generating new ideas.

Project management is a structured but flexible process for producing a new end result. Its success depends upon effective application of communication skills in a two-step sequence: first plan, then produce. This sequence is the genesis of every successful project life cycle.[39] For

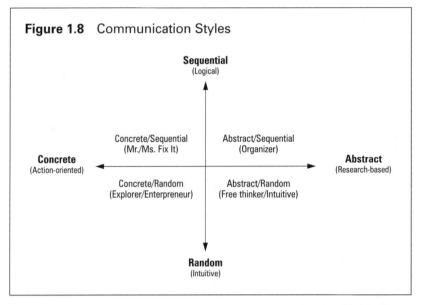

Figure 1.8 Communication Styles

Sequential
(Logical)

Concrete/Sequential
(Mr./Ms. Fix It)

Abstract/Sequential
(Organizer)

Concrete
(Action-oriented)

Abstract
(Research-based)

Concrete/Random
(Explorer/Enterpreneur)

Abstract/Random
(Free thinker/Intuitive)

Random
(Intuitive)

Source: Vijay K. Verma. 1995. Flying to Project Success on Wings of Communication. 1995. *Proceedings of the Project Management Institute Seminar/Symposium.* Upper Darby, PA: Project Management Institute, p. 566. Data adapted from *Interpersonal Communication Skills Workbook* used in seminars presented by Career Track of Boulder, CO.

example, the planning phase includes the concept and development phases of a typical four-phase life cycle, whereas the production phase includes execution and finishing. While four phases are considered typical, in many industries projects are broken down into five, six, or even as many as nine phases. In some projects, for example, a pre-formulation (feasibility study) phase is included in the planning phase.

The planning phase of a project involves the development of project goals, technical requirements and plans for implementation. The main focus is on flushing out customer needs, which may require a number of iterations and reruns to optimize project effectiveness. Visioning, intelligence-gathering, and creativity are all important elements of this phase, which places an emphasis on free thinking, exploring new ideas and encouraging creativity.

In the production phase, the focus is on efficiency in meeting customer needs within specified constraints. This is achieved through effective communication with emphasis on organizing logically, evaluating alternatives and fixing problems without losing sight of details and administrative issues. Figure 1.9 shows the phases of a sample project life cycle with the factors that should be emphasized during each cycle and the most suitable blend of communication styles to optimize productivity during each phase. Project managers should recognize that the characteristics of each communication style have their place in the different phases of the project

Human Resource Skills for the Project Manager

Figure 1.9 Communication and the Project Life Cycle

Phase		Major Attributes/ Emphasis	Communication Style/Blend
Plan (Flesh out customer requirements)	Feasibility Study (pre-formulation)	• Sense of vision • "Big picture" (conceptual) • Analysis	Absract/Random and Abstract/ Sequential
	Conceptual (Formulation)	• Listening • Creativity • Alignment	Abstract/Random
	Development	• Participative/ acceptance and commitment • Integration • Cooperative	Concrete/Random
Produce (Meet customer requirements)	Execution	• Re-alignment and organization • Teamwork and synergy • Trust	Abstract/Sequential and Concrete/ Random
	Finishing	• Transfer of product and information	Concrete/ Sequential

Source: Vijay K. Verma. 1995. Flying to Project Success on Wings of Communication. 1995. *Proceedings of the Project Management Institute Seminar/Symposium.* Upper Darby, PA: Project Management Institute, p. 566.

life cycle, and identify the appropriate team members to supply those necessary styles. In addition, the individual manager should learn to be flexible in adapting his or her personal communication style as much as possible to suit the requirements of the different phases of the project life cycle. Self-assessment Exercise A in the Appendix will help the project manager determine his or her preferred communication style.

Summary

Communication carries a special importance in project management, since most of the problems in a project environment can be traced to some kind of communication problem. The communication skills of project managers are often put to the test by overlapping areas of responsibility, gray lines of authority, delegation problems, lack of motivation, complex organizational structure and conflicts with and among various project participants. Effective communication helps to gain interpersonal acceptance and commitment and can also serve as a good motivating factor. It is the key to integration and interface management.

Communication is a process that requires a two-way effort. It can be verbal, nonverbal or written in a formal or informal mode. To be an effective communicator, the project manager must thoroughly understand the goals and processes of interpersonal communication, plan properly to design and implement communication strategies and use feedback to ensure the accuracy of the message. The macro-barriers (related to environment) and micro-barriers (related to a specific situation) of communication in a project must be identified and remedied to achieve effective interpersonal communication. Appropriate communication efforts may be blocked due to these barriers, leading to chaos and project management problems. Project managers pay attention to the nonverbal elements of communication, such as vocal tones, facial expressions, and body language to complement the verbal message wherever necessary and possible.

Communication in a project environment can be of several types, including interpersonal, informal, project management information system, and communication with the community. Along with informal communication, project managers must manage the formal channels of communication and maintain communication links across the organization interfaces. For example, upward communication is important to report project status to top management and resolve priority conflicts, while downward communication directs, implements and evaluates the efforts of team members, and lateral communication is used to negotiate resources, functions, and resolve conflicts with functional managers and other project stakeholders.

Project participants spend a significant amount of their time in project meetings. When well planned and well managed, these meetings can be very productive. Project managers, who often act as chairpersons of meetings, should plan, direct, manage, and control the meetings by following the guidelines outlined in this chapter.

Effective communication is the key to high team performance and can be achieved by creating openness (task and relationship) in communication, developing trust to achieve accuracy in communication and providing positive support and counseling to project team members when needed. Project managers must create an environment that facilitates effective communication, encourages new ideas and creativity in problem solving, and minimizes closed communication.

Listening is a vital component of communication because it helps in identifying problem areas; in negotiating effectively, in resolving conflict, making decisions and solving problems. Just as they "read between the lines," project managers must be able to "listen between the words." For effective listening, they must recognize the importance of verbal and nonverbal listening behaviors (including body language). They should use gestures and body language consciously (with consideration for cultural differences) to put people at ease and enhance communication.

Perceptions form our personal reality. Therefore, project managers must recognize the role of perception in gaining understanding and try to overcome perceptual differences both as a speaker and a listener. They should create an environment that minimizes barriers to effective listening. Active listening requires patience, self-control, empathy and a willingness to see things from the other person's point of view. In addition to improving communications, it generally facilitates the development of mutual trust, respect and good working relationships, enhancing overall team performance.

There are four communication styles resulting from the blending of the thinking or decision-making dimension and the action style dimension. These styles—concrete-sequential, abstract-sequential, concrete-random and abstract-random—each have their strengths and are each appropriate to different phases of the project life cycle. Project managers must learn to identify these styles in themselves and in others and to maximize the benefits of each style by utilizing it at the appropriate time in the project life cycle.

Outline

Persistent effort to achieve comes from the heart, not from the head.

— Anonymous

Motivation in a Project Environment

IN ALL PROJECTS, in all industries, *people* use their human skills to define the goals, prepare the plans, and implement those plans in order to meet project goals within specified constraints. Project managers, who are expected to get the work done through project teams and other project stakeholders, must emphasize the human factors in project management to create an environment that encourages open and effective communication; an environment in which everyone involved in the project feels motivated and committed to produce their best. Most project participants want job satisfaction; a sense of accomplishment, achievement and growth; and enough financial compensation and other rewards to live the kind of life they feel is important. Job satisfaction is the general attitude of a person toward his or her job. In the most general sense, it is a pleasurable or positive emotional state resulting from the appraisal of one's job or job experience.[1] This positive feeling occurs when the work is in harmony with needs and values of the individual and provides challenges and opportunities that they can take pride in. Satisfied project team members do their best at work and produce quality results. Therefore, project managers must understand the dynamics of human behavior so that they can create an environment in which project team members feel motivated.

This chapter deals with the definition of motivation, basic motivational processes, what motivation depends upon, and the importance of a project manager's own motivation in a project. General theories of motivation and some practical guidelines to help motivate people in a project environment are discussed, along with motivational factors related to project task, personal drives, project manager, and the organizational climate. ■

General Overview of Motivation

Motivation is an intrinsic phenomenon. Extrinsic satisfaction only leads to movements, not motivation.

— Frederick Herzberg

Overall project success is dependent upon the motivation and performance of project team members and other stakeholders. A highly motivated project team means substantial cost savings, better quality, and higher team productivity, satisfaction and morale. Lack of motivation leads to conflict, stress, low morale and productivity, and sometimes to a total failure in meeting project objectives. While it is well known that motivated and satisfied project team members always do their best and produce quality results, it is important to also recognize that motivation is an *internal* phenomenon that causes individuals to contribute extra effort *voluntarily*. Therefore, project managers must understand the dynamics of human behavior in order to continually motivate the project team members.

What is motivation?

In general, motivation refers to the internal drives within a person that cause that person to willingly devote extra effort in a specific, goal-directed manner. Motivation has been variously defined as:

- The process of inducing an individual to work toward achieving project objectives while also satisfying personal objectives. Motivation helps people energize themselves to overcome political, bureaucratic, and resource barriers to change.[2]
- The inner state that causes an individual to behave in a way that ensures the accomplishment of their goals; or the creation of a work environment that provides people with the opportunity to gain maximum psychological, social and economic satisfaction.[3]
- A drive within a person, fueled by human needs or wants, to achieve personal objectives.[4]

These definitions have some elements and underlying ideas in common. For example:

- Motivation influences productivity.
- Motivation is an intrinsic and internal phenomenon or process.
- Motivation encourages people to achieve their objectives.
- Motivation involves psychological, social and economic satisfaction.
- Motivation means the creation of an environment that helps everyone achieve work-related objectives while gaining the maximum personal satisfaction.

Basic motivational process

The best way to determine what motivates people? Ask them.

— Anonymous

In spite of a slight increase in productivity, tough global competition has led to painful downsizing, concessions in union agreements, financial re-

Human Resource Skills for the Project Manager

structuring, and the closing or modernizing of obsolete plants and facilities. All these changes, which force companies to do more with less, emphasize the need for project managers to understand people and to develop new ways to motivate their "human capital." While everyone may not agree on what motivates people, there is general agreement that the organizational and work environment must provide an atmosphere in which:[5]

- People have a desire not just to join an organization but also to remain and grow in it.
- People want to fulfill their responsibilities and perform the tasks assigned.
- People want to go beyond routine performance and demonstrate some creativity and innovation in their work.

Therefore, to be effective, project managers must understand the motivational process and stimulate project participants to be high-performance workers on an individual as well a group basis. At the same time, project managers should try to get everyone's commitment to contribute creatively to the project team and to the organization as a whole. In establishing a motivational environment, project managers must ensure that team members' personal goals are, as far as possible, congruent with organizational goals.

One motivational principle states that people's performance is dependent upon their self-motivation and level of ability: that is, performance is a function of ability and motivation. According to this principle, in order to perform a task satisfactorily, it is necessary to have both the ability and the desire to attain a high level of performance.[5]

Ability, or a person's talent to perform the task, may include intellectual competencies such as technical, analytical and communicating skills, and manual competencies such as physical strength, stamina, and dexterity. However, having ability in terms of intellectual and manual skills is not sufficient. A personal desire to achieve high performance plays a very important role in the motivational process and hence influences overall productivity. A manager can facilitate this process by minimizing roadblocks that hinder the full use of a team member's ability.

To understand the motivational process, one must understand what drives human behavior, what direction this behavior takes, and how to maintain positive behavior.[5] In addition, it is important to identify the core phases and any complications in this process.

The six core phases in the motivational process. Since motivation is an internal phenomenon, it is triggered by needs and wants that create drives within people. Motivated, they are willing to put in extra effort and take action to satisfy their objectives and meet their needs and wants. To understand the motivational process, one must understand the dynamics of human behavior to determine why and how individuals behave in certain ways to satisfy their needs. There are six core phases in the motivational process.[5]

1. Identify the person's needs. Needs are deficiencies that act as energizers. These deficiencies may be expressed as psychological needs (the need for recognition or opportunity to work on a visible/high-profile project), or they may be physiological needs (food, clothes, shelter), or social affiliation needs (friendship)

2. Create drives. Needs give rise to wants or desires that create drives within people, that is, a state of unrest or dissatisfaction that the person wants to reduce or eliminate.

3. Select goal-directed behavior. Stimulated by such an inner drive, a person develops a course of action to achieve a goal that will meet the need and ease the state of unrest. This goal, a specific result that the individual wants to achieve, acts as a force to make the person work harder and achieve high performance. Thus, we say that motivation is goal-directed.[6]

4. Perform the task. By exerting extra effort and performing tasks that will help them reach their goals, people achieve high performance. Successful accomplishment of desirable goals leads to a reduction in need deficiencies and the tensions or dissatisfactions created by them. For example, the goal of advancement or promotion and an expectation that working long hours will help get that promotion may create tension or a state of unrest; the promotion itself relieves both the need and the tension.

When people believe that specific behaviors may relieve tension, they act, directing their behavior toward the goal of reducing this tension or state of unrest. For instance, project managers who are high achievers may try to work on high-profile projects in the hope of gaining more visibility and more influence on important organizational goals.

5. Receive feedback. People are personally satisfied when they receive positive feedback and when project goals are achieved successfully. Also, receiving recognition or rewards for achieving high performance reinforce that their behavior is appropriate and should be repeated. Likewise, punishment or negative feedback received for major or repeated failures suggest that they should not repeat the behavior, since it is likely to produce undesirable results.

6. Reassess needs and goals. Once people receive feedback in the form of either rewards or punishments, they reassess their needs and goals and make appropriate adjustments in their strategies, actions, and behaviors.

Figure 2.1 shows the motivational process in which needs act as motives for human behavior and the core phases in this process.[4,5]

Complications in the motivational process. The general model just described presents an oversimplified view of the motivational process. In the real world, of course, the process is not so clear-cut. Some common complications in the motivation process are:[5]

Figure 2.1 Effect of Needs on Human Behavior; Core Phases of the Motivation Process

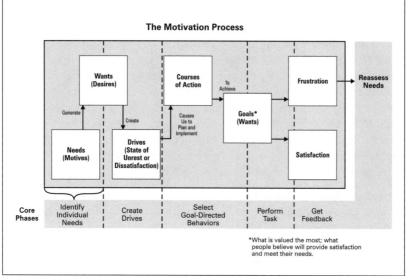

The Motivation Process

*What is valued the most; what people believe will provide satisfaction and meet their needs.

Motives can only be inferred and cannot be seen. For example, some project team members may have similar abilities and training but may still produce higher-quality results than others. This is because of differences in their levels of motivation, which can be seen only after comparing their outputs.

Needs are dynamic in nature. The needs of individuals change with time and circumstances and may sometimes conflict with each other. For example, project participants who put in longer hours in order to get a promotion may find that this conflicts directly with their needs for affiliation and their desire to be with their families.

People rank and select their motives differently. People differ in terms of what motivates them. For example, some people may want more money while others may want opportunities to work on selected projects or appropriate recognition for achieving high performance.

People apply different energy levels in pursuing their motives. A need itself or its relative importance may change with time and circumstances, affecting the level of effort that people are willing to put forth to satisfy that need. Therefore, the project manager must communicate informally and develop effective interpersonal relationships to stay on top of what motivates people, how much, and why.

Theories of Motivation

Preconceived notions are the locks on the door to wisdom.

— *Merry Brown*

Motivation is dynamic and complex. What motivates a few or most of the team members in one project may not be so successful in other projects. Project managers must appreciate that the effectiveness of their motivational techniques depends upon the situation, the organizational environment and the behavior of people—all of which keep changing.

There are several motivational theories and tactics.[7] Understanding them can help the project manager in motivating project participants. The major theories of motivation can be grouped into two categories:[5] *content theories* attempt to determine the link between intrinsic factors and certain behaviors, whereas *process theories* explore how personal factors interact and influence each other to produce behaviors.

Content theories of motivation

Content theories deal with the factors within a person that energize, direct, and stop behavior. These theories focus on identifying the specific factors that motivate people. Some of these factors may be:

• Good salary, working conditions and friendly co-workers
• Food, clothes and shelter to satisfy basic physiological needs
• Job security or working in a financially stable industry
• Need for advancement and growth
• Need for achievement, power and affiliation.

Four of the most widely recognized content theories of motivation are Maslow's Hierarchy of Needs Theory; Alderfer's Existence, Relatedness, Growth (ERG) Needs Theory; Herzberg's Motivator-Hygiene Theory; and McClelland's Achievement Motivation Theory.[5]

Although these theories are general in nature, their concepts are valid in a project environment as well. Project managers should understand the various theories of motivation along with their strengths and weaknesses. Extensive literature is available about these theories, but a brief discussion of each is given below.

Hierarchy of Needs Theory. Maslow[8] developed a very useful model to explain the motivational process in relation to the way that human needs change throughout the developmental life cycle. This model, the oldest among the content theories of motivation, is universally applicable and still valid in understanding the process of motivation.

Maslow suggested that within every human being there exists a hierarchy of five types of needs. Some assumptions underlying this hierarchy include:

• Motivation springs from an unsatisfied need. When one need is satisfied (or, as Maslow said "substantially satiated"), another need emerges

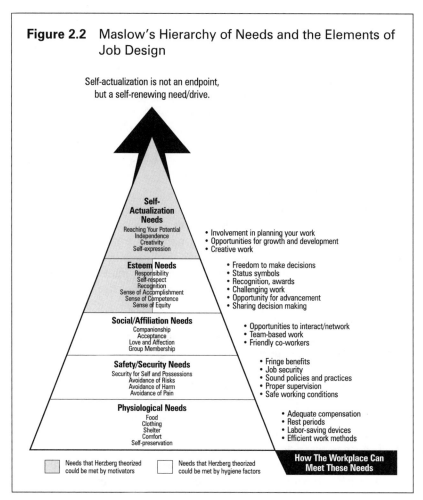

Figure 2.2 Maslow's Hierarchy of Needs and the Elements of Job Design

Self-actualization is not an endpoint, but a self-renewing need/drive.

Self-Actualization Needs
Reaching Your Potential
Independence
Creativity
Self-expression

• Involvement in planning your work
• Opportunities for growth and development
• Creative work

Esteem Needs
Responsibility
Self-respect
Recognition
Sense of Accomplishment
Sense of Competence
Sense of Equity

• Freedom to make decisions
• Status symbols
• Recognition, awards
• Challenging work
• Opportunity for advancement
• Sharing decision making

Social/Affiliation Needs
Companionship
Acceptance
Love and Affection
Group Membership

• Opportunities to interact/network
• Team-based work
• Friendly co-workers

Safety/Security Needs
Security for Self and Possessions
Avoidance of Risks
Avoidance of Harm
Avoidance of Pain

• Fringe benefits
• Job security
• Sound policies and practices
• Proper supervision
• Safe working conditions

Physiological Needs
Food
Clothing
Shelter
Comfort
Self-preservation

• Adequate compensation
• Rest periods
• Labor-saving devices
• Efficient work methods

Needs that Herzberg theorized could be met by motivators

Needs that Herzberg theorized could be met by hygiene factors

How The Workplace Can Meet These Needs

Source: Hierarchy of Needs adapted from Abraham Maslow's *Motivation and Personality*, 1970, Harper and Row.

in its place; thus, at any given time people are struggling to satisfy some unsatisfied need.

• Lower-level needs must be substantially satisfied before higher-level needs can be addressed. Generally people do not skip a level in between.
• The dynamics of needs are complex and several needs may affect behavior at any one time.
• Higher-level needs can be satisfied in more ways than lower-level needs.

Figure 2.2 illustrates the five sets of needs and the management tactics that address them.[8]

1. Physiological needs include the basic needs for food, water, and shelter. People must concentrate on satisfying these needs before they are able to worry about higher-level needs. Project managers should recognize that most people cannot be concerned about their work until their physiological needs are satisfied. Managers who focus on these needs ensure that workers are physically safe, comfortable, and adequately compensated.

2. Safety and security needs include the needs for safety, stability, and protection from physical and emotional harm. People who are motivated primarily by safety needs value their jobs as a defense against the risk of being unable to satisfy basic needs. Meeting this level of needs also means protection from violence or sexual harassment in the workplace, and addressing job safety issues. Managers who feel that safety needs are important and want to use them to motivate people tend to emphasize policies, rules, job security, and fringe benefits. While these elements are important, an overemphasis on safety needs can cause managers to be less likely to encourage creativity and innovation, and the team members, in turn, simply follow the rules and instructions without taking any individual initiative.

3. Social or affiliation needs include the needs for affection, friendship, acceptance, love, and a feeling of belonging. Social needs emerge after both physiological and safety needs are satisfied. People who feel motivated by these needs value their work as an opportunity for finding and establishing friendly interpersonal relationships. Project managers and team leaders who are so motivated tend to act in a supportive or even permissive manner. They try to create a participative climate and emphasize team members' acceptance by their co-workers, team-based norms, and extracurricular activities (company picnics, summer barbeques, Christmas parties and sports programs).

4. Esteem needs include internal factors such as self-respect, self-worth, autonomy, and a personal sense of achievement, as well as external factors such as status, recognition, and attention. People who get "turned on" by esteem needs want others to accept them on their own merits and to perceive them as competent and intelligent. Project managers who consider these needs when motivating their team members give them public rewards and recognition for superior performance. These managers use lapel pins, trophies, appreciation certificates or letters, articles in the company newsletter, achievement lists on bulletin boards, or attendance at conferences and seminars. By promoting their team members' pride in their work and creating within them a sense of ownership of their jobs, the project manager enhances their commitment and productivity.

5. Self-actualization needs are the highest-level needs in the hierarchy. They are the source of a person's drive to become what he or she is capable of becoming. Self-actualization is not an end point but a lifelong process. As the self-actualized person strives for higher goals, the need for self-actualization increases further. People who strive for self-actualization

Human Resource Skills for the Project Manager

experience acceptance by others and have increased problem-solving ability. Managers who emphasize self-actualization tend to promote self-directed work teams and give more autonomy to their team members in designing their own jobs. They offer them special challenges and assignments that enhance their unique skills. Project managers may be normally limited in giving opportunities and therefore they must be open, flexible and willing to consider opportunities that may satisfy self-actualization needs.

Each level of needs influences human behavior. Therefore, project managers and their overall organization are wise to assist project team members and other participants in their search for satisfaction in every category of needs. Maslow identifies the goals that people typically seek for the satisfaction of needs and suggests the types of behavior that will help achieve these goals. Studies have shown that the fulfillment of needs differs from person to person depending upon job description, age, race, and the size of the organization. Yet people normally progress from one level of needs to the next without skipping any levels. This also means that if a self-actualized person is suddenly put in a situation where, for example, physical safety is threatened, he or she can fall back lower to a lower motivational level (Level 1 or 2).

ERG Needs Theory. Alderfer developed a theory based upon the concept that the individual has three sets of basic needs: Existence, Relatedness, and Growth, which can be described as follows:[9]

Existence needs are similar to Maslow's physiological and safety needs. They include material needs that can be satisfied by air, water, food, clothes, shelter, salary, fringe benefits and working conditions.

Relatedness needs are similar to Maslow's social needs and can be met by establishing and maintaining interpersonal relationships with superiors, co-workers, subordinates, friends and family.

Growth needs are similar to Maslow's esteem and self-actualization needs and refer to an individual's efforts to explore opportunities for personal development and growth by contributing to creativity and productivity at work.

The categories of needs suggested by Alderfer are similar to those in Maslow's theory. However, the two theories differ in terms of how people satisfy the different sets of needs. According to Maslow, unfulfilled needs act as motivators and people progress to higher-level needs only after the preceding lower-level needs are satisfied. ERG theory suggests that, in addition to this fulfillment progression process, there also exists a frustration-regression process. This means that if, for example, an individual is frustrated in trying to satisfy growth needs, frustration will lead to regression and relatedness needs will re-emerge as a major motivating force.

This theory provides an insight for project team leaders. For instance, if a project team leader sees that the satisfaction of growth needs of a par-

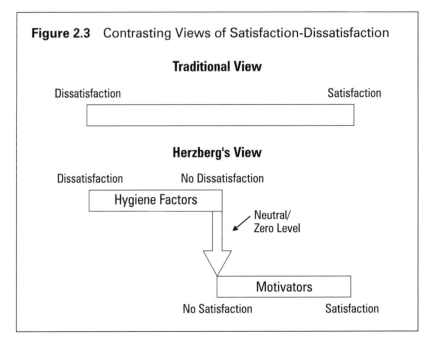

Figure 2.3 Contrasting Views of Satisfaction-Dissatisfaction

Traditional View

Dissatisfaction   Satisfaction

Herzberg's View

Dissatisfaction   No Dissatisfaction

Hygiene Factors

Neutral/
Zero Level

Motivators

No Satisfaction   Satisfaction

ticular team member is limited due to tasks assigned to him or her, then the team member could be encouraged to satisfy lower-level needs, i.e., relatedness or existence needs.[10] However, sometimes highly persistent and self-motivated project personnel may continue to give importance to a certain level of needs and keep trying to satisfy that in spite of frustrations and failures.

Both Maslow's and Alderfer's theories of need offer good insight about motivation. Although both theories refer to different categories of needs, both theories agree that satisfying needs is an important part of motivating people in a project environment.

Motivator/Hygiene Theory. Herzberg's motivator-hygiene theory is one of the most controversial theories of motivation, due to two features.[5] First, it stresses that some job factors lead to satisfaction, whereas others can only prevent dissatisfaction and are not sources of satisfaction. In contrast to a traditional view, Herzberg's view postulates that job satisfaction and dissatisfaction do not exist on a single continuum; instead, there is a neutral (zero) level (representing no dissatisfaction), that separates the two continuums (see Figure 2.3).[11] Herzberg further suggested that this zero level may escalate as people expect and demand more in order to merely stay at the "no dissatisfaction" level.

Herzberg[12] suggested that there are two types of factors associated with the motivation process, namely *hygiene factors* and *motivators*. Hygiene factors relate to the *work environment* while motivators relate to *work itself*.

Hygiene factors, if provided appropriately, prevent dissatisfaction. Likewise, if not provided, they can create dissatisfaction. Good hygiene is necessary but not sufficient to achieve worker satisfaction. These factors may bring about peace, but not necessarily motivation. They will be placating people rather than motivating them. These factors include:

- Compensation
- Company policies and administration
- Working conditions
- Relationships with supervisors and subordinates
- Relationships with peers
- Level of supervision (too much or too little).

Though the absence or inappropriate administration of these factors leads to unhappiness, their presence does not guarantee workers' contentment. Since they can only prevent dissatisfaction, they are also called *maintenance factors*. These factors usually are helpful in motivating workers only on a temporary, short-term basis. After a while, worker satisfaction caused by such measures goes back to a zero level and that zero level escalates each time, creating a higher threshold of "no dissatisfaction."

Motivating factors (motivators), by contrast, increase job satisfaction and are more permanent. Some examples of motivators are:

- Opportunity for advancement
- Opportunity for achievement
- The challenge or variety inherent in the work itself
- Sense of responsibility
- Opportunity for recognition
- Opportunity for personal growth.

While motivating factors can be used in traditional organizations, project work situations are characterized by desirable motivating and hygiene factors. Generally, people are interested in working on projects because they want challenging work assignments; flexibility, variety, and more autonomy; and the opportunity to earn more money. Most participants in a project could be motivated through:

Job Enrichment. Expanding a job vertically by adding planning and evaluating responsibilities is a very effective approach, as it offers challenges to project participants. Job enrichment programs must be designed and administered very carefully. A successful job enrichment program:

- Relaxes some controls while retaining accountability
- Increases an individual's accountability for his or her own work and gives visibility
- Gives a person a complete natural unit of work (module, area, division, etc.)
- Grants more autonomy or additional authority to allow increased freedom

- Keeps the worker (not just the supervisor) informed of progress and status
- Offers challenging assignments opportunities
- Offers specialized tasks or a variety of tasks.

These changes motivate the worker by giving him or her increased responsibility, authority, recognition, and information power, as well as opportunities for professional and personal growth,] and achievement.[3]

Flexible Time. In most cases, project team members are professional, creative, self-motivated and self-responsible. In light of these attributes, they should be given greater flexibility to choose their working hours within company policies and overall constraints. Although participants should be available to optimize the communication among themselves, contractors, and other external stakeholders to achieve the desired level and rate of progress at all times, the choice of starting and finishing times can be as flexible as the project phase and organizational situation allows. Table 2.1 shows the advantages and disadvantages of using flextime programs.[3]

Money and motivation. Herzberg's motivational theory seems to suggest that money is a hygiene factor and does not work as a long-term motivator. It does appear to be a hygiene factor in that an inappropriate level of monetary compensation in project environments causes dissatisfaction in project participants, leading to lower morale and productivity. However, money (given as a bonus/incentive to beat the schedule and budget, etc.) also acts as a positive reinforcement to high performance in a project environment. Inappropriate remuneration systems can act as demotivating factors and create an unhealthy project climate, dragging down the performance level of everyone associated with the project.

Sometimes, it is easy to get so caught up in setting goals, creating enriched jobs and encouraging participation that one forgets that money is one of the major reasons that most people work. Therefore, merit increases based on performance, bonuses on completing projects successfully under budget and ahead of schedule, and other pay incentives should be considered in motivating project managers and project team members.

A review of 80 studies[13] that evaluated motivational methods and their impact on employee productivity supports the importance of money to increase productivity. These studies highlighted the following points regarding the increase in productivity:[13]

- Goal setting alone increased productivity by 16 percent
- Efforts to enrich jobs yielded 8 to 16 percent increase in productivity
- Employee participation in decision making produced a median increase of less than 1 percent
- Monetary incentives led to an average increase of 30 percent in productivity.

This does not imply that management should focus solely on money. However, it is obvious that money is a very important incentive for moti-

Human Resource Skills for the Project Manager

Table 2.1 Flextime: Pros and Cons

Advantages	Disadvantages
Improved employee attitude and morale	Lack of supervision during some hours of work (problems not resolved quickly)
Suitable schedule for working parents	Key people unavailable at certain times
Workers avoid peak traffic periods	Understaffing at times may impact customer service
Suitable for "early birds" who work best before office interruptions begin	Difficulty accommodating employees whose output is others' input
Easy scheduling of personal appointments (medical, dental, etc.)	Employee abuse of flexibility
Accommodation of employee's leisure time activities	Difficulty in planning work schedules
Increased efficiency	Problems in keeping track of hours
Decreased absenteeism	Difficulty in scheduling meetings at mutually convenient times
Decreased turnover	Difficulty in coordinating projects
Workers gain sense of independence, ownership of job with a team	Problems when working interdependently

Source: Edward G. Thomas. 1987. Workers Who Set Thier Own Time Clocks. *Business and Society Review* (Spring): p. 50. Reprinted by permission of the publisher.

vating project participants. If money is removed completely as an incentive, people are not going to show up for work. The same can't be said of goals, enriched work, or opportunities for participation.

The motivator/hygiene theory has some drawbacks and has been criticized on several points:[11]

- The theory seems reasonable, because when things are going well and the motivational level of all project participants is high, managers and team members take the credit themselves. However, when things fail, they blame it on external factors.
- The reliability of Herzberg's methodology in drawing conclusions has also been questioned. Researchers who interpreted the responses might have interpreted similar responses differently, making it impossible to accurately assess the data.

- No overall measure of satisfaction was utilized. The study ignores the fact that a person may dislike part of his or her job, yet consider it acceptable due to personal constraints or circumstances. In this sense, it ignores situational variables.
- The theory is inconsistent with previous research.
- Herzberg assumed a definite, clear relationship between satisfaction and productivity. However, his research methodology focused only on satisfaction, not on productivity. Therefore, his research is only relevant under the assumption that there is a close relationship between satisfaction and productivity.[12]

Herzberg's theory is very popular in spite of these criticisms. Job satisfaction is one of the key factors that increases motivation in people. In terms of job satisfaction, motivating factors (motivators) influence the degree of job satisfaction and hygiene (maintenance factors) influence the degree of job dissatisfaction. Job enrichment is among the important techniques for motivating project participants and much of the enthusiasm for job enrichment can be attributed to Herzberg's findings and recommendations.

Figure 2.2 shows how Herzberg's theory intersects with Maslow's Hierarchy of Needs, indicating which levels of the hierarchy can be satisfied by desirable motivating factors or hygiene factors. For example, esteem needs can be satisfied by a hygiene factor (a private parking space or other status symbol) as well as by a motivating factor (such as a reward for outstanding performance).

Achievement Motivation Theory. According to McClelland's theory, there are three relevant motives or needs in work situations:[14]

1. *The need for achievement.* The drive to excel, strive to succeed and achieve performance standards.

2. *The need for power.* The need to influence the behavior of others to make them behave in a way that they would not behave otherwise.

3. *The need for affiliation or association.* The desire for friendly and close personal relationships at work.

Achievement motivation theory suggests that people generally have some achievement motives and that they are motivated according to the strength of their desire either to achieve high levels of performance or to succeed in competitive situations.

This theory supports the view that there is a correlation between achievement, power, and affiliation motives and the overall motivation and performance achieved in a project. High achievers perform well in jobs that offer personal responsibility, moderate challenges, and feedback. Effective project managers generally have a high need for power and relatively low for affiliation. High achievers have three major characteristics:[14]

1. They like to select their own goals.
2. They set difficult but achievable goals.

68

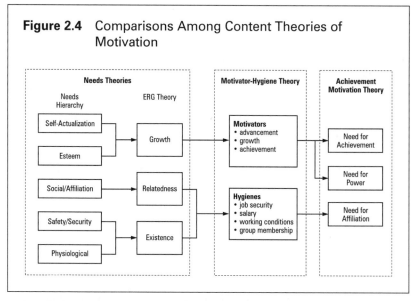

Figure 2.4 Comparisons Among Content Theories of Motivation

3. They prefer assignments that provide immediate feedback.

High achievers are aware of their strengths and limitations. They are self-confident and place a high price tag on their services. They believe that monetary incentives must match their achievement and adequacy, and if this is not done, lack of money may create dissatisfaction. When achievement motivation is successful in a project, project participants like to meet high-performance challenges. However, achievement motivation does not operate when high achievers are performing routine, structured, or boring tasks or when there is no competition.

This theory also suggests that, to motivate project participants, project managers should use the following guidelines:

- Provide periodic feedback because feedback enables project participants to modify their performance to meet project objectives.
- Provide good role models of achievement to be followed.
- Modify the self-images of employees. High achievers have high levels of self-confidence and seek tough challenges and responsibilities.
- Encourage project team members to formulate plans and explore ways to attain them. Empower them to make the decisions for which they are the best qualified.

ALL FOUR CONTENT THEORIES OF MOTIVATION are interrelated. Figure 2.4 shows a comparison among content theories and indicates similarity in some of the components of each theory.[5]

Process theories of motivation

Process theories of motivation attempt to explain and analyze how personal and intrinsic factors interact and influence each other to produce certain types of behavior. Process theories of motivation emphasize the decision-making processes used by individuals and the role of rewards on future performance. These theories suggest that in order to improve project teams' performance, project managers should try to create proper work environments, match skills with tasks and establish clear performance to reward linkages. Project managers must recognize high performance when it occurs and recognize and reward it (if possible) as soon as possible. Since individuals will work harder to obtain rewards that satisfy their important needs than to obtain rewards that do not meet their important needs, project managers must stay in touch with their team members in order to be fully aware of their high-priority personal needs and goals.

The six well-known process theories of motivation are: Theory X-Theory Y; Contingency theory; Goal-setting theory; Expectancy theory; Reinforcement theory; and Equity theory.[5]

Theory X-Theory Y. McGregor developed Theory X and Theory Y, which describe how managers deal with their subordinates.[15] He summarized the two predominant yet opposite sets of assumptions made by managers about human nature and their effect on the motivational level of their employees.

The main assumptions under Theory X are that most people:[4,15,16]
- Dislike their work and will try to avoid it
- Lack ambition and have little capacity for problem solving and creativity
- Prefer constant directions and avoid taking responsibilities and initiatives
- Are motivated only by Maslow's lower level needs (physiological and safety)
- Are self-centered, indifferent to organizational needs and resistant to change.

Theory X assumes that people follow the path of least resistance and are largely motivated by money, position, and punishment. The real tragedy of Theory X is that it is a self-fulfilling prophecy about people. Managers who believe in this theory tend to be authoritarian and suspicious. They impose tight organizational structures, rigid rules/policies, and strict supervisory controls because they believe that subordinates are immature and lack a sense of responsibility.[16]

Theory Y, on the other hand, implies a humanistic and supportive approach to managing people. The main assumptions under Theory Y are that most people:[15,16]
- Meet high performance expectations if appropriately motivated and if the work climate is supportive

- Are creative, imaginative, ambitious and committed to meet organizational goals
- Are self-disciplined, can direct and control themselves, desire responsibilities, and accept them willingly
- Are motivated by Maslow's higher levels of needs (esteem and self-actualization).

Managers who subscribe to Theory Y tend to establish less rigidly structured organizations and impose limited supervisory controls. They provide more freedom and the opportunity to participate in planning and decision making. They emphasize opportunities for development and growth.[16]

In a project environment, most project team members are self-motivated and fit in with Theory Y assumptions. Consequently, project managers should encourage creativity, autonomy and high participation, and try to provide challenging assignments and opportunities for professional development and growth. Theory X may be reserved for crisis situations requiring an authoritarian management style.

Theory Z. In the mid-70s, there was a surge of interest in Japanese styles and philosophies of management. Researchers looking into the motivation of Japanese workers, and the attitudes of Japanese management towards them, noted that McGregor's theories did not seem to fit with the realities of the Japanese workplace. In response, Ouchi developed a third theory, Theory Z, which, although not an extension of Theory X-Theory Y, can be related to McGregor's concepts.

Ouchi noted that in Japanese organizations, which are characterized by lifetime employment, consensus decision making, and collective responsibility, management views workers in an egalitarian light, meaning that they are deemed trustworthy and capable of working without close supervision. This is also a characteristic of Theory Y managers; however, because of the unique social underpinnings of the Japanese workplace, Theory Z also postulates that high levels of trust, confidence, and commitment to workers on the part of management lead to high levels of motivation and productivity on the part of the workers.[17]

Ouchi contrasted these Japanese organizations (which he termed "Type J" organizations) with traditional American organizations (Type A) in which short-term employment, autocratic decision making, and explicit, formal controls were the norm. He then postulated that, to the extent that the egalitarian assumptions of Japanese organizations could be incorporated into American organizations, the productivity of American workers could be improved. He called this hybrid organization a "Type Z" organization.

Since most projects are done by skilled people who are generally self-motivated and capable of achieving high performance, the Type Z organization, in which people are motivated by their needs for self-esteem and self-actualization, seems most conducive to project management. (It is generally hard to create a Type J organizational climate in a project environment because of practical difficulties regarding lifetime employment, consensus decision making, and collective responsibility.) And, in fact, many of the companies held up as examples of the Type Z organization—IBM, Hewlett-Packard, Eastman Kodak—place a heavy emphasis on the use of project management practices.[18]

Contingency Theory. This theory, developed by Morse and Lorsch, was built upon McGregor's Theory Y and Herzberg's theory of hygiene and motivating factors. The research study behind this theory attempted to determine how the fit between an organization's characteristics and its tasks relates to an individual's motivation and suggested that this organization and task fit influences and is influenced by the effectiveness of task performance and individuals' feelings of competence.[19]

This theory implies that people have a central need to achieve a sense of competence and that this need continues to motivate people even after competence is achieved. The ways of fulfilling this need vary from person to person, depending upon how this need interacts with other needs and the strengths of those other needs. Good fit between task and organization leads to competence and hence motivation.[4,19] For example, people working on projects that involve highly structured and organized tasks (assembly lines in manufacturing organizations) perform better under formal procedures, well-defined directions and formal organizational structures. On the other hand, people working on projects with non-routine, unique and unstructured tasks (in high-tech and R&D industries) perform better with less formal control and in a freer form of organizational structure that encourages open communication, creativity and innovation.

Contingency theory suggests that project managers should ensure that tasks assigned to project participants match their skills and that the organizational climate (degree of control, organizational structure) is conducive to help them meet their needs and achieve a sense of competence. Project managers should tailor jobs to fit people and/or provide appropriate training opportunities to develop their skills, knowledge, and attitude in order to enhance their level of competence. Both tasks and people must be analyzed before an appropriate fit can be made.[4,19]

Project managers must know their people well in terms of their strengths and goals in order to assign tasks appropriately. Project participants will feel motivated depending upon how well their tasks match their skills and level of commitment. Genuine support from management can help them meet their need for increased competence.

Goal-Setting Theory. This theory, developed by Latham and Locke,[20] implies that the intention to work toward a goal is a major source of job motivation. It views motivation as coming from an individual's internal drive and desire to achieve goals. For example, clear, specific and challenging goals generally motivate project team members and others involved in a project. Project participants must be invited to participate in setting goals and formulating plans and implementation strategies in order to gain their acceptance and commitment to meet those goals.

Expectancy Theory. This theory, originally developed by Victor Vroom,[21] assumes that people think seriously about how much effort they should put into a task before doing it. Motivation takes place if there is an expectation of a favorable outcome. It is based on the concept that people choose behaviors that they believe will lead to desired rewards or outcomes, and it suggests that the strength of a tendency to act in a certain way depends upon:

- The strength of their expectation that the act will be followed by a desired outcome/good performance (effort-performance linkage)
- The expectation that good performance will be rewarded (performance-reward linkage)
- Attractiveness of the reward to the individual (valence).

The linkage, also called expectancy, is the belief of an individual that his or her act or effort will result in a given outcome. The value of expectancy ranges from 0 (no relationship perceived) to +1 (complete certainty that the act will be followed by desired outcome). Project managers must try to strengthen both linkages in order to help team members achieve what they value the most. However, it must be realized that the *importance* or *value* of what people want may change from time to time, depending on their personal situations. Project managers should try to ascertain the most important needs that team members want to satisfy through informal communication and by developing better understanding and interrelationships. Later, Porter-Lawler developed a model to illustrate the expectancy theory of motivation, which is shown in Figure 2.5.[22]

For example, when facing schedule delays and cost overruns, project team members may develop several alternatives for completing the project successfully on schedule and within budget. However, before putting forth extra effort, they ask themselves the following questions:

- Can we do it? (effort to performance linkage)
- If we do it, what will be the consequences for us? (performance to reward/outcome linkage)
- Is it really worth the effort required? (valence).

Thus, project team members search out their own justification and seek a sense of accomplishment and recognition in exchange for becoming motivated.

Figure 2.5 Porter and Lawler Model of Motivation

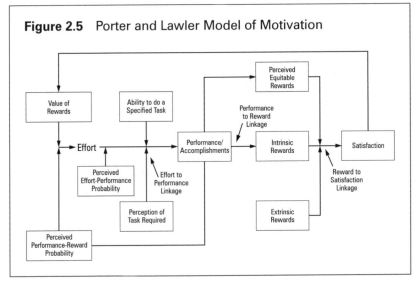

Adapted from: L.W. Porter and E.E. Lawler. 1968. *Managerial Attitudes and Performance*, Homewood, IL: Richard D. Irwin, Inc., p. 17. Reprinted by permission of the publisher.

Reinforcement Theory. This theory is based on Skinner's[23] behavior modification theories. *Reinforcement,* a key element of this theory, is any event that increases or decreases the likelihood of a future response. Reinforcement theory suggests that human behavior is shaped by the previous positive or negative outcomes experienced by a person.

This theory emphasizes the pattern in which rewards are administered and it states that a desirable behavior will be repeated if rewarded and that undesirable behavior can be discouraged by punishment. It stresses that only positive, not negative, reinforcement should be used, and only to reward desired behavior.[23]

Positive reinforcement occurs when a pleasant stimulus is presented to a person. Typical positive reinforcements in project environments include promotions, autonomy, opportunities to work on high-profile projects, opportunities for professional development and training, etc. However, which reinforcements work best in motivating particular project participants depend upon their needs and wants. To complicate the issue further, an individual's needs and wants may change with time. Therefore, project managers must stay in constant touch with their team members and encourage open and informal communication with them. For example, if project participants (including project managers) are genuinely recognized by their superiors, the probability that they will repeat a behavior, leading to similar or even higher performance, is increased. In a project environment, praise is often used as a most readily available pos-

74

itive reinforcement. However, it is only effective if it is genuine—mere lip service or predictable, continuously applied praise does not reinforce. Other tangible positive reinforcements are money, letters of commendation, time off, and promotions.

Equity Theory. This theory of motivation, developed by Adams,[24] is based on the notion that people are motivated by their desire to be treated equitably. In organizations, employees get pay and other benefits (outcomes) for their services (inputs). Equity theory proposes that there is considerable evidence that team members compare their job inputs and outcomes with those of others on the project, and that inequities can influence the degree of effort they exert.[24] Their perception of unfair allocation of rewards can lead to conflict and problems, requiring considerable effort from the project manager, functional manager and the human resource manager to solve them. Also, when individuals perceive that they are over-rewarded, they may be motivated to work harder in order to justify their rewards. Project managers must be cautious that all project participants are compensated fairly for their contributions to project success because any sign of inequity will turn demotivate people.

These theories outline different ideas and observations about how employees are motivated in general. Project managers must recognize the strengths and weaknesses of each theory and use them only as a guideline to develop their own motivational strategies.

Based on the various theories of motivation, the following general suggestions can be made to motivate project team members:

- Establish goals using a participative style.
- Ensure that goals are realistic and attainable.
- Ensure that tasks assigned are interesting, varied and involve some challenge, responsibility and learning opportunities.
- Emphasize that everyone's contribution is important to the project and show how their contribution fits into the "big picture."
- Provide enough information, support and authority to do the job.
- Recognize individual differences.
- Individualize rewards.
- Link rewards to performance.
- Check the system for equity.
- And above all: Don't ignore the importance of *money*.

Motivation and Project Management

If a project is to succeed, it must have both a motivated project manager and a motivated project team. A project team takes its attitude from the project leader, so one of the greatest motivational tools the project manager possesses is enthusiasm, positive attitude and confidence.[25] If the project leader/manager is enthusiastic and positive so will be the team, and if he or she is negative it will lead to low team morale. Enthusiasm, confidence, and the "motivation to manage" on the part of the project manager will stimulate the productivity of project team members and lead to a similar attitude in project team members. And it is well-recognized that enthusiastic and confident people are generally more productive.

In addition, by being positive toward change rather than negative, an enthusiastic attitude can take away the deadening effect wrought by changes. To encourage positive "change management," therefore, top management should provide an appropriate environment to support and motivate project managers because this will lead to increased motivation among project teams as well. Sometimes the only way to do this is by following the axiom "*Act* enthusiastic and you will *be* enthusiastic." Even in tough situations, a positive attitude has a way of rubbing off on others.

The project manager must be self-motivated and able to motivate project team members and others associated with the project. To do this, project managers must have a good understanding of the motivational process, of their own "motivation to manage," and of the factors upon which motivation depends.

The project manager's "motivation to manage"
In a project environment, project managers must be motivated to manage their projects effectively. The motivation to manage and its associated attitudes cause one to:[26]
- Choose a project management career
- Be successful as a project manager
- Move rapidly up the corporate ladder.

The following six components are all part of the project manager's motivation to manage.[27]

1. *Favorable attitude toward authority,* which helps project managers obtain support for their actions by creating good relationships between themselves, their superiors and functional managers
2. *Desire to compete with other managers* and to achieve excellence
3. *Assertive motivation,* or an ability to take charge, make decisions and even take disciplinary action when necessary
4. *Desire to exercise power*; that is, to influence project team members and others involved in a project by using informal authority and positive reinforcement; studies show that successful project managers have a higher need for power than for affiliation[28]
5. *Desire for a distinctive position,* acquired by taking positions of high visibility and by initiating things that invite attention, discussion and popularity
6. *Sense of responsibility* with respect to getting the work out, staying on top of routine demands, and gaining some satisfaction from it. Project managers should manage their projects by using effective reporting and control.

76

To be successful, the project manager must have the motivation to manage and must continually evaluate himself or herself as a project manager in order to achieve a proper fit between personal motivations and job duties. If the project manager feels a lack of motivation, he or she may choose to select jobs that are more appropriate to his or her motivation to manage—or attempt to change that motivation.[26] The motivation to manage can be increased through self-assessment and by preparing an action plan to optimize motivation. (See Self-assessment Exercise B in the Appendix.)[26]

What does motivation depend upon?

When you have a true desire to play, excelling is not work.

— *Anonymous*

Motivating employees in a project environment is easier said than done. Before devising strategies to motivate project participants, it is important to identify the factors upon which motivation depends. Some of these factors are:[29]

Project culture. Project participants frequently work long hours, sometimes under great stress. And the project manager does not always have the ability to reward them for their contributions to the extent that he or she would like to. However, the culture of projects, which often stresses openness, teamwork, effective communication, and a clear understanding of plans and expectations, can provide powerful intrinsic motivation to succeed.

Project reward system. Many of the rewards of working on projects are other than monetary. Nevertheless, such rewards as recognition by peers and other stakeholders, the gaining of status through project performance, and the ability to influence that results from that status must be considered powerful intrinsic motivators. In addition, those who succeed in the high-performance project environment often receive promotions and the increase in remuneration that comes with them.

Work content. People excel at what interests them. In the project environment, participants can be motivated by the intellectual challenge of their tasks, by the challenge and change involved in working on a variety of projects, by work-related travel opportunities and by meeting people (networking).

Environment. The working conditions created by the organizational climate can be motivating or de-motivating. Two factors that increase the likelihood that participants will feel motivated are the availability of support systems and enthusiastic project managers.

Supervision. Both the quality and the quantity of supervision impact on the motivational climate of a project. Talented, experienced, or technically proficient project participants must be well-managed without being over-managed.

Previous success. One motivational factor that is purely intrinsic to the individual (or to the team, if they have worked as a team previously) is the level of satisfaction achieved on previous projects. Was performance rewarded? Were achievements documented? Having worked hard and been motivated to succeed, and then receiving no rewards for that commitment weakens the morale on new projects.

Competition. Competition can be a good motivating factor. For instance some organizations may actively pursue offshore opportunities and look for international collaborators in order to compete in the global market. Sometimes in a large project, different teams acting as business units (e.g., R&D, production or marketing) may be motivated to cut their costs and improve quality to win internal competitions.

Believing in what you do is perhaps the most powerful intrinsic motivator. When work tasks and objectives are congruent with the personal values and the professional or social ethics of the participants, then even money becomes a secondary reason for going to work every morning.

Guidelines for Creating a Motivational Project Environment

The people who get on in this world are the people who get up and look for circumstances they want, and, if they can't find them, make them.

— Anonymous

The previous sections have outlined the importance of motivating project personnel and discussed some theories that can help project managers understand what motivates people to succeed. In addition to a motivated project manager, it is important that all project team members and others involved in a project are also motivated in order to optimize performance. In choosing the motivation techniques that he or she will use, the project manager must consider and integrate variables and factors associated with:

- The job itself or associated tasks
- The individual's personal drives
- The project manager's personal drives
- The overall organizational climate.

The following practical guidelines have proven successful in motivating employees in a variety of projects in different industries.

Factors related to project tasks/jobs

Managers can design jobs with built-in potential motivators by incorporating Herzberg's essentials of a "good" job.[12]

1. **Direct feedback.** Prompt and objective information about individual performance in daily work
2. **Client relationship.** An individual customer to be served inside or outside the organization
3. **New learning.** Continued opportunity for acquiring skills that are valued by the employee

4. **Scheduling.** Opportunity to pace one's own work and to time one's own work breaks within the constraints set by management deadlines
5. **Unique expertise.** Some job aspects that leave room for doing one's "own thing"
6. **Control over resources.** Some degree of control, such as providing an independent mini-budget.
7. **Direct communications authority.** An open communications system with direct access to relevant information centers
8. **Personal accountability.** Personal inspection of output equates the level of accountability for work performance with personal competence.

Factors related to personal drives

I was always looking outside myself for strength and confidence, but it comes from within. It is there all the time.

— Anonymous

As discussed earlier, motivation is an internal process; most of the time, project personnel will be motivated when they are ready to be motivated. Therefore, the project manager must take time to understand employees' needs and what turns them on or off. Table 2.2 shows factors that play a positive or a negative role in motivating participants in a project. The project manager, with the support of top management, must create an environment that enhances motivating factors and eliminates conditions that may keep people from producing their best work.

Factors related to project managers

Project managers play a very important role in motivating project team members and others involved in the project. They can use the following list of motivational ideas while managing their projects.[30]

- *Use appropriate methods of reinforcement.* Recognize employees when they do good work.
- *Eliminate unnecessary threats and punishments.* It is better to avoid or withdraw from unpleasant situations that may reduce your motivation.
- *Assign project personnel some responsibility and hold them accountable.* Giving people appropriate responsibility is always a good motivator.
- *Encourage employees to set their own goals.* People tend to know their own capabilities and limitations better than anyone else.
- *Relate tasks to personal and organizational goals.* Explain the "big picture" to project stakeholders and show them how it relates to their personal goals.
- *Clarify expectations and ensure that project team members understand them.* This avoids the frustration of not being sure what is expected.
- *Encourage project participants to engage in novel and challenging activities.* Provide opportunities for project participants to try new tasks. This fosters creativity and innovation.

Table 2.2 Motivating Factors in the Project Environment

"Turn Ons"	"Turn Offs"
Opportunities for intellectual growth and advancement	Lack of challenging assignments
Sense of accomplishment or achievement	Personal accomplishments not valued
Variety of projects/assignments	Routine, boring jobs/tasks
Open communication and access to information	Poor communication, information not readily accessible
Recognition and rewards (monetary and otherwise)	No recognition for good performance
Status and flexibility	Restrictive company policies and administration
Direction and support for meeting project goals	Lack of support/resources
Enthusiastic project manager	Negative attitude by project manager
Cohesive, harmonious teams	No team spirit
High levels of trust and respect	Lack of trust among project participants

- *Don't eliminate anxiety completely.* A certain level of anxiety is fundamental to motivation. Sometimes the best work is done under pressure.
- *Don't believe that "liking" is always correlated with positive performance.* A task can be intrinsically boring, yet the consequences are highly motivating.
- *Individualize your supervision.* To maximize motivation, treat people as individuals.
- *Provide immediate and relevant feedback.* This will help project team members improve their performance in the future. Inform employees how they might improve their performance with informational feedback.
- *Exhibit confidence in your project team.* This results in positive performance.
- *Show interest in each team member and their knowledge.* People need to feel important and personally significant.
- *Encourage individuals to participate in making decisions that affect them.* This increases their acceptance and hence their commitment to implement those decisions. People who have no control over their destiny become passive.
- *Establish a climate of trust and open communication.* Lack of trust and open communication are common obstacles to high motivation.

- *Minimize the use of statutory position powers.* Try managing democratically, encouraging input and participation. Inappropriate use of position power turns people off.
- *Listen to and deal effectively with employee complaints.* Handle problems before they become blown out of proportion. People are motivated when interests are looked after.
- *Emphasize the need for improvements in performance, no matter how small.* Frequent encouragement to improve performance in the early stages and throughout the project life cycle will yield continuous improvement as confidence and proficiency are obtained.
- *Demonstrate your own motivation through behavior and attitude.* Be positive: it's contagious. Walk your talk and set examples.
- *Criticize behavior, not people.* This is more effective in resolving conflict. When criticized personally, people become defensive, which reduces objectivity.

Factors related to organizational climate/environment

The organization's climate can impact the effectiveness of project personnel and the degree to which they can be motivated. Management must formulate strategic plans, establish clear goals, and encourage a participative, open management style and effective communication. It must encourage new ideas with some tolerance for failure, develop an equitable reward/recognition system, create an environment that provides the opportunity to excel and grow, and discourage bureaucracy. It should focus on building trust and confidence among all project participants.

To create a favorable working climate, one in which everyone working on various projects feels motivated, top management must implement policies like the following.[30]

- *Make sure that accomplishment is adequately recognized.* People need to feel important. Also remember that what gets rewarded gets done.
- *Provide people with flexibility and choice.* Permit employees to make decisions when possible.
- *Provide an appropriate mix of extrinsic rewards and intrinsic satisfaction.* Employees need to obtain personal satisfaction in addition to extrinsic rewards. Ensure that the reward systems are equitable to everyone working on the project.
- *Design tasks and environments to be consistent with employees' needs.* Different people need different activities. Use good common sense in making the proper "fit."
- *Make sure that effort pays off in results.* If effort does not result in accomplishment, effort will be withheld.
- *Be concerned with short-term and long-term motivation.* People should receive reinforcement in short-term and long-term assignments.

Management must demonstrate a sincere respect for all individuals working on the project and a willingness to train them, to set reasonable and clear expectations for them, and to grant them the practical autonomy that makes it possible for them to step out and make effective contributions to the project. Such "people orientation" should be genuine rather than using gimmicks and lip service that are ineffective and may lead to conflict and misunderstanding.[31]

Of all the ways that the project manager can obtain better performance from his team members, one motivator stands out above the rest: recognition. Recognition alone will not work, but in combination with other necessary factors, it works extremely well and therefore project managers should:

- *Recognize* and help eliminate barriers to individual achievement. If barriers are not dealt with, project team members may remain underachievers.
- *Increase* the likelihood that team members will experience accomplishment. "Nothing succeeds like success."
- *Help* project team members to see the integrity, significance and relevance of their work in terms of organizational output. Communicate the vision clearly and help them see the whole picture, not just pieces.

Figure 2.6 shows practical motivational techniques in a nutshell.

Putting it All Together (From Theory to Practice)

The will to win goes dry without positive reinforcement.

— *Anonymous*

Motivating project participants is challenging because motivation is, to a great extent, an internal phenomenon. Project managers are challenged to turn theories of motivation into practices. While there are no all-encompassing, definite techniques, project managers will find the following suggestions very useful in motivating project participants.[11]

Set goals and get everyone's acceptance and commitment (buy-in). Goals set in a collaborative manner motivate people and provide them something to shoot for. Individual goals must also match project goals. Participation in goal-setting generally reduces any resistance to the tasks required to reach those goals. It helps gain their acceptance and hence their commitment to meet goals. The process of participation should be genuine, not window-dressing, and should fit organizational culture.

Follow SMART goal setting. Ensure that goals are *Specific, Measurable, Attainable, Rewarding* and *Results-oriented* and have a *Timeline*. What gets measured gets done. Employees should perceive that increased efforts will lead to higher performance and then to more rewards. They should be able to expect and get regular and timely feedback.

Match people to jobs. People are motivated when they are working on jobs that they are capable of doing and that they *want* to do rather than

Human Resource Skills for the Project Manager

Figure 2.6 Motivational Techniques in a Nutshell

Manifest confidence when delegating
(helps build mutual trust)

Open communication
(increases mutual understanding and respect)

Tolerance for failure
(develops creativity)

Involve project participants
(increase acceptance and commitment)

Value the efforts and recognize good performance
(what gets rewarded, gets done)

Align project objectives to individuals objectives
(people are eager to satisfy their needs)

Trust your team members and be trustworthy
(vital for motivation)

Empower project team members appropriately
(especially for decision making and implementation)

have to do. Performing such jobs makes them feel challenged and gives them a chance to shine.

Recognize individual differences. As the song says, "different strokes for different folks." People differ in terms of attitudes, personality and other personal variables and are therefore motivated by different factors. For example, expectancy theory applies more accurately to people who believe that they have control over the events in their lives.[32]

Link rewards to performance. Rewards play a significant role in motivating people. Rewards and recognition should be visible and tied to specific outstanding results. This reinforces people positively and motivates them to maintain a high level of performance. Pay increases, promotions, letters of appreciation, publicity about performance, bonuses, and lump sum increases (rather than those spread over the entire year) are examples of effective rewards to enhance motivation.

Individualize rewards. Different needs motivate different people in different ways. Project managers should know their team members well enough to determine what specifically turns them ON and then ensure that they can deliver the rewards that satisfy their most important needs.

They can determine this by practicing "management by walking around;" that is, by talking informally to their team members.[31] Some of the common rewards that project managers can use are pay, promotions, opportunity to work on challenging assignments and to participate in goal setting and decision making.

Check the system for equity. Employees should perceive that the rewards they get are according to the results they produce. Experience, ability, effort, and other inputs should justify differences in pay, responsibility and other obvious outcomes.[33]

Don't ignore money. Although Herzberg's theory of motivator and hygiene factors suggested that money is not a motivating factor, it should not be completely ignored. Money is, after all, a major reason why most people work. This does not mean that management should focus solely on money, but even people who come to work in the absence of goals, job enrichment or participation will not show up for work if money is removed as an incentive. Still, it should be recognized that some people work for self-respect and sense of self-worth, irrespective of money. This is evident from the large number of volunteers who work on community and social projects.

DIFFERENT PEOPLE ARE MOTIVATED by different factors. The key to motivating project participants is a project manager who stays in touch with people and is aware of what "turns them on" as individuals and then does his or her best to provide appropriate environments and outcomes.

Summary

Motivation is the inner state that causes an individual to behave in a way that ensures the accomplishment of both personal and project or organizational goals. To be effective in motivating project participants, project managers must ensure that project goals and personal goals are aligned as much as possible.

Success in motivating project team members and other personnel associated with the project will lead to improved productivity, better quality, higher morale, and overall success in meeting project goals and objectives. It will result in substantial cost savings because a lack of motivation leads to conflict, strikes, lower productivity, stress, and ultimately a complete failure of the project. Better motivation leads to job satisfaction, which helps project participants satisfy their needs and fulfill their intrinsic and extrinsic expectations about work. In such a workplace, employees will help each other win and create a *real* team spirit and feelings of trust, respect and confidence in each other.

According to a basic motivational principle, people's performance depends upon their level of motivation (a personal desire to achieve high performance), and their level of ability (competence and skills to perform the task). There are six core phases in the motivation process which in-

84

clude identifying needs, creating drives, selecting goal-directed behavior, performing the task, receiving feedback, and reassessing need deficiencies. Project managers can follow this process in principle, but they must be aware of its complications and limitations.

There are two types of theories of motivation (content theories and process theories), which outline different ideas, observations, and how people are motivated in general. The content theories of motivation are based on intrinsic factors that lead to certain behavior. These theories include the Hierarchy of Needs Theory, the Existence, Related and Growth needs (ERG) Theory; the Motivator/Hygiene Theory; and the Achievement Motivation Theory. The process theories of motivation are based on how personal factors interact and influence to produce certain behavior. These include Theory X-Theory Y; Contingency Theory; Goal-Setting Theory; Expectancy Theory; Reinforcement Theory; and Equity Theory. Project managers must evaluate the strengths and weaknesses of these theories and use them only as guidelines to develop their own motivational strategies.

It is important to have both a motivated project manager and a motivated project team.

The project manager's own motivation to manage, enthusiasm, positive attitude, and confidence will stimulate the productivity of project team members. In a project environment, motivation depends upon project culture, project reward system, work content, work environment/climate, competition, previous success experiences and personal attitude and values.

In a project environment, motivation can be both a problem and an opportunity to inspire high performance. Project managers must be able to turn motivational theories into practice. Motivational techniques in a project environment must consider various factors, such as the job or tasks, the personal drives of individuals, project managers (their motivation to manage and people skills) and overall organizational climate. Some useful techniques in motivating project participants include setting goals that are specific, measurable, attainable, rewarding and have a timetable, and then getting everyone's acceptance and commitment. Project managers should try to recognize individual differences and match jobs assigned to people according to their skills and interests. They should link rewards to performance, individualize the rewards to get maximum impact, design an equitable system and, above all, *not ignore money.*

Conflict is the gadfly of thought. It stirs us to observation and memory. It instigates invention. It shocks us out of sheeplike passivity, and sets us at noting and contriving ... Conflict is a "sine qua non" of reflection and ingenuity.

— *John Dewey*

Understanding Conflict

CONFLICT IS AS INEVITABLE in a project environment as change seems to be. When project team members interact during the course of completing their tasks and responsibilities, there is always a potential for conflict. In fact, it is virtually impossible for people with diverse background skills and norms to work together, make decisions and try to meet project goals and objectives without conflict. Another basic cause of conflict stems from the incompatibility or incongruence between goals of the individuals working on a project and organizational goals and expectations. Also, the tremendous change presently occurring in work places is a primary underlying reason for conflict.

Conflict is the offspring of disagreement between individuals.[1] It refers to any situation in which there are incompatible goals, thoughts or emotions within or between individuals or groups. There are three different views of conflict: traditional, contemporary and interactionist. Conflict can occur at four different levels: intrapersonal, interpersonal, intragroup, and intergroup.

Project managers must identify, analyze and evaluate both positive and negative values of conflict and their effect on performance. They must learn how and when to stimulate conflict and how to use it to increase the performance of project team members. While conflict is inevitable in a project environment, it need not have destructive consequences. Attitudes and conflict management styles play an important role in determining whether such conflict will lead to destructive or mutually beneficial outcomes.[2]

There are different categories of conflict and various sources of conflict in a project environment. The sources of conflict vary according to the project life cycle. For effective management of conflict, project managers must be able to identify and analyze the sources of conflict and their relationship to the project life cycle. ∎

Basic Concepts of Conflict

Instead of looking on conflict and discussion as a stumbling block in the way of action, we think it an indispensable preliminary to any wise action at all.
— *Pericles*

Conflicts of interest among project participants can often be resolved through negotiation. But first of all, one must analyze how and why conflict occurs. To understand conflict situations, it is necessary to define *wants*, *needs*, *goals* and *interests* and how they are related.[3]

Wants are a desire for something; everyone has a unique set of wants. *Needs* are a necessity for survival; needs are more universal. *Goals* are an ideal set of affairs that we value and work to achieve; goals are set on the basis of our wants and needs. *Interests* are the potential benefits to be gained by achieving our goals.

A cooperative relationship exists among project participants when their goals are mutual and compatible with each other. However, when their goals are opposite, they are in a competitive relationship and their interests come into conflict.

Conflict refers to any situation in which there are incompatible goals, thoughts, or emotions within or between individuals or groups that lead to opposition and disagreements. In other words, conflict occurs when individuals or groups have incompatible goals, and when they block each other's efforts to attain those goals.[4]

As applied to human behavior, conflict can also be a disagreement between individuals that can range from a mild disagreement to a win-lose emotion-packed confrontation.[5]

In today's project environment, conflict is inevitable because of the various competing objectives, personal goals, requirements for resources, and divergent views that exist and must be integrated to meet overall goals of the project. Whether conflict is constructive or destructive in a project environment depends upon how the project manager and members of the project team view the conflict and deal with it. This section deals with differing views of conflict, levels and types of conflict, values of conflict and the importance of stimulating constructive conflict in a project environment.

Views of conflict

Over the years three distinct views have evolved about conflict in projects and organizations.[6]

The traditional view assumes that conflict is bad and always has a negative impact on projects or organizations. This view argues that performance declines as the level of conflict increases, as shown in Figure 3.1, and therefore it must be avoided. In this view, conflict is closely associated with such terms as violence, destruction, and irrationality. This traditional view dominated management literature during the late 19th century and continued to do so until the mid-1940s.

88

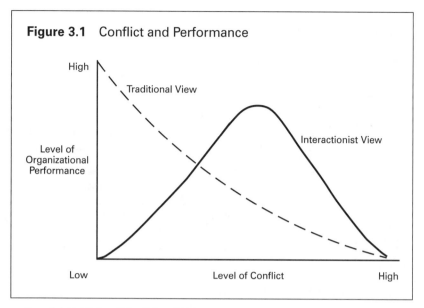

Figure 3.1 Conflict and Performance

Source: Frederick A. Starke and Robert W. Sexty. 1992. *Contemporary Management in Canada.* Scarborough, ON: Prentice-Hall Canada: p. 474. Reprinted by permission of the publisher.

Because the traditional view considered conflict in a negative light, attention was given to reducing, suppressing or eliminating it. It was the manager's responsibility to free the project of any conflict. The most common reaction of traditional managers has been to suppress conflict by using an authoritarian approach. While this approach has worked sometimes, it has not generally been effective because, when suppressed, the root cause of conflict is ignored and never found and the potentially positive aspects of conflict cannot emerge.

The traditional view of conflict is widely held because institutions that have a strong influence on our society concur with this view.[6] This negative view of conflict played a role in the development of labor unions. Violent or disruptive confrontations between workers and management led people to conclude that conflict was always detrimental and should therefore be avoided.

The behavioral or contemporary view, also known as the human relations view, argues that conflict is natural and inevitable in all organizations and that it may have either a positive or a negative effect. This approach advocates acceptance of conflict and rationalizes its existence. Since projects may sometimes benefit from conflict, project managers should focus on managing conflict effectively rather than simply suppressing it or eliminating it. The behavioral view dominated ideas on conflict from the late 1940s through the mid-1970s.

Figure 3.2 Conflict Views and Managerial Actions

View	Possible States	Managerial Actions
Traditional	A = D, where D = 0 A > D, where D = 0	Do nothing Resolve conflict
Behavioral	A = D, where D $\geq$ 0 A > D, where D $\geq$ 0	Do nothing Resolve conflict
Interactionist	A = D, where D > 0 A > D, where D > 0 A < D, where D > 0	Do nothing Resolve conflict Stimulate conflict

Key: A = Actual level of conflict
D = Desired level of conflict

Source: Copyright 1978 by The Regents of the University of California. Reprinted from the *California Management Review,* Vol. 21, No. 2, p. 68. By permission of the Regents.

The interactionist view is the current theoretical perspective on conflict and assumes that conflict is necessary to increase performance. While the behavioral approach *accepts* conflict, the interactionist view *encourages* conflict on the basis that a harmonious, peaceful, tranquil, too-cooperative project organization is likely to become static, apathetic, stagnant and non-responsive to meet the challenges of change and innovation. This approach encourages managers to maintain an ongoing minimum level of conflict—enough to keep projects self-critical, viable, creative and innovative.

Figure 3.2 shows a summary of these three views in terms of actual and desired levels of conflict.[6] According to the traditional view, conflict is bad and should therefore be avoided: the desired level is always zero. If actual conflict rises above zero, it should be resolved. The behavioral view differs only in terms of the desired level of conflict, which could be above zero. However, the managerial implications are the same as those in the traditional view, i.e., "do nothing" or "resolve the conflict." If the desired level of conflict is above zero, then there are three possible outcomes:

1. Actual level of conflict is greater than the desired level (A>D)
2. Actual level of conflict is equal to the desired level (A=D)
3. Actual level of conflict is less than the desired level (A<D).

This third possibility, which was completely overlooked by both the traditional and behavioral views, is addressed by the interactionist view of conflict. In this view, conflict management implies not only conflict

90

resolution but also conflict stimulation. According to both the behavioral and interactionist views, there is an optimal level of conflict that maximizes project/organizational performance (see Figure 3.1). A project with no conflict whatsoever has little incentive for innovation, creativity or change because its participants are comfortable with the status quo and they are not concerned about improving their performance.[6]

Four levels of conflict

Conflict can be viewed differently at different levels and should be analyzed from various perspectives, ranging from individuals to that of the group. Conflict can occur at the following four levels in a project:[7]

Intrapersonal conflict, also known as role conflict, stems from unmet personal or professional expectations within the individual. This level of conflict may not affect the project, as long as it does not influence other project participants negatively. However, it can reduce the motivation and productivity of that particular individual. Individuals experience such a conflict when faced with certain dilemmas at work, such as being required to act against their moral values or receiving conflicting demands from two different bosses (typical in a matrix organizational structure).

Interpersonal conflict can occur between specific team members or between one person and the entire group. Interpersonal conflict is most often caused by differences in personality, style, communication skills, or competing personal ambitions. Analyzing the *intrapersonal* conflict present in group members may help determine why individuals try to block the attainment of each other's goals.

Intragroup conflict refers to a conflict between a single person and a group of people (such as his or her project team). It may occur, for example, in a union environment when what an individual wants to do (e.g., produce more) is against what the group norm dictates (e.g., restriction of output). It can also occur when what a boss wants (e.g., obedience from subordinates) differs from what a group of subordinates want (e.g., participation and flexibility). In both cases, the group is likely to win because it is more able to block the goal attainment of the individual than vice versa.

Intergroup conflict can arise between groups of people within the project team or between the project team and groups outside the project. Intergroup conflict occurs when one team or group is pitted against another and are normally caused by the interpersonal frictions between individual group members or between influential project leaders. Labor-management disputes are a common example of an intergroup conflict that can be partially resolved by dealing with the conflict on a personal basis through those influential leaders (union and management).

Only one or a combination of several of these types of conflict may exist in a project. For example, an intrapersonal conflict over a tradeoff issue between quality and cost or quality and schedule could set off an interpersonal conflict. This may cause respective staff groups to rally around the major participants and lead to an intergroup dispute. Therefore, the project manager should carry out a thorough analysis and assessment of the conflict before taking any action in order to reduce its negative impact.

Conditions leading to conflict

Due to competing departmental objectives, personal goals and needs for resources, conflict is unavoidable in today's work environment. The diverse mix of viewpoints within the project team must be integrated and directed toward the project objectives. Conflict that arises from this clash of viewpoints can be constructive or destructive, depending upon how the project manager views the conflict and deals with it.

The primary aim of every project manager should be to manage conflict constructively to optimize project team performance and accomplish project objectives successfully. This can be achieved by understanding the conditions leading to conflict, the potential results of conflict, and the various methods of dealing with conflict in an organizational or in a project environment. Although divergent ideas and disagreement may arise whenever project participants interact with each other, Filley identified nine conditions that predispose an organization toward conflict.[5,8]

- *Ambiguous roles, work boundaries, responsibility and authority* are likely to occur when two or more individuals, sections or departments have related or even overlapping responsibilities with ambiguous roles and poorly defined authority. This is typical of matrix structures that violate the rule of unity of command, as some individuals may have two bosses.
- *Inconsistent or incompatible goals* may lead to conflict when the individuals or the units define and establish their own missions and purposes within the organization. Incompatible goals arise when individuals or departments are dependent on others and yet perceive each other as having opposing goals. For example, a design engineer may want to enhance his or her reputation by producing a unique, state-of-the-art design, while the project manager is generally more concerned with completing the task on budget, within schedule and is prepared to accept a standard design as long as it meets the client's requirements.
- *Communication problems* create the most misunderstanding and the most intense conflicts. The misinterpretation of a design drawing, a misunderstood change order, a missed delivery date or a failure to execute instructions are generally the results of a breakdown in communication. A high percentage of the frictions, frustrations and inefficiencies in working relationships are also traceable to poor communication. Communication problems block the efforts of the individuals and parties involved to explain their viewpoints and negotiate for their needs to achieve project success.

92

- *Dependence on another party* can lead to conflict when one discipline or unit is dependent on the other for activities and resources. Each party may be more interested in meeting its own deadlines than in being sensitive to the needs of other parties who may be working on tasks and activities that are crucial to project success.
- *Specialization or differentiation* creates a condition leading to conflict due to professional egos. Modern high-technology organizations are characterized by pools of technical experts or specialists responsible for unique tasks. These *specialists* possess their own viewpoints, language, goals, and ways of doing things.
- *Need for joint decision making* can lead to conflict as people may have quite different opinions and points of view but conform to pressures for joint decision making. This condition is especially prevalent when different technical groups have to work together with management groups.
- *Need for consensus* creates a condition for conflict when project teams having a diverse mix of team members with divergent talents, backgrounds, and norms must agree among themselves. It is very similar to the need for joint decision making. Such a condition arises when no decision maker is available to evaluate and select among several alternatives and enforce the selected solution. When several people with different backgrounds, norms, and goals must reach consensus on a course of action, the resulting conflict may be very difficult to manage.
- *Behavior regulations* lead to high levels of conflict as individuals tend to resist tight boundaries placed on their actions. Such situations may involve safety and security concerns (policies, rules and procedures) about which the individuals have views different from those of the management. If management tries to impose or enforce its ideas, team players may feel they are in a conflict with the very organization they attempt to serve. This can lead to frustration and conflict.
- *Unresolved prior conflicts* tend to build up and create a tense atmosphere, which can lead to even more intense and destructive conflict. In general, the longer a conflict lasts without reaching a satisfactory resolution, the worse it becomes. The use of positional power to resolve conflict (a *forcing approach*) leaves bitter feelings and generates more intense conflict at a later date. If one party is not willing and committed to resolve a conflict, those people involved can generate more difficulties until they are completely unable to work together as a team. Consequently, the failure to manage and deal with conflict quickly leads to more serious problems in the future.

These nine antecedent conditions of conflict exist in every organization at all times, to a greater or lesser extent, and do not exist in isolation in any organization. The extent to which a combination of these conditions exists creates the conditions for conflict and determines its intensity within the organization and project team. They are very commonly found in matrix organizational structures. These antecedent conditions simply set the stage for personal disagreement that may lead to a minor or a serious conflict. Project managers must be aware of these conditions and create an atmosphere that is likely to prevent or at least dampen the negative outcome of these conditions.

Conflict and Performance

Difference of opinion leads to inquiry, and inquiry to truth.
— *Thomas Jefferson*

Conflict, if not managed appropriately, can be destructive and detrimental to project performance. It can drastically lower team morale and productivity and hamper the decision-making process, making it long, complex and difficult. It can create tension among individuals, and cause the formation of competing coalitions within the project organization leading to lower commitment, incompatible goals and unnecessary power struggles. But while conflict in a project is inevitable, its results do not always have to be destructive. Constructive conflict management is one of the keys to accomplishing project goals and objectives within severe constraints. This section deals with positive and negative values of conflict and the effects of conflict on performance.

The positive and negative value of conflict

Conflict is natural in a project, which is characterized by a unique set of activities carried out by a diverse mix of people. Conflict can be positive or negative in terms of its influence on the performance of project participants. Project managers must try to create an environment where constructive (positive) conflict is stimulated and negative conflict, which can have detrimental effect on project success, is resolved effectively at an early stage. Table 3.1 shows the main positive and negative values of conflict, which are also described below.[8,9]

Diffusion of more serious conflict. Minor conflicts, if not managed effectively in a timely manner, can lead to major conflicts and to serious and undesirable consequences. Conflict resolution techniques can help nip the evil in the bud, prevent more destructive outcomes, and promote better understanding among project participants. Games or minor competitions can provide entertainment and release tension among the parties involved, helping to channel aggressive behavior and reduce major conflicts and disruptions.

Major stimulant for change. Assuming that there is enough trust and respect between the project participants, any conflict encourages them to look into themselves, analyze the situation rationally and feel positive about it. It helps them overcome resistance to change and makes them more supportive and committed to manage change effectively to accomplish project goals.

Fosters creativity and innovation. The process of managing conflict, if done constructively, can lead to a clarification of facts. Conflict can also stimulate the search for new methods or solutions. In the case of disagreement over a choice between two alternatives, team members may agree to

Table 3.1 The Value of Conflict

Positive Aspects	Negative Aspects
Diffuses more serious conflicts	Can lead to more hostility and aggression
Fosters change and creativity as new options are explored	Desire to "win" blocks exploration of new opportunities
Enhances communication if both parties are committed to mutual gain	Inhibits communication; relevant information never shared
Increases performance, energy, and group cohesion	Causes stress; creates in unproductive atmosphere
Balances power and influence if collaborative problem solving techniques are emphasized.	May cause loss of status or position power when both parties take it as a contest of wills and strive for a win-lose outcome.
Clarifies issues and goals	Real issues overlooked as positions become confused with personalities

explore new and better alternatives or to search for another solution mutually acceptable to both. The project manager must try to keep the group's attention on the facts of the situation and keep the emotional content low.

Enhances communication. A positive view of conflict encourages both parties to communicate more effectively by listening to each other and trying to understand the other person's perspective. Communication is further enhanced when the parties involved are mature enough to understand that their primary purpose is to meet the project's objectives, regardless of whose ideas are finally used.

Clarifies issues and goals. Project teams are composed of people with diverse backgrounds, norms and personalities, who may have different objectives and values that they think are important. A positive approach to conflict management will motivate the team members to clarify their positions on the various issues, policies, goals and objectives.

Increases performance, energy and group cohesion. Conflict and disagreements are almost sure to happen among project team members with different ideas and skills. However, a team approach is the key to project success. Project managers must channel this conflict in a manner that emphasizes the importance of team effort and convinces everyone to help each other win in spite of individual differences. The concept of "synergism" must be reinforced, promoting an atmosphere of pulling together, helping each other and believing in the basic goals of the team.

Balancing of power and influence. Conflict situations can reveal the relative power and influence of the parties. After the conflict is resolved, the losing party loses status and influence while the winning party gains status and tends to feel increase in their power and influence. This can create a negative impact or it can lead to constructive competitive feelings, encouraging both parties to try harder and improve their performance. Therefore, project managers must be extremely careful as to how they deal with conflict in a project. Conflict resolved through coercion, control and suppression clearly demonstrates a superiority of power of one party over another, which should be discouraged. Project managers must try to create an equal power balance because it leads to creative problem-solving methods and the effective resolution of conflict in a project environment.

IT IS SOMETIMES EASIER TO SEE THE NEGATIVE IMPACTS of conflict than its positive impacts. If conflict is not properly managed, it causes trouble and friction among project participants, which leads to lower productivity. It also leads to "coffee-break" talk, false rumors and criticisms, and further erosion of confidence and morale. Following are some of the major drawbacks of conflict.

Conflict causes stress. In extreme cases, or for particularly sensitive people, conflict causes stress that affects individuals both emotionally and physically, leading to back pains, ulcers, high blood pressure and heart disease. It brings on sleepless nights, frustrations, irritable outbursts, and loss of self-confidence and self-esteem, taking its toll in physical and mental strain.

Conflict creates an unproductive atmosphere. Conflict and clashing views in a project may lead to breakdown or lack of communication. The resulting confusion and ambiguity can lower productivity.

Conflict tends to distort behavior. In conflict situations, people's sense of values may change. They may be strongly urged to find the facts—or project priorities may be twisted and random decisions made. Decisions may be implemented in an authoritarian style due to excessive emotional involvement. Loyalty may become more important than making rational management decisions.

Conflict may cause loss of status or position power. In conflict situations, sometimes people tend to show off their position, power and status. Therefore, conflict and disputes, depending upon how they are managed and who the parties are, may label the parties as winners or losers. The losing party may tend to feel some loss in status or position power that ultimately may affect the winners as well because they have to work with the losing party as a team in order to achieve an optimum level of project success.

Conflict, if not managed properly, can increase confusion and ambiguity; while communication and sharing of relevant information between parties declines. Personal relationships may become more tense, resulting

96

in the loss of energy, productivity and enthusiasm contributed by the project team. Excessive conformity to group demands and viewpoints, or intense competitiveness, may keep people from adapting to changing environmental demands and coming up with creative and innovative solutions to project problems. Project managers should focus on handling conflict in such a way that the positive impacts are maximized while reducing the negative outcomes.

Conflict and outcomes

The potential values of conflict described earlier indicate that conflict is neither good nor bad but can have either a positive and negative impact on a project, depending upon how it is handled. The application of conflict resolution techniques can lead to either of two outcomes. A *functional outcome* is one that satisfies the parties involved in the conflict and increases overall project performance. A *dysfunctional outcome* creates dissatisfaction. It either makes one party unhappy or reduces the overall project performance. The two criteria used to determine whether a conflict is functional or dysfunctional are:
• The degree to which an individual or the group is satisfied with the outcome
• Overall project performance after the outcome is implemented.

In a project environment, stimulating healthy conflict can lead to positive results. But how much conflict is enough? Project managers must evaluate the situation and determine an appropriate level of conflict to achieve a functional outcome and optimize project performance.

The influence of a certain type and level of conflict on performance may vary from project to project in an organization and even within different areas of the same project. Its influence depends upon the cohesiveness of working relationships among project participants and their commitment to negotiate using a win-win strategy. Functionality or dysfunctionality may thus be a matter of judgment.

The relationship between conflict and performance (as shown in Figure 3.3) poses challenges to project managers.[9] Neither too little nor too much conflict is desirable. Project managers must create an environment where conflict is stimulated only to healthy levels that increase performance. Conflict must be created only when it can help to derive the full benefit of team members, functional managers and other support personnel, yet reduce it before it becomes destructive. Since it is not easy to measure whether a certain level of conflict is functional or dysfunctional, project managers must be cautious in creating an environment where the level of conflict corresponds to an optimum performance. Various conflict management techniques and practical guidelines to manage conflict in a project environment are discussed in the Chapter Four.

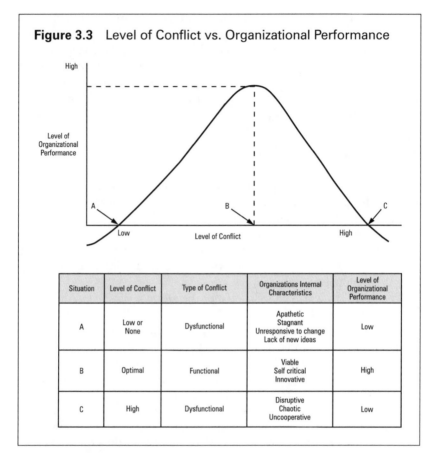

Figure 3.3   Level of Conflict vs. Organizational Performance

Situation	Level of Conflict	Type of Conflict	Organizations Internal Characteristics	Level of Organizational Performance
A	Low or None	Dysfunctional	Apathetic Stagnant Unresponsive to change Lack of new ideas	Low
B	Optimal	Functional	Viable Self critical Innovative	High
C	High	Dysfunctional	Disruptive Chaotic Uncooperative	Low

Source: Stephen P. Robbins and Robin Stuart Kotze. 1986. *Management Concepts and Practices (Canadian Edition)*. Scarborough, ON: Prentice-Hall Canada, p. 485. Reprinted by permission of the publisher.

About Conflict in a Project

It's best that we should not all think alike. It's the difference of opinion that makes horse races.

— Mark Twain

Sources of conflict in a project include the project manager, the project team, the clients or customers, other internal stakeholders (contractors, staff and service personnel, functional managers, senior managers) and external stakeholders (general public, press, personnel from regulatory, financial, political and technology areas) who are not directly part of the project. Any or all of these parties can be involved in a conflict.

There are numerous causes of conflict. The most common and well documented sources of conflict include incompatible goals, structural relationships, limited resources, communication problems and individual differences.[10,11] For effective management of conflict, project managers must understand the different categories of conflict, reasons for conflict in project management and their relationship to the life cycle of the project.

Categories of conflict

In general all potential conflict can be summarized in one of three categories, although it is common for a particular conflict situation to be based on two or more categories of conflict.[12]

1. *Goal-oriented conflicts* are associated with end results, performance specifications and criteria, priorities and objectives.
2. *Administrative conflicts* refer to the management structure, philosophy and techniques and are mainly based on definition of responsibilities and authority for tasks, functions and decisions.
3. *Interpersonal conflicts* result from differences in work ethics, styles, egos and personalities of the participants.

Reasons for conflicts in project management

Although conflicts occur in everyday life in all human relations, project environments are particularly vulnerable to generating conflict. There is no shortage of reasons for this. Thamhain and Wilemon[13,14] have identified seven major sources of conflict in project management based on their research conducted in a private manufacturing company. Their work was later confirmed by Eschmann and Lee[15] in the military area and by Peter Stoycheff[16] in the educational environment.

The reasons for conflict in a project, whether group-oriented or interpersonal, are many.[12,13]

Project priorities or goal incompatibility. Goal conflicts involve differences in project priorities and criteria for evaluating results. Goal conflicts also refer to differing views on the necessary sequence of tasks or events. There may be considerable difference between the goals, expectations and performance criteria perceived by project managers and functional managers, leading to conflicts between project tasks and functional responsibilities. Priority conflicts can be resolved by formulating strategic plans participatively and developing a master plan and the first two or three levels of work breakdown structure in collaboration with the client, project team, and other project stakeholders.

Administrative procedures. These refer to differences regarding how the project will be managed. They include conflict over reporting systems (e.g., recipients, frequency, number and contents of reports and forms) and how reports should be used in managing the project. Conflicts may be caused by disagreements over the levels of administrative support required for a project. However, procedural conflicts can be minimized by designing a project organization appropriately and clearly defining the roles, responsibilities and reporting relationships.

Technical opinions and performance tradeoffs. These are related to disagreements over technical issues, performance specifications, technical tradeoffs in terms of budget, cost and quality and general performance issues. Project team members may disagree on the best way to do things. Moreover, if new technologies are involved, especially in R&D projects, the differences can be more intense and the players more opinionated. Conflicts over technical issues can be reduced by regular project reviews, frequent testing and integration.

Task uncertainty and information requirements. Disagreements in this area are related to uncertainties in accomplishing tasks due to unpredictable technology. This is particularly true in the case of high-tech and pure-research projects. The higher the degree of task uncertainty, the greater the need for reliable information critical to the task and the higher the possibility of conflict over the task and the information required to complete it. If tasks are of a routine nature, the degree of conflict is low and will usually be centered on *who* completes the task and *when* rather than *what* and *how* to complete the task.

Role uncertainty. This refers to disagreements between the relative responsibility, authority and accountabiliy of the project manager, project team members and functional managers in an organization. These issues are typical sources of conflict in a matrix project environment.

Differences in time horizons. Some project participants may have a long-term view of various project issues, while others have a short-term view. Conflicts may develop regarding the importance of each view depending upon how strongly the individuals feel about the issue.

Human resources. The management of project human resources, including staffing and personnel utilization, is a common and major cause of conflict in a project.

- How many people are required?
- Where do they come from (internally or externally)?
- How many people can we hire and for what tasks?
- Who has to do the routine "grunt" work and who gets to do the final tasks?

Questions such as these are often controversial and open to heated debate. Major conflicts can be reduced by developing a detailed work breakdown structure and a matching organizational breakdown structure.

Resource allocation. Other projects or groups in the organization may need to utilize the same people, equipment or facilities, causing conflicts, especially if resources are in short supply. Such situations force top management to make tough priority decisions and the "losing" party may feel unhappy and lose status and positional power in the eyes of others. Sometimes priority decisions are simply based on overall critical path analysis and projects with poor discipline in project planning and control may have to be "rescued" through extra allocation of resources. This frustrates and demotivates those project managers who practice timely planning and appropriate project management and control. This is especially experi-

100

enced by people involved in R&D activities, where poorly managed but high-profile research projects get higher priority for resources at the cost of other projects that are being well-managed, but have a lower profile. Conflicts over resources can be minimized by proper planning and monitoring, providing required training to both technical experts and project management staff, selecting support staff early, and above all, by motivating project participants to produce their best.

Costs and budgets. The budget is one of the most important constraints of a project. It is an important yardstick for measuring overall performance. Some common issues related to budgets include:

- Is there ever enough money for any project?
- Don't most projects cost more than they should or were projected to cost?
- Why can't we have enough financial contingencies to deal with unpredictable problems?

There are often disagreements over cost estimates. Conflicts over cost can be reduced by generating preliminary product requirements, feasibility studies with sound cost estimates, and marketing plans, and by analyzing financing arrangements and resource requirements.

Schedules. Like budgets, schedules are also a constant source of conflict, tension and anxiety. Disagreements related to schedules center on the sequencing and prioritizing of schedule items and on time estimates, especially when people want a higher priority for their projects' activities ahead of those of others. Some human problems caused by inappropriate priority decisions associated with budget and schedules are similar to those explained under human resources conflicts. Schedule conflicts can be minimized by establishing a master project schedule from detailed schedules of subprojects (major work packages), identifying and tracking major milestones, and involving project stakeholders responsible for various tasks. Scheduling information should be communicated in a user-friendly format and in a timely manner.

Communication problems. Breakdown in communication is the most common and obvious source of conflict. A lack of trust, respect and effective listening skills can develop into serious communication problems. People may misinterpret messages, leading to conflict and misunderstanding. Communication is too important to be covered by administrative procedures alone. Project managers and their project teams must possess effective communication skills in resolving project conflicts. They must learn effective listening skills and create an atmosphere to encourage open communication.

Personality. Although project managers attempt to build cohesive project teams, interpersonal differences associated with individual styles, perceptions, attitudes and egos are guaranteed to clash at times, even among friends. When we add other human behavioral dimensions such as power, self-esteem, motivations and status to the equation, we are likely to see serious conflicts among project team members.

Personality conflicts are quite common. However, they can be reduced by using effective team-building approaches, training team members in managing conflicts effectively, emphasizing the importance of cohesive teamwork, encouraging open communication, and building trust among project participants. Management must have reasonable tolerance for failure in order to encourage creativity and innovation.

Conflict throughout the life cycle of the project

According to a classic study involving a survey of about 100 project managers conducted by Thamhain and Wilemon,[13] seven sources of conflict were ranked as follows:

1. Schedules (includes task uncertainty and information requirement)
2. Priorities (goal incompatibility and differences in time horizon)
3. Human resources (staffing and resource allocation)
4. Technical issues (technical opinions and performance tradeoffs)
5. Administrative problems (managerial and administrative issues outlining how the project will be managed; may include role uncertainty, authority and responsibility of each project participant, and reporting relationships)
6. Personality (includes interpersonal disagreements)
7. Cost.

The predominant sources and intensities of conflict vary over the life cycle of the project. Figure 3.4 shows ranking of conflict intensity arising from seven sources of conflict[5,13] in four phases of the project cycle:

- Conceptual phase (project initiation or formation)
- Development phase (planning or project build up)
- Execution phase (implementation or main program), and
- Finishing phase (termination or phaseout)

Following are some highlights based on the survey of 100 project managers conducted by Thamhain and Wilemon on the sources of conflict through the four phases of the project life cycle.[5,13,14]

Conceptual/Initiation phase (Formation). Front-end and strategic planning is done in this phase. In this phase, the project manager must launch the project within the larger "host" organization. The three predominant sources of conflict, in order of importance, are project priorities, administrative procedures, and schedules. Other sources, in order, are manpower, cost, technical issues and personality.

Frequently, when goals are being set, conflicts develop between the priorities assigned to the project and the priorities that are believed to be important by other functional and staff personnel. To eliminate the negative impact of this conflict, project managers should carefully evaluate their positions as early as possible and plan for the impact of their projects on the groups that support them.

The second source, administrative procedures, is associated with several management issues, including:

Human Resource Skills for the Project Manager

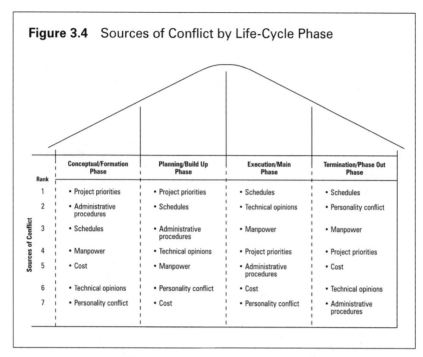

Figure 3.4 Sources of Conflict by Life-Cycle Phase

Rank	Conceptual/Formation Phase	Planning/Build Up Phase	Execution/Main Phase	Termination/Phase Out Phase
1	• Project priorities	• Project priorities	• Schedules	• Schedules
2	• Administrative procedures	• Schedules	• Technical opinions	• Personality conflict
3	• Schedules	• Administrative procedures	• Manpower	• Manpower
4	• Manpower	• Technical opinions	• Project priorities	• Project priorities
5	• Cost	• Manpower	• Administrative procedures	• Cost
6	• Technical opinions	• Personality conflict	• Cost	• Technical opinions
7	• Personality conflict	• Cost	• Personality conflict	• Administrative procedures

(Sources of Conflict)

Source: John R. Adams and Nicki S. Kirchof. 1982. *Conflict Management for Project Managers*. Drexel Hill, PA: Project Management Institute, p. 22.

- Project organization structure
- Reporting relationships and procedures
- Authority of the project manager
- Control over human and other resources
- Establishment of schedules, performance specifications and performance criteria.

Most of these areas are negotiated by the project manager, and to minimize the problems, clear procedures should be established as early as possible.

Schedules represent another area where established groups must show some flexibility in accommodating a new project. Most project managers feel that this causes conflict because it involves a re-orientation of present operating patterns and "local" priorities in support departments. The situation gets worse when these support groups are committed to other projects. Similarly, negotiations over support personnel and other resources can lead to potential conflict in this phase. Therefore, effective communication, planning and negotiating skills are needed to avoid destructive conflict emanating from these potential conflict sources.

Development/Planning phase (Build-up). In this phase, the project plan is mapped and major planning decisions are made. The three sources ranked highest in conflict intensity during this phase (see Figure 3.4) are project priorities, schedules, administrative procedures. These were also ranked highest in the conceptual phase; in fact, some of these conflicts are an extension of conflicts that arise during the first phase. Other sources of conflict beyond these three are technical issues, manpower, personality and cost. Conflicts develop in the conceptual phase over the establishment of schedules, whereas in the planning phase, conflicts arise over the enforcement of these schedules.[5,13,14]

Conflict over administrative procedures becomes less intense in the planning phase, indicating that administrative problems are diminishing, most likely because these were resolved in the conceptual phase.

Conflict over technical issues becomes more evident in this phase (rising from sixth rank in the conceptual phase to fourth in the planning phase). This is primarily due to disagreements with support groups that cannot meet the technical requirements and have to increase their efforts, affecting the project manager's cost and schedule objectives.

The project managers surveyed by Thamhain and Wilemon pointed out that personality conflicts are especially difficult to handle. Even small and infrequent personality conflicts can become more disruptive and detrimental to the overall project or program than intense conflicts over non-personal issues.

Conflict over cost was still indicated to be low in this phase because:
- Most project managers feel no conflict over the establishment of cost targets.
- Some projects are not mature enough for arguments over the cost estimates to emerge and cause disagreements between the project managers and their supporters.

Execution/Implementation phase. The implementation phase shows a different conflict pattern. The three highest ranking sources of conflict in this phase are schedules, technical issues and manpower. Additional sources of conflict in order are priorities, administrative procedures, cost and personality (see Figure 3.4).

In the implementation phase, meeting project schedules becomes very critical to project performance. In large projects, the interdependency of various support groups dealing with complex technology frequently results in slippage in schedule. A slippage in schedule of one group may cause a "domino" effect and affect other groups if they are on the critical path. Therefore, schedules become a greater source of conflict, especially later in the implementation phase, as more pressure is put on team members to meet schedules and deadlines.

While conflicts over schedules often develop in the earlier phases, the emphasis changes with time. For example in the concept phase, conflicts occur over the "establishment" of schedules; in the planning phase conflicts are over "enforcement" of schedules; in the implementation phase more intense conflicts develop over the "management and maintenance" of schedules.[5,13]

A high level of conflict develops over technical issues during this phase for two main reasons:

1. The various subsystems (such as configuration management, commissioning procedures) are actually integrated for the first time during this phase. Due to the complexities of this integration and interface management process, conflicts may develop over the lack of sufficient system integration and/or poor technical performance of one subsystem, affecting performance of other subsystems in the project.

2. A prototype of complex technical components is usually designed and tested during this phase to eliminate technical problems. However, this prototyping process may not proceed smoothly or produce successful results. Consequently, it can generate intense conflict in the main program phase over reliability and quality control standards, various design problems, and testing procedures. All these technical problems can severely impact the project and cause conflicts for the project manager.

Human resources utilization reaches its highest level in the implementation phase. If support groups are also providing personnel to other projects, severe tensions can develop over the availability of human resources and other project requirements. Conflicts over priorities decline in this phase as efforts are made to resolve priority issues in the conceptual and planning phases.

Finishing/Termination phase. This phase reveals an interesting shift in the dominant source of conflict in a project environment. The top three ranked sources include schedules, personality, and human resources.

Schedules still ranked the highest because schedule slippages that develop in the implementation phase tend to carry over into the termination phase. Delays in schedules become cumulative and impact the project most severely in the final stages of a project.

Personality conflict, previously ranked lower, is ranked second in this phase because:

• Project participants tend to be tense, concerned and uncertain about future assignments.

• Interpersonal relationships may be strained due to pressure on project participants to meet stringent schedules, budgets and performance objectives.

Disagreements over staffing and allocation of human resources may develop because of new projects phasing in, creating competition for personnel during the critical phase-out stage. Such problems jeopardize proper documentation, training and orientation, especially in computer and research projects. Conflicts over priorities are directly related to other project start-ups in the organization. The situation is worsened when some personnel may leave the project organization prematurely because of prior commitments that may cause stoppage in the schedule of current project or because of an opportunity for a better assignment elsewhere. In either case, the combined pressure on schedules, human resources, and personality, make projects more vulnerable to conflicts over priorities.

Cost, technical issues, and administrative procedures, are again ranked lowest because, one hopes, by the time the project reaches this phase, most of these issues have been resolved.

It should be pointed out that while cost control is difficult in the termination phase, it does not cause intense conflicts. Nevertheless, the low level of conflict over cost should not imply that the cost performance carries any less weight than other factors when evaluating the overall performance of a project manager. In fact, cost performance is one of the key evaluation criteria in appraising the performance of project managers. In some projects, conflicts over cost are low because:[14]

- Some project components are purchased externally on a fixed fee basis and the contractor bears the burden of cost escalations.
- Cost control may not be the highest priority. Participants recognize that costs are difficult to control due to unexpected problems throughout the project life cycle. Therefore, budgets are adjusted for increase in the cost of material and personnel over the life of a project.
- Some projects, especially high-tech and R&D, are managed on a cost-plus basis. In each project, original cost estimates cannot be rigidly adhered to due to continuous changes in the scope of the projects.

In addition to the seven reasons for conflict in project environments suggested by Wilemon and Thamhain, there are four additional conflict sources that should not be overlooked.

- *Communication problems* are the most common and obvious sources of conflict. The intensity of conflict may vary depending upon the degree of breakdown in communication and the players involved. Conflicts due to communication problems can be very high in all phases of the project life cycle.
- *Differences in time horizon* may surface when goals and priorities are discussed and become more dominant during the concept and planning phase of the project. Some people may look at the issues from a long-term point of view, while others may have a short-term outlook. As the project progresses, plans and procedures become well laid out and the project participants are more concerned with completing the task within the budget, schedule and human resources constraints.
- *Role uncertainty* can be included in administrative procedures along with other managerial issues and therefore conflict is likely to occur mostly in the concept and planning phases.

Human Resource Skills for the Project Manager

Figure 3.5 Trend of Conflict Intensity over the Four Project Life Cycle Stages

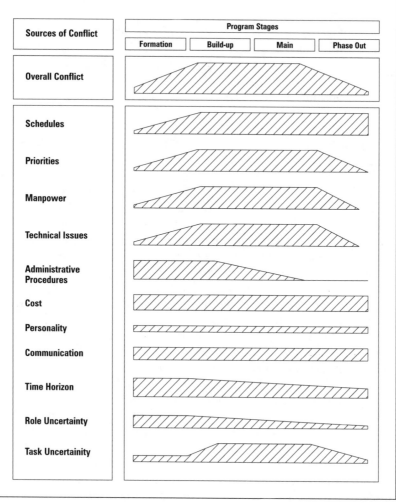

Source: Hans J. Thamhain and David L. Wilemon. 1975. Conflict Management in Project Life Cycles. *Sloan Management Review* (Spring): pp. 31-50. Reprinted by permission of the publisher.

- *Task uncertainty and information requirements* can be included in the schedule and therefore conflict of this nature is more likely to dominate during the planning stage of the project life cycle. However, it can cause some conflict during the implementation and termination phases as well.

Conflicts caused by communication problems are common and occur in all four phases of the project life cycle. Therefore, communication should not be overlooked as a potential source of conflict.

Table 3.2   Ranking the Sources of Project Conflict

Thamhain & Wilemon (1975)	Posner (1986)
1. Schedules	1. Schedules
2. Priorities	2. Cost/Budget
3. Human resources	3. Priorities
4. Technical issues/Performance tradeoffs	4. Human resources
5. Administrative procedures issues/Performance	5. Technical tradeoffs
6. Personality	6. Personality
7. Cost/Budget	7. Administrative procedures

Figure 3.5 shows a graphical summary of the relative conflict intensity for each of the seven sources of conflict, as indicated by Thamhain and Wilemon[13,14] over the four phases of the project life cycle. Additional sources of conflict (as outlined above) have been added based on the author's experiences on a variety of projects.

The work of Thamhain and Wilemon has been confirmed by other investigators working in a variety of project environments.[15, 17] Posner did a study in 1986 similar to that done by Wilemon and Thamhain in 1975, and came up with a slightly different ranking of sources of conflict over the project life cycle. Table 3.2 shows a comparison between the rankings of conflict sources reported by these two studies, and Table 3.3 shows a comparison of conflict source rankings for each phase of the project life cycle.[13, 17]

As shown in Table 3.2, the major difference in Posner is the pattern of conflict over costs, changing from seventh to second place. Conflict over administrative procedures has dropped from fifth to last position. These differences can be explained by a variety of changes in circumstances and ways of managing business, programs, and projects. Differences over cost can be attributed to tough global competition. Also, a shift in government contract pricing strategy (from a more flexible cost-plus basis to more rigorous fixed-price approach) has increased emphasis on cost issues. The decreased intensity of conflict over procedures can be explained by wider acceptance of project management concepts, strategies and techniques.[18]

INDIVIDUAL CONFLICTS, OF COURSE, VARY by project and by the players involved. However, project managers must be aware of the primary sources of conflict and its relative intensity during each phase in the life cycle of the project. They should analyze the reasons for these conflicts and plan in advance to minimize their negative impact.

Table 3.3   Conflict Source Ranking
           by Phase of the Project Life Cycle

Thamhain & Wilemon (1975)	Posner (1986)
Conceptual/Initiation Phase	
1. Priorities	1. Schedules
2. Administrative procedures	2. Cost/Budget
3. Schedules	3. Priorities
4. Human resources	4. Human resources
5. Cost/Budget	5. Technical issues/Performance tradeoffs
6. Technical issues/Performance tradeoffs	6. Personality
7. Personality	7. Administrative procedures
Development/Planning Phase	
1. Priorities	1. Human resources
2. Schedules	2. Priorities
3. Administrative procedures	3. Schedules
4. Technical issues/Performance tradeoff	4. Technical issues/Performance tradeoffs
5. Human resources	5. Cost/Budget
6. Personality	6. Personality
7. Cost/Budget	7. Administrative procedures
Execution/Implementation Phase	
1. Schedules	1. Schedules
2. Technical issues/Performance tradeoffs	2. Priorities
3. Human resources	3. Cost/Budget
4. Priorities	4. Technical issues/Performance tradeoffs
5. Administrative procedures, Cost/Budget, Personality	5. Human resources
	6. Administrative procedures
Phaseout	
1. Schedules	1. Schedules
2. Personality	2. Cost/Budget
3. Human resources	3. Personality
4. Priorities	4. Priorities
5. Cost/Budget	5. Human resources
6. Technical issues/Performance tradeoffs	6. Administrative procedures
7. Administrative procedures	7. Technical issues/Performance tradeoffs

Summary

Conflict is a part of project life. This is because projects are done by people or teams of people with a diverse mix of backgrounds, norms and skills and involve many interactions between people and groups. Conflict occurs when individuals or groups have incompatible goals, thoughts or emotions and, in working together, make decisions to accomplish their objectives. Conflicts in themselves are neither good nor bad. They can have both positive or negative effects. Effective conflict management focuses on minimizing negative conflict.

Resolving conflicts of interests requires negotiation. To manage conflicts successfully, it is important to analyze how and why conflicts of interests occur, basic concepts of conflicts and their effects on performance of project participants. There are three views of conflicts, namely traditional, contemporary and interactionist. The traditional view assumes that conflict is bad and should be suppressed, while the contemporary view assumes that conflict is inevitable between humans and should be managed. The interactionist view suggests that conflict is a necessary part of work and therefore should be stimulated to foster creativity and innovation. Conflicts can occur at four levels: intrapersonal, interpersonal, intergroup, and intragroup.

Although project participants may have divergent ideas and disagreements when they interact with each other, there are nine predominant antecedent conditions, that predispose an organization toward conflict. These antecedent conditions of conflicts are common in most organizations to a greater or lesser extent. It is the degree to which a variety of these conditions exist in combination that leads to conflict and determines its intensity within the organization and project team. These conditions tend to be more apparent in projects that are organized in matrix forms and are frequently used to create change using modern and high technology through a diverse mix of specialized pool of human resources in highly complex and uncertain situations. The project manager must be able to identify these conditions and avoid potential destructive results of conflict by controlling and channeling conflict into areas that can be positive to project success.

Conflict can have either positive or negative effects on performance. On the positive side of the ledger, conflict can diffuse more serious conflict, act as a major stimulant for change, increase creativity and innovation, enhance communication, clarify goals and issues, increase performance energy and group cohesion, and balance power and influence. Detrimental effects of conflict include increased stress, unproductive atmosphere, distorted views of behavior, and loss of status/position power. Conflicts have a significant impact on performance of project participants. Project managers should resolve conflicts to achieve functional outcomes and minimize dysfunctional outcomes. They should allow conflict only to a level where it increases the performance of project participants.

For effective management of conflict, the project manager must understand the different categories of conflict, reasons or sources of conflict and their relationship to the project life cycle. There are 11 main reasons for conflict in a project: priorities, administrative procedures, technical issues, task uncertainty, role uncertainty, differences in time horizons, staffing and allocation of human resources, costs, schedules, communication problems, and personalities.

The predominant sources and intensities of conflict vary over the four major project life cycle phases (conceptual, planning, execution and termination). A 1975 survey by Wilemon and Thamhain described the relative intensity of seven major sources of conflict over the four phases of project life cycle. This was updated in 1986 by Posner, with slightly different ranking of intensity for seven major sources of conflict. Individual conflicts, of course, vary by project and the players involved. However, project managers must be aware of the primary sources of conflict during each phase. Conflicts caused by communication problems are the most common and happen in all phases of the project life cycle. Thus, effective communication is essential to project success.

Destructive conflict can be highly detrimental to the productivity of the project team and hence project outcome. It can drastically affect the quality of decisions and the decision making process, making it long, complex, and difficult. It can lead to the formation of unhealthy and competitive coalitions within the organization, thus reducing commitment of project participants to the objectives of the project and those of overall organization. In essence, destructive conflicts can lead to a number of divisive, frustrating distractions that degrade the quality and quantity of efforts normally applied toward organizational goals. Moreover, in addition to causing project failures, conflicts lead to tension, stress and poor working relationships, which lessen mutual trust and cooperation. Therefore, it is vital that project managers understand the basic concepts of conflict, categories of conflict, negative and positive values of conflict, and how conflicts influence the performance of project team members. They must identify, analyze and evaluate various reasons for conflict as the project progresses through its life cycle and use appropriate strategies to manage conflicts effectively.

chapter

4

Outline

Conflict Management Techniques   114

Practical Guidelines for Managing Conflict in a Project   127

Summary   142

Human Resource Skills for the Project Manager

The test of the first-rate intelligence is the ability to hold two opposed ideas in the mind at the same time, and still retain the ability to function.

— F. Scott Fitzgerald

4

Managing and Resolving Conflict in a Project Environment

ECAUSE THE WAY conflict is managed can significantly impact project success, the ability to manage conflict is one of the most important skills a project manager must possess. An American Management Association study of middle- and top-level executives revealed that the average manager spends approximately 20 percent of his or her time dealing with conflict.[1] The importance of conflict management is also reinforced by a research study of managers that analyzed 25 skills and personality factors to determine which, if any, were related to managerial success. Of the 25 factors, the ability to handle conflict was most positively related to managerial success.[2]

Effective conflict management requires a combination of human skills. The first step in managing conflict is an ability to understand and correctly diagnose it.[3] Conflict management therefore consists of a diagnostic process; a selection of interpersonal style, communication and negotiating strategies; the development of trust and respect; and structural interventions designed to avoid unnecessary conflict and reduce or resolve excessive conflict.

Structural conflicts in a project environment can be resolved by changing procedures, personnel, authority structures, and reporting relationships. Project managers must be aware of various interpersonal conflict resolution modes and their strengths and weaknesses in order to choose an appropriate approach according to circumstances. Project managers must follow some practical guidelines to manage conflict in a project, which involve preparing for the conflict, facing the conflict and then resolving the conflict by developing win-win strategies. They must also recognize that it is sometimes good to *stimulate* conflict in order to encourage self-evaluation, creativity, and innovation. ■

Conflict Management Techniques

People are trying to either shun conflict or crush it. Neither strategy is working. Avoidance and force only raise the level of conflict ... They have become part of the problem rather than the solution.

— DeCecco and Richards

According to both the contemporary and interactionist views, conflict is inevitable in projects and there is an optimal level of conflict that maximizes overall performance. Two important implications of these views are that:

- Conflict in projects is good because it stimulates creativity, innovation, improvements, and higher productivity.
- Management of conflict should become a key project management activity and project managers must develop appropriate skills to effectively manage conflict.

Conflict management involves intervention by top management or project managers (depending upon the intensity and nature of conflict) to stimulate or decrease the level of conflict between the parties involved. Conflict management should encourage constructive conflict and discourage destructive conflict.[4] Projects are designed to meet defined goals and objectives, so conflict that facilitates the achievement of goals should be encouraged, and conflict that obstructs goal attainment should be discouraged.

Conflict management techniques include stimulating an appropriate level of conflict; altering organizational structures; using various interpersonal styles and choosing an appropriate conflict resolution approach.

Stimulating conflict

He that wrestles with us strengthens our nerves and sharpens our skills. Our antagonist is our helper.

— Edmund Burke

The whole notion of stimulating conflict is difficult to accept because conflict traditionally has a negative connotation. However, the interactionist view encourages conflict. There is evidence that, in some situations, an increase in conflict actually improves performance.[5]

Robbins designed the following set of questions to which affirmative answers suggest a potential need for conflict stimulation.[6]

- Are you surrounded by "yes people"?
- Are project team members afraid to admit ignorance and uncertainties to you?
- Is there too much emphasis on reaching a compromise that may lead to losing sight of values, long-term objectives, or the project's welfare?
- Are project managers more concerned in maintaining the impression of peace and cooperation in their project, regardless of the price?
- Is there an excessive concern by decision makers for not hurting the feelings of others?

- Do project managers believe that popularity and politics are more important for obtaining organizational rewards than competence and high performance?
- Are project managers unduly enamored of obtaining consensus for their decisions?
- Do project team members show unusually high resistance to change?
- Is there a lack of new ideas, creativity, and innovation?
- Is there an unusually low level of turnover among project team members?

General management and project managers can stimulate conflict in the following ways:[7]

Accept conflict as desirable on certain occasions. The project manager may block launching project activities unless sufficient front-end planning has been done and a basic framework with clear project priorities, scope definition, and administrative procedures has been established. To a degree, conflicts at the front end should be viewed positively, since a project manager's opportunity to participate in setting the project's budget and schedule (including arguing for objectives that may cause conflict) is likely to decrease conflicts down the road.

Bring new individuals into an existing situation. Thoughtful questions and comments from newcomers or outsiders may provide a different, fresh perspective. It may encourage long-time team members to remove their blinders and think of new ways of doing things. For example, a project manager may bring in an outside expert to increase team effectiveness by introducing modern styles of team management such as empowerment, team partnering and a win-win conflict resolution strategy.

Restructure the organization. The project organization structure may have to be changed to suit the circumstances. New reporting relationships may create uncertainty, but may also motivate project participants to discover innovative and creative ways to get things done.

Introduce programs designed to increase competition. A manager of projects may introduce competition to encourage work package managers to accomplish their work packages ahead of schedule and under budget without compromising quality. Competition can lead to productive conflict, as individuals or groups try to outdo each other. A project manager must understand the difference between competition and conflict in order to get positive results. Management may establish rewards, awards or recognition for winners of such competitions. Managers of some work packages may come into conflict with each other as they try to win, but overall organizational output will probably increase.

Introduce programmed conflict.[8] Some project participants may be keen in pushing their ideas. Project managers should play "devils advocate" and use dialectical inquiry to develop and clarify opposing points of view. These approaches are designed to program conflict into processes of planning, decision making, and risk analysis, and thus make conflict legitimate and acceptable.

Conflict stimulation can play a positive role in organizations with large programs or projects (especially R&D organizations) where it is important to foster creativity and innovation. Stimulating conflict is considered a proactive approach that requires "upfront" initiative aimed at minimizing the impact of potential negative conflict and avoiding costly "patching up" operations later in the project cycle.

Resolving structural conflicts

Structural conflict resolution techniques focus on the structural aspects of the project organization that may be causing the conflict. These techniques emphasize that certain structural features of project organization can cause conflict even if the project team members behave (as individuals) in a reasonable manner. Some structural conflict resolution techniques are briefly described below.[9]

Procedural changes mainly refer to changing work procedures to avoid conflict. For instance, a project manager or technical expert on the project team may evaluate and select a vendor for a technical contract. The purchasing department may then follow their traditional departmental procedures, causing delays that may lead to conflict. Such disputes can be avoided by involving the purchasing department in the process of evaluating bids for complex technical contracts and thereby ensuring their cooperation and prompt service when needed to expedite the contract.

Personnel changes involve transferring individuals into or out of the project in order to resolve personality conflicts. For example, a personality conflict between two high-performing technical experts may be reducing overall project output. One of the experts is transferred to another project and both are then able to make a significant and positive contribution to their new projects and to the organization as a whole.

Authority changes clarify or alter lines of authority and responsibility to reduce conflict. Such situations usually arise in matrix structures, where functional managers may over-exercise their authority over personnel who have been assigned to a specific project manager for the duration of the project. Clarifying or changing authority lines or reporting relationships in such circumstances will reduce typical structural conflicts between the project manager and the functional manager.

Layout changes rearrange work space to resolve conflict. This becomes essential when two project teams harass or disturb each other continually. It may be effective to build a physical separation between them to eliminate interaction.

Resource changes involve increasing resources so that the disputing parties can each have what they need. For example, a conflict may develop between two project managers (each handling a large but tight project) over the priorities for purchasing and accounting personnel. A manager of projects can resolve such conflicts by getting an authorization to hire separate accounting and purchasing personnel for each project so that both project managers get what they need.

THE ABOVE METHODS ARE USED to resolve, prevent or reduce structural conflicts. However, project managers should analyze the sources and intensity of conflict before taking action.

Interpersonal conflict resolution techniques

Part of my job as a coach is to keep the five guys who hate me away from the five guys who are undecided.

— *Casey Stengel*

Interpersonal conflict resolution techniques focus on the human interaction in a conflict situation. These techniques are based upon the recognition that the choice of a conflict management strategy depends upon the intensity of the conflict and the relative importance people place on maintaining good relationships versus achieving goals. Like a leadership style, the specific method to resolve conflict also depends upon a number of situational variables. The "best" approach will be the one that both minimizes the obstacles to project completion and helps to develop cohesive and effective project teams.

Main conflict resolution modes. There is no "right" way to settle a conflict. Individuals attempt to manage interpersonal conflict in a variety of ways.[10] The choice of an appropriate style for resolving conflict depends upon a broad range of factors such as:
- The relative importance and intensity of the conflict
- The time pressure for resolving the conflict
- The position taken by players involved
- Motivation to resolve conflict on a long-term or a short-term basis.

Conflict management possibilities are also dependent upon the ratio of assertiveness to cooperation among the parties involved in the conflict, as well as on the type of conflict being handled. Conflict resolution techniques range from the power-based "steamroller" approach to a more defensive, diplomatic and tactical approach. Intermediate views suggest variations of avoidance, give-and-take negotiation, collaboration and problem solving.

Blake and Mouton presented five general techniques for resolving conflict:[11]
1. Withdrawing
2. Smoothing
3. Forcing
4. Compromising
5. Collaborating/confronting/problem solving (also referred to as negotiating).

Some authors have suggested that there is a subtle difference between collaborating and confronting/problem-solving. For the purposes of this discussion, we will consider them as six separate techniques (as shown in Table 4.1). Blake and Mouton's five techniques are shown in Figure 4.2 and used for comparison with the Thomas-Kilmann model (see Figure 4.1, pages 124–25).

Despite the minor differences in definitions and terminology, these studies of conflict resolution modes offer an analytical base for handling specific project situations. The project manager must analyze the situation and select the appropriate mode for managing conflict within their project organizations in order to create a climate conducive to achieving a constructive outcome.[7,12,13]

Withdrawing (avoidance, denial or retreat) involves giving up, pulling out or retreating. It also refers to refusal to deal with the conflict. It involves ignoring conflict as much as possible. This style is appropriate when a "cooling off" period is needed to gain better understanding of the conflict situation and also when the other party involved in the conflict is both unassertive and uncooperative. Withdrawal is a passive, stopgap way of handling conflict and generally fails to solve the problem. Therefore, this style should not be used if the conflict deals with an issue that is of immediate concern or is important to the successful completion of the project.

Smoothing, or accommodating, is an appeasing approach. It involves emphasizing areas of agreement while avoiding points of disagreement. Smoothing is appropriate to keep harmony and avoid outwardly conflictive situations. It works when the issues are more important than personal positions and aspirations of the parties involved. Since smoothing tends to keep peace only in the short term, it fails to provide a permanent long-term solution to the underlying conflict. Generally, conflict reappears again in another form.

Both smoothing and withdrawing styles incline towards ignoring or delaying tactics, which do not resolve conflict but will temporarily slow down the situation. Project managers must remember that if the conflict is not handled and resolved in a timely manner it will likely lead to more severe and intense conflict in the future.

Forcing (using power or dominance) implies the use of position power to resolve the conflict. It involves imposing one viewpoint at the expense of another and is characterized by a win-lose outcome in which one party overwhelms the other. Forcing is used when there is no common ground on which to bargain or negotiate, and when both parties are uncooperative and strong-willed. Project managers may use it when time is of the essence, an issue is vital to the well-being of the project, and they feel they are right based on the information available. Under such circumstances project managers take the risk and simply dictate the action in order to move things forward. This approach is appropriate when quick decisions are required or when unpopular issues such as budget cuts, fast-tracking or staff cutbacks are essential in a project.

Forcing usually takes less time than compromise and negotiation but it leaves hard feelings because people dislike having others' views imposed on them. Conflict resolved by force may develop again and haunt the enforcer at a later date. Although forcing definitely resolves the conflict quickly, it should be used only as a last resort.

Compromising is primarily "bargaining"—receiving something in exchange for something else. It involves considering various issues, bargaining, using tradeoff negotiations and searching for solutions that bring some degree of satisfaction to both parties involved in the conflict. In this mode, neither party wins but both get some degree of satisfaction out of the situation. Temporarily, both parties may feel hurt because they had to give up something that was important to them, but compromising usually provides acceptable solutions. A definitive resolution to the conflict is achieved when a compromise is reached and accepted as a just solution by both parties involved in the conflict. The only problem with compromising in a project situation is that, sometimes, important aspects of the project might be compromised in order to achieve personal objectives.

Collaborating is an effective technique to manage conflict when a project situation is too important to be compromised. It involves incorporating multiple ideas and viewpoints from people with different perspectives. It offers a good opportunity to learn from others. Active collaboration by both parties in contributing to the resolution makes it easier to get their consensus and commitment. Collaboration is not very effective when more than a few players are involved and their viewpoints are mutually exclusive.

Confronting or problem solving (negotiating) implies a direct confrontation where disagreement is addressed directly. Conflict is treated as a problem in this process and both parties are interested in finding a mutually acceptable solution. This approach requires a give-and-take attitude between the parties, meaning that both parties are somewhat assertive and somewhat cooperative. It involves pinpointing the issue and resolving it objectively by defining the problem, gathering necessary information, generating and analyzing alternatives and selecting the best alternative under the circumstances. Confrontation requires open dialogue between participants, who must be mature, understanding, and competent—both technically and managerially.

In most cases, confronting or problem solving may take longer than other techniques, but they provide final solutions by ultimately resolving the underlying problems.

Table 4.1 summarizes these six interpersonal conflict resolution techniques. However, a survey of management literature suggests some additional techniques for resolving conflict.[9]

Table 4.1 Conflict Management Styles

Style	Description	Effect
Withdrawing/ Avoiding	Retreats from an actual or potential conflict situation	Does not solve the problem
Smoothing/ Accommodating	Emphasizes areas of agreement rather than areas of difference	Provides only short-term solution
Compromising	Searches for and bargains for solutions that bring some degree of satisfaction to all parties	Does provide definitive resolution
Forcing	Pushes one viewpoint at the expense of others; offers only win-lose solutions	Hard feelings may come back in other forms
Collaborating	Incorporates multiple viewpoints and insights from differing perspectives; leads to consensus and commitment	Provides long-term resolution
Confronting/Problem Solving	Treats conflict as a problem to be solved by examining alternatives; requires give-and-take attitude and open dialogue	Provides ultimate resolution

Majority rule. The side with the most votes gets its way. (Example: At a committee meeting, to select a project management system, a dispute may be settled by voting.).

Consensus. The parties involved in conflict must attempt to reach a consensus on what should be done to resolve the conflict. (Example: At a strategic planning meeting dealing with a number of programs/projects, projects are prioritized in order of importance after a lengthy discussion in which members of the management team indicates their preferences.)

Mediation and arbitration. These are normally used to resolve conflicts between labor and management or other contractual disputes. In *mediation*, a neutral third party tries to help parties involved in the conflict to work out a resolution. In *arbitration*, a neutral third party imposes a binding solution on both parties involved in the conflict.

Superordinate goal. In this technique, an agreed-upon goal is used to override the conflict. (Example: A general contractor in a project may

Human Resource Skills for the Project Manager

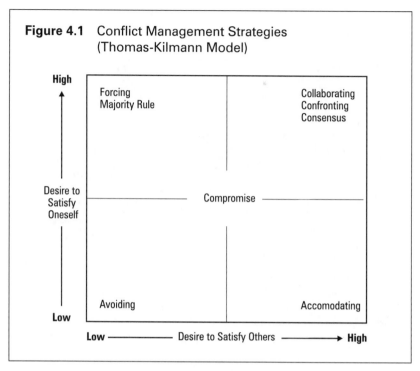

Figure 4.1 Conflict Management Strategies
(Thomas-Kilmann Model)

Source: K.W. Thomas. 1976. Conflict and Conflict Management. In *Handbook of Industrial and Organizational Psychology*, M.D. Dunette, ed. Chicago: Rand McNally: p. 900. Used by permission of Marvin D. Dunnette.

share cost overruns with some subcontractors to achieve a superordinate goal of staying within overall budget for that specific work package.)

Choosing a conflict resolution approach

By blending the breadth of the sun and the shade, true harmony comes into the world.

— *Tao Te Ching*

In project management, which conflict resolution techniques should be favored and which should be avoided? The effectiveness of each technique varies widely, depending upon the situation. (See Self-Assessment Exercise C in the Appendix to determine your preferred style.) The result of any conflict resolution approach depends upon how the project manager manages the conflict. Destructive conflicts have a significant negative impact and project managers must control and channel the conflict resolution process for constructive results. Choosing an appropriate conflict resolution approach involves:

- Analyzing and evaluating conflict resolution techniques
- Understanding the dynamics of handling two-party conflicts
- Choosing the best conflict resolution approach (negotiating to solve problems by using win-win strategy).

Figure 4.2 Conflict Resolution Modes

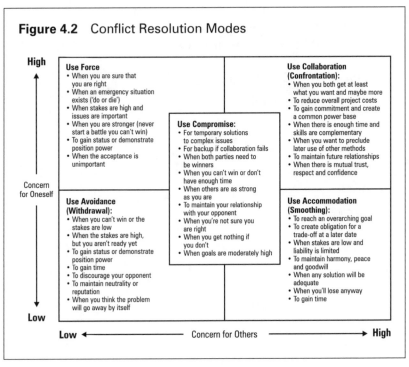

Source: Data based on information from the work of Paul Dinsmore, *Human Factors in Project Management,* AMACOM, 1990, pp. 149-166.

Analyzing and evaluating conflict resolution techniques. Conflict resolution techniques can be evaluated by using two models, one developed by Thomas and Kilmann[14] and another developed by Filley,[11,14] which are briefly described below.

Thomas-Kilmann conflict model involves comparing several of the interpersonal techniques outlined in the previous section by analyzing two essential dimensions of conflict (shown in Figure 4.1):[14]

- Desire to satisfy oneself (concern for one's own views)
- Desire to satisfy others (concern for other's views).

The terms applied to conflict resolution techniques or modes in Thomas-Kilmann model vary slightly from those used by Blake and Mouton.[15] *Avoiding* or *withdrawing* corresponds to both a weak desire to satisfy oneself and a weak desire to satisfy others. *Accommodating* or *smoothing* represents a strong desire to satisfy others but a weak desire to satisfy oneself. *Compromising* corresponds to a medium level of desire to satisfy both others and oneself. *Collaboration* or *confrontation* is characterized by a high concern for others and high concern for one's own views. *Forcing and majority rule* are represented by a strong desire to satisfy oneself and a weak desire to satisfy others. Figure 4.2 shows that, according to the

122

Figure 4.3 Styles of Conflict Resolution

Blake & Morton	Filley's Model		
Conflict Resolution Mode	Conflict Resolution Style	Concerns for	
		Personal Goals	Relationships
Forcing	Win—Lose	High	Low
Smoothing	Yield—Lose	Low	High
Withdrawing	Lose—Leave	Low	Low
Compromising	Compromise	Medium	Medium
Collaborating/ Confronting/ Problem Solving	Integrative	High	High

Source: John R. Adams and Nicki S. Kirchof. 1982. *Conflict Management for Project Managers*. Drexel Hill, PA: Project Management Institute, p. 13.

Thomas-Kilmann model, each conflict resolution mode is appropriate under specific situations.

Filley's model, similarly, classifies the styles of handling conflict in terms of concern for personal goals and concern for relationships.

Based on these concerns, Blake and Mouton's five styles (see Figure 4.3) correspond to five interpersonal conflict resolution modes that Filley identified as:[15,16]

- *Win-lose style* (high concern for personal goals and low concern for relationships) refers to a "tough battler" who wants to meet his or her own goals at all costs.
- *Yield-lose style* (low concern for personal goals and high concern for relationships) represents a "friendly helper" who places high values on maintaining relationships with others and low values on achieving his or her own goals.
- *Lose-leave style* (low concern for both personal goals and relationships) implies a person who sees conflict as a hopeless, useless and punishing experience.
- *Compromise style* (moderate concerns for both personal goals and relationships) implies a compromiser who will try to find a position where each side benefits and ends up with something.
- *Integrative style* (high concern for both personal goals and relationships) emphasizes problem solving. An integrative-style person is a problem solver. He or she will try to satisfy his or her own goals as well as the goals of others.

Figure 4.4 Conflict Management Results in Two-Party Conflict

		1st Party's Conflict Handling Mode				
		Problem Solving	Forcing	Compromising	Smoothing	Withdrawing
2nd Party's Conflict Handling Mode	Problem Solving	Quick Agreement	Forcing Over 50%	Problem Solver	Problem Solver	Problem Solver
	Forcing		Stalemate	Forcer	Forcer	Forcer
	Compromising			Agreement	Compromise	Compromise
	Smoothing				Stalemate	Smoothing Over 50%
	Withdrawing					Stalemate

Source: John R. Adams and Nicki S. Kirchof. 1982. *Conflict Management for Project Managers*. Drexel Hill, PA: Project Management Institute, p. 42.

The first three styles—*win-lose, yield-lose and lose-leave*—are not effective because of their extremes. They generally lead to project failure, whereas the last two—*compromise and integrative*—lead to project success.

Both models emphasize the long-term concern for maintaining relationships, which plays a significant role in choosing a suitable conflict resolution technique. Forcing, smoothing, withdrawing, majority rule and the superordinate goal technique are generally less effective because they fail to deal with the basic cause of the conflict. But in some circumstances, these may be useful because they impose a period of peace while the parties involved in conflict think about thei r next moves. The most appropriate technique is the one that clears the path for moving the project on the right track and removing the barriers to project success. However, it is not easy to choose the best approach because each situation is unique and the players involved have different personalities.

Dynamics of handling two-party conflicts. Most conflicts in a project environment occur between two parties. The results of a two-party conflict do not depend only on the conflict resolution approach used by one party, for instance the project manager. Rather, the results are dependent upon the interplay of conflict handling techniques chosen and used by both parties.[16] In examining and preparing for a conflict resolution, the project manager should try to determine in advance the conflict resolution technique that the other party may use. Based upon this information, the project manager can work out a strategy and select a mode that is most likely to resolve the conflict.

Figure 4.4 shows conflict management results in two-party conflicts. This figure assumes that both parties have equal power at the beginning of the conflict. Note that a quick agreement is generally reached when parties have a problem-solving or confrontation attitude. Agreement also occurs when both parties are in a compromising frame of mind. However, stalemates predominate when both parties have a forcing, smoothing or withdrawing attitude. It is obvious from Figure 4.4 that confrontation is a strong and effective resolution technique to use against conflict handling modes by the other party. This is true except when the other party chooses a forcing mode, which may tend to overpower the confronting mode. Forcing is effective except when used against another forcing party, which results in a stalemate. Compromise yields to the problem solver or forcer, but reaches an agreement with the compromiser, smoother or withdrawer. Smoothing, on the other hand, wins over withdrawing, but yields to confrontation, forcing or compromising. Withdrawal yields to all other types of resolution techniques with the exception of withdrawal itself, which results in a stalemate.[16]

The project manager should review the concepts outlined in Figure 4.4 when preparing to handle conflict. The project manager must take time in studying the behavior of all other parties associated with the project so as to accurately predict each potential "opponent's" likely response to the conflict situation.

The best conflict resolution approach. Each conflict situation is unique. Therefore, it is difficult to recommend the best conflict resolution approach due to the many variables and the dynamic nature of conflict. Of the approaches discussed above, some are more suited to certain situations than others. Which conflict resolution approach is the best depends upon:

• Type and relative importance of conflict
• Time pressure
• Position of the players involved
• Relative emphasis on goals versus relationships.

Forcing, smoothing, withdrawing, majority rule and the superordinate goal techniques are generally not effective in resolving conflicts because they fail to deal with the real cause of the conflict. But, sometimes, they may be appropriate when it is important to create a period of peace and harmony while the parties involved in the conflict think about their next move.

Techniques like compromise, mediation and arbitration are usually used in labor-management disputes but they have some potential problems. For example, in compromising, each party gives up something and neither gets exactly what it wants. In arbitration, both parties may be unhappy with the arbitrator or with the binding decision.

The best solution for managing project conflicts is the confronting/problem solving, or negotiation, mode. Since project management involves solving problems as the project progresses through its life cycle, this type of conflict management is very practical. This approach aims for a win-win strategy, which is best for both the project and the parties involved. Project

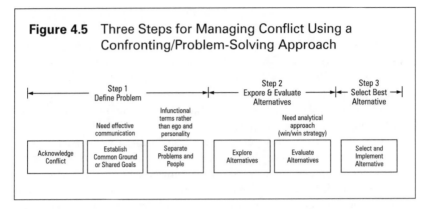

Figure 4.5 Three Steps for Managing Conflict Using a Confronting/Problem-Solving Approach

managers should acquire proper training in the procedures, nuances, and skills of professional negotiation.

Conflicts are managed effectively if they are resolved on a permanent basis. The relationship between the desire for achieving goals and the desire for maintaining good long-term relationships has a significant impact on the choice of a conflict resolution style. Some guidelines and important steps for negotiating effectively to resolve conflicts and solve problems in a project environment are outlined below.

Confronting/problem solving (negotiation) focuses on optimizing overall project goals. Its goal is to arrive at an acceptable agreement that resolves conflicts or disagreements and helps move the project ahead. This method may involve using the other resolution modes of collaboration and compromise as part of the process. This approach emphasizes that both parties must accept the end result of the negotiation and feel committed to make it work.[12] In fact, *winning (especially at the cost of others) never resolves the conflict and therefore should never be a goal of true negotiation.*

Project managers may use the following simple three-step approach (see Figure 4.5) to resolve conflicts through problem-solving negotiation.[12]

1. *Define the problem.* This is the first and most important step to ensure successful conflict resolution. It involves the following steps:
   - Acknowledge that conflict exists
   - Establish common ground or shared goals through effective communication
   - Separate the problem from the people.
     The problem should be defined in clear, objective and functional terms, not in terms of egos, emotions and personality traits.
2. *Explore and evaluate alternatives.* The people involved should list as many alternatives as possible. The alternatives should be analyzed and ranked by using an objective criteria, not opinions and attitudes. It involves an open, in-depth tradeoff analysis. Win-win strategy to meet project goals should be emphasized as the major goal of negotiation.

Human Resource Skills for the Project Manager

Some people involved in this process may have different goals and their own hidden agendas. Project managers must use effective communicating skills, actively listening to everyone involved in the negotiation process. Both verbal and nonverbal components of communication should be recognized.

3. *Select and implement the best alternative.* Project managers must clearly explain the possible outcomes of negotiation and how and why a specific alternative has been selected. They should try to get the acceptance and commitment of everyone involved in the conflict by emphasizing how the negotiated settlement will help everyone individually and, above all, the project as a whole.

IN MOST SITUATIONS, MANAGERS SEE THEMSELVES as compromising or negotiating a conflict, while they view the other parties as opponents, competing, forcing their viewpoints, uncompromising, uncooperative and keen to win at any cost. This is why conflicts continue in so many projects and, if not managed effectively, lead to project failure. Project managers must convince project participants of a team perspective in which individuals win only when the team wins. Project managers must inspire teamwork by establishing a clear, compelling shared vision.

The causes and sources of conflicts must be understood as a first step to managing the conflict effectively. Project managers must try to create a climate conducive to open dialogue, open communication, and, above all a commitment to reaching a mutually acceptable solution with a focus on win-win results by using an objective problem-solving approach.

Practical Guidelines for Managing Conflict in a Project

Nine-tenths of the serioius controversies that arise in life result from misunderstanding.

— Louis .D. Brandeis

Conflict is caused by disagreement between individuals. It is a basic element of human behavior and is inevitable in all endeavors involving people. Most projects involve interactions between people and groups. When a project team of great diversity interacts to complete their tasks, there is always the potential for conflict. In fact, it is virtually impossible for people to work together, make decisions, give and accept delegation and attempt to meet project goals without conflict.

Both the project manager and the project team must resolve conflict as soon as possible. Sometimes, a project manager may decide to stimulate conflict to foster challenge and creativity among project team members. Identification, analysis and evaluation of the conflict before taking action is the key to effective management of conflict in project management. Some practical guidelines for managing conflicts effectively in a project, based on the concepts and techniques described in the previous sections, include preparing for conflict, facing conflict, and then resolving conflict.[17]

Preparing for conflict

According to the traditional view, conflict has a negative impact on project performance because it creates unpleasant situations, stress and may spoil interpersonal relationships. Therefore, preparing for conflict is the first step in managing conflict.[17]

Expect conflict. The project manager should expect that the sources of conflict will vary with the phases of the project. According to Wilemon and Thamhain's survey of 100 project managers,[11] there are seven major sources of conflict: schedules, priorities, human resources, technical issues, administration, personality and cost. The predominant sources and intensity of conflict vary over the life cycle of the project. Wilemon and Thamhain showed the ranking of conflict intensity arising from seven sources of conflict in four typical phases of the project life cycle—conceptual phase (initiation phase), planning/project build up phase, implementation/main program phase, and termination/phase-out phase. In addition to these seven sources of conflict, four additional sources have also been also identified: communication problems, differences in time horizon, role uncertainty, task uncertainty/information requirements.

Project managers may also find that the focus of conflict will vary with the attributes of the team and of the project goals. With an experienced team, the focus of conflict is within the team itself. If the project goals are vague and loosely defined, the focus of the conflict will likely be between the team and upper management or between the project team and the client, or both. The project manager should analyze the reasons or sources of conflict, how they vary with the phases of the project cycle, and the focus of the conflict before taking any action.

Plan ahead to handle conflict. After analyzing the sources, intensity and focus of conflict, project managers should plan how to deal with conflict. Some planning tools include:[17]

Developing a framework within which to view conflicts objectively. Conflicts among project participants may arise as the project teams progress through stages of team development. In such circumstances, conflicts come from the need of each person to answer the following questions in order to establish their positions clearly.[18]

- *Am I in or out?* In this type of conflict, people are likely to ask themselves whether they belong to the team or not. They raise issues that are unimportant in themselves just to break the ice and initiate communication.
- *Where do I stand? (Am I up or down?)* Are people at the top or at the bottom of a hierarchy? How will the group make decisions? How much responsibility does each team member have? How much authority, influence, and control does each individual on the project team have?
- *Am I near or far?* This question raises the issues of openness and affection. Team members must decide how close they want to get to other team members without feeling stuck with them. Emotions and

Human Resource Skills for the Project Manager

perceptions may express themselves positively (openly expressed positive feelings and warmth) or negatively (open hostility and jealousy).

Analyzing key players involved in the situation. This analysis should consider the whole project and should involve identifying the key players and their personalities. Who are the people or groups that are contributing to the conflict? Project managers should analyze their personalities, interpersonal habits, values and convictions. This knowledge will help create a cooperative and accommodating atmosphere. All key players should be willing to accept resolution of the conflict, otherwise it will continue or become even more intense and reduce project performance.

Preparing a communication strategy. Comments should be based on job description, job environment, chains of command and channels of communication. This will help individuals involved in the conflict situation be more objective and prepared to deal with the situation.

Planning ahead by the project manager involves answering the question: "Is the conflict primarily related to goals, authority or personalities or some combination of these?" These conflicts should be defined in objective terms, with a minimum of personal biases and opinions.

Prepare for stress management. Conflict can cause stress that varies in intensity depending upon the sources and intensity of conflict. Stress, if not managed in a timely manner, can cause severe physiological and psychological problems. Effective stress management is discussed in detail in Chapter Six.[17]

After preparing for the conflict, the project manager is able to face it.

Facing the conflict

Not everything that is faced can be changed, but nothing can be changed until it is faced.

— James Baldwin

Although conflict is one of the things we dislike the most, it is inevitable. Most often, when we try to avoid conflict, it will seek us out. Some people wrongly hope that conflict will go away if it is ignored. In fact, conflict ignored is more likely to get worse, which can significantly reduce project performance.

Sometimes people do not recognize conflict or else they avoid it. Such avoidance never resolves conflict but rather multiplies it. The best way to reduce conflict is to confront it. To face conflict effectively, project managers should do the following:[17]

Serve as a lightning rod. Hill compared managers of successful projects with those of projects that failed and found that the managers of successful projects:[19]

- Personally absorbed aggression
- Communicated and listened effectively
- Counseled their teams to maximize their output

- Encouraged openness, emotional expression, and new ideas
- Served as role models in planning, delegating, etc.
- Minimized potential conflict whenever possible
- Stimulated conflict to foster creativity and innovation.

In each of these behaviors, high-performing project managers faced the conflict without taking it personally. They often dealt objectively with hostility without responding in a hostile manner. Thus, project managers take the heat themselves, then ground it so that it harms neither them nor its source. Project managers can do this by:[17]

- Putting themselves on hold, rather than fighting back
- Screening out distractions to focus energy directly on the conflict and the people involved
- Giving the situation more time by allowing a cool-down period and time to think
- Responding to both emotional and factual contents of the situation.

The project managers surveyed by Wilemon and Thamhain felt that personality conflicts were often disguised as conflicts over other issues, such as technical issues and manpower, etc.[13] These "disguises" will persist if project managers only deal with facts. They should deal with feelings as well. Positive feelings, if expressed, can increase project performance. Even negative feelings, if expressed constructively, may help clarify confusion or remove a bottleneck in a project. To "name without blame," project managers must express feelings as feelings, not as facts. They must accept responsibility for their own feelings and avoid judging people based on feelings and impressions alone.

"Surface" the real issues. Conflicts that remain below the surface can have negative impacts on a project in many ways, such as:[17]
- Distorted or withheld information
- Slipped schedules
- Unplanned absences from project meetings
- Lack of initiative to solve problems
- Not working together as a real team.

A successful conflict manager should handle these burning issues gently but firmly. To "surface" the real issues, project managers may:[17]

Treat the surface issue as "real" two or three times. Project managers should give people two or three chances to bring the conflict into the open by themselves. However, if this fails, the project manager should approach the person and urge them to discuss the conflict in the open with the aim of resolving it as soon as possible.

Make the conflict visible to other parties involved. To resolve the conflict, project managers must make the conflict visible to other parties involved in the situation. They can do this by using effective communication techniques and planning aids such as Linear Responsibility Charts. LRCs are quite effective in resolving conflicts over administrative aspects of pro-

Human Resource Skills for the Project Manager

ject management such as procedures, task breakdowns, and assignments of responsibility and authority. Project managers may choose to prepare an LRC for each phase of the project life cycle.

Surfacing the real issues primarily involves getting all the background information associated with the conflict. This may uncover important aspects of the project which if not identified immediately will lead to serious consequences and even project failure. Project managers must use interpersonal skills, information and other resources to respond to:

- Real doubts (if any) about the value of the project
- Real questions about cost effectiveness (What is causing major cost deviations? Why?)
- Real questions about schedule (What is causing the real delay and how much; what options are available?)
- Real concerns about the way the project is being run, and how the project affects other projects or systems already ongoing.

Give ample support. Block described the importance of support in a work relationship.[20] Most people want to feel secure and worthwhile and receive encouragement, recognition and praise. Unfortunately, some project managers confuse support with agreement and, consequently, in a conflict (disagreement) situation, they withhold support when it is needed the most.

Conflict handling starts with identification of two dimensions: the *cooperativeness dimension* represents the degree to which the person wants to satisfy the concerns of the other party; the *assertiveness dimension* represents the degree to which the other party wants to satisfy his or her own point of view or concerns (e.g., one specialist may push his or her own solution to technical problems in a project without listening to other views seriously).

The project manager's job becomes very complicated when conflicts are buried. The project manager must surface the real issues that affect project performance by giving people two to three chances to make the conflicts visible to other parties and giving sufficient support in bringing conflicts into the open and resolving them using a problem solving approach.

Resolving the conflict

I never let the sun set on a disagreement with anybody who means a lot to me.
— *Thomas Watson, Sr.*

Due to the dynamic and sometimes unpredictable nature of projects, a substantial amount of management time is dedicated to resolving conflicts. In some cases, disagreements can be handled by a straightforward decision; in other situations a combination of time and skills is required. The project manager, the project team, and all other stakeholders involved in a conflict situation must work together in managing the conflict with an aim to achieving a win-win situation for everyone.

As outlined in previous sections, effective conflict management requires an extensive effort at the "front end." Good conflict managers size up possible clashes before contacting the parties and then they work out appropriate actions to resolve potential problems. To resolve conflicts, project managers should do the following:[17,21]

- Look for win-win alternatives
- Cut losses when necessary
- Formulate proactive conflict management strategies
- Plan properly as a solution for handling conflicts.

Look for win-win alternatives. Of the interpersonal conflict resolution styles outlined earlier, *confronting* (negotiating and problem solving) is the most effective approach because it starts with an understanding by both parties that they must search for solutions that bring satisfaction to all the parties involved in the conflict. It emphasizes the need to look for win-win solutions. Project managers must create a cooperative and assertive environment to achieve such an outcome. They must encourage open communications among all project stakeholders. Project managers should use the following guidelines to achieve a win-win situation.

Do the doable. Project managers must be able to evaluate the situation and spend their efforts and energy in doing only whatever is really possible. "It's no use in trying to teach ducks to sing—it will only frustrate you and confuse the ducks!"

Build on earlier market analyses. Using the strategy of only doing the doable, project managers should build on earlier analyses of situations to give some insight into the conditions that would meet the other party's criteria for a win-win solution.

Use the assertive model. Build on the strengths of all parties while minimizing their weaknesses. Building mutual understanding and trust will help in reaching a win-win solution.

Look at things right side up. It is a mistake to assume that the person is the problem and start attacking the person instead of the problem. To look at things right side up and achieve win-win solutions, project managers should try the following techniques.[17]

Separate the person from the problem and from his or her own behavior. Sometimes people blame others for their failures or inefficiencies:

"If I had an efficient staff, the project would be finished on time."

"If you would leave me alone, I could work this out!"

In the first case, the project manager sees the staff as the problem, rather than the slippage in schedule; in the second, the speaker sees an individual as the problem, rather than his own difficulty concentrating. Such perceptions fail to separate the people from the problem and therefore they don't help arriving at sensible solutions. Such views only lead to more frustration. Project managers should be able to find acceptable solutions by refocusing on the conflict picture by answering, for example, the following questions:[17]

Q: What is happening that I don't like?

A: Wasting too much time debating over priorities and over administrative aspects.

Q: What is not happening that I would like?

A: Not committing sufficient time and resources to meet the project schedule.

Q: What should happen for me to be able to say "This situation is no longer a problem"?

A: The following needs would have to be met:
- Need to define objectives with agreed-upon priorities
- Need to define interfaces and agreed upon in writing
- Need to have a plan with required resources identified and made available
- Need to eliminate barriers to communication to ensure effective flow of information.

Concentrate on outcomes instead of positions. Some project managers may confuse outcomes with positions. When people get locked into a contest over positions or methods, the most aggressive one wins and the other team members and the project suffer. Therefore, project managers should focus on outcomes rather than on the positions of the parties involved with an aim of optimizing overall project performance.

Avoid "catastrophizing." Catastrophizing is an "upside down" approach and leads only to lower team morale and confidence, increased frustration and eventually to potential project failure. Some of the common catastrophizing remarks that describe inconvenience, difficulty, or frustration are:

"This is going to be a disaster."

"We will never get this done on time."

"This project is driving me crazy."

"I can't stand the project structure."

Instead of catastrophizing, encourage project participants to be more positive and to suggest solutions that are manageable and helpful.

Picture things going well. Visualize and imagine positive results. It is difficult to move onto something better without knowing what "better" is. To develop a clear picture of "better," the project manager should:[17]
- Picture things going as he or she wants them to
- Enlist the support of others and try to get their commitment
- Deal with obstacles positively (use a problem solving approach!).

Identify priorities and verbalize them. Priorities rank very highly as a source of conflict throughout the project life cycle. Sometimes, people compromise so much in a conflict that no one wins and everyone is dissatisfied. Successful project managers evaluate the priorities up front and identify the "must haves" and "nice to haves." While resolving conflicts, he or she may compromise on "nice to haves" in order of importance. Project managers can rank priorities by asking the following questions:

Which features would contribute most to project success?

Which features would contribute the least?

Cut your losses when necessary. Sometimes, a project may have gotten "too deep in the hole," which leads to conflicts. Should the project be continued or should someone review the situation, try to estimate the bottom line to completion and then make a rational decision whether or not to abandon the project? The project manager should avoid making such decisions based upon ego and emotion. Cutting losses can actually yield a savings which can be used for other business opportunities.

In most cases, only senior management or the project director or sponsor is authorized to cancel projects. However, a few project managers may also have the authority to cancel projects if necessary. In all cases, the persons with such authority should cut their losses and resolve such situations by using the following guidelines.[17]

Keep a mental file of things that don't fit. It is easy to see what you expect to see instead of what is real. Project participants may say one thing but act differently. Project managers must watch out for the degree of real commitment and interest in doing certain things on a project. When words and behavior don't match, behavior should be believed more— even if it is the words you *want* to believe.

Project managers should pay attention to nonverbal communication while getting feedback to their questions, because actual behavior more closely correlates with the nonverbal component than the verbal component of communications. By ignoring this concept, the project manager is more likely to accept passive resistance—the beginning of a hidden "sink hole."[17] Not all sink holes are hidden of course, some of them are right out in the open! But the behavior may be so difficult and complex to measure that the project manager may simply not believe their eyes or ears and thereby misjudge the situation completely.

Follow the rule of two (or three). Successful project managers would prefer to cut their losses before costs skyrocket. They may not be able to recognize the inconsistency right away, but they should confront the situation and address it directly if it occurs a second or third time.

Establish a system for cutting back investment of money, time, effort and ego. This follows the common management principle, "Plan your work and work your plan." When something goes wrong in the project, people may go through the stages of grief: denial, anger, bargaining, depression, stress and—hopefully—acceptance. Project managers who become emotionally upset over losses on their projects are also vulnerable to loosing their self-esteem.[17]

Human Resource Skills for the Project Manager

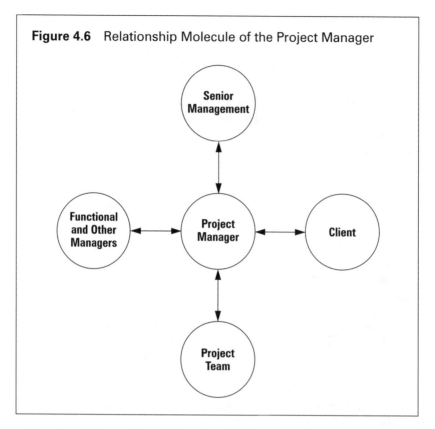

Figure 4.6 Relationship Molecule of the Project Manager

Senior Management

Functional and Other Managers

Project Manager

Client

Project Team

People who have planned ahead to handle their losses are better off because they can turn to their written plans and take necessary action accordingly. Even though it may be difficult to implement the actions, at least the difficult step of "deciding what to do" was done when they could think more clearly. To cut losses before it is too late, the project manager's plan should answer the following questions.[17]

- *How much money* should be invested before expecting some return?
- *How much time* should be allowed before following another course of action?
- *How much energy* and ego should be invested before being satisfied that the best shot has been given? (This limits the spillover into personal life as well as the effect on other projects.)

Although we all hope for the best, we must be prepared for the worst. It is important for the project manager to continually evaluate project progress and outcomes so that he or she can be better prepared to deal with losses before being exposed to more losses. He or she is more likely to anticipate loss by keeping a mental file of things that don't fit, confront the situation the second or third time it occurs and keep a system in place for cutting back investment if the losses become too costly. Project managers should have a "contingency plan" to deal with losses, or cut costs in other areas. It should be emphasized that sometimes project managers may be too egotistic to be objective in cutting their losses at the appropriate time.

Formulate proactive conflict management strategies. Conflict can be resolved or kept under control by using a proactive approach to managing conflict. This requires acting before conflict actually occurs to minimize its impact. Before formulating proactive conflict management strategies, it is important to understand the project manager's "relationship molecule" that shows the major project participants with whom the project manager usually interacts throughout the project life cycle (see Figure 4.6).

Project managers must establish good understanding, trust and rapport with all the project stakeholders with whom they interact to minimize the probability of conflict. The following ideas for proactively managing conflicts with major project stakeholders are summarized in Table 4.2.[21]

Minimizing conflict with senior management involves knowing their requirements and styles. Conflicts with a boss can be minimized using the following ideas.[21]

- *Place yourself in the boss's shoes.* Understand and be sympathetic to the challenges, problems and pressures of senior management.
- *Analyze the boss's thinking pattern.* Try to be consistent with the boss's way of thinking (analytical or intuitive).
- *Don't only take problems to the boss, take solutions as well.* Explore alternatives and suggest recommendations; try to make the boss's job easier.
- *Keep the boss informed of your progress and plans.* It will help the boss be your effective mentor. Also you can get better support from your boss.
- *Listen and observe.* These are key ingredients of communications. Look for both verbal and nonverbal components of the message. "Listen between the lines."
- *Consult the boss on policy, procedures and criteria.* It will help clarify management philosophy and your boundaries related to administrative issues—and you may also need it to protect yourself.
- *Don't steamroll the boss.* Be patient and give time for thinking and evaluating your propositions; timing is vital.

Minimizing conflict with project team members involves knowing your team members well, developing rapport and trust. Some practical ideas to minimize conflict with team members include:[21]

- *Discover your team members' personal and professional goals.* Whenever possible, match tasks to their interests and personal goals. This is a key to motivation.
- *Clarify your expectations.* Clarify what you want, when you want, and why you want; ensure that your communication is well understood.

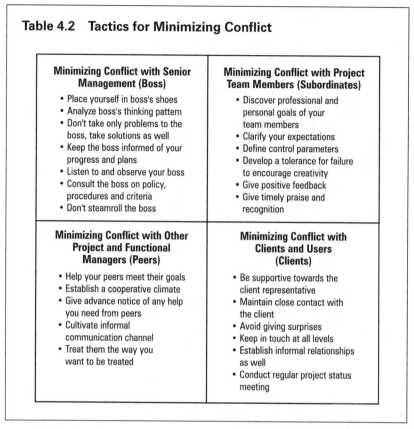

Table 4.2   Tactics for Minimizing Conflict

Minimizing Conflict with Senior Management (Boss)	Minimizing Conflict with Project Team Members (Subordinates)
• Place yourself in boss's shoes • Analyze boss's thinking pattern • Don't take only problems to the boss, take solutions as well • Keep the boss informed of your progress and plans • Listen to and observe your boss • Consult the boss on policy, procedures and criteria • Don't steamroll the boss	• Discover professional and personal goals of your team members • Clarify your expectations • Define control parameters • Develop a tolerance for failure to encourage creativity • Give positive feedback • Give timely praise and recognition
Minimizing Conflict with Other Project and Functional Managers (Peers)	**Minimizing Conflict with Clients and Users (Clients)**
• Help your peers meet their goals • Establish a cooperative climate • Give advance notice of any help you need from peers • Cultivate informal communication channel • Treat them the way you want to be treated	• Be supportive towards the client representative • Maintain close contact with the client • Avoid giving surprises • Keep in touch at all levels • Establish informal relationships as well • Conduct regular project status meeting

Source: Data based on information from the work of Paul Dinsmore, *Human Factors in Project Management,* AMACOM, 1990, pp. 149-166.

- *Define control parameters.* Clarify performance appraisal techniques, discuss forms, frequency and intensity of controls with your project team members. Exercise controls based on facts, not on opinions.
- *Develop a tolerance for failure.* To err is human: use mistakes as opportunities for training to improve in the future. Remember failures form a launch pad for success. Use postmortem strategy sessions to learn lessons for the future.
- *Give positive feedback.* Demonstrate your confidence in your project team. Avoid criticisms. When you need to point out a mistake, balance your comments with positive feedback.
- *Give timely praise and recognition.* Most project team members are self-motivated high achievers. They thrive on praise, challenges and opportunities to grow. Appropriate and timely recognition and praise can do wonders. It will create positive reinforcement and motivate them to maximize their performance.

Minimizing conflict with your peers involves treating your peers with respect—the way you want to be treated. Conflict with your peers can be minimized by using the following guidelines.[21]

- *Help your peers meet their personal and professional goals.* Support their objectives. Look for areas of mutual interest rather than conflict.
- *Establish a cooperative atmosphere.* Remember the strengths of a team approach. You need each other to succeed. Do favors without expecting any immediate return. The law of reciprocity suggests that if you are cooperative with your peers, they are more likely to collaborate with you.
- *Give advance notice about any help you need.* Your peers may have their own constraints. Justify your requests in terms of project goals and objectives; be accommodating to your peer's requirements.
- *Cultivate informal communication channels.* Formal communications are slow and cold. Informal communications increase comfort level and understanding, and therefore help solve problems effectively. Have lunch together, develop social encounters, and discuss topics other than daily work.

Minimizing conflict with clients and users involves effective communication with them and responding to their needs promptly.[21]

- *Be supportive towards the client's representative.* Supply them necessary data and information because you will need their help throughout the project.
- *Maintain close contact with the client.* Avoid communication gaps. Clients require attention and importance; when they don't get it, they tend to become more demanding and sometimes unreasonable.
- *Avoid surprises.* Don't spring surprises, unless you have good news. Don't let problems build up, let your client know about them and what you are doing to solve them.
- *Keep in touch at various levels.* Most projects have an organizational structure that mirrors that of the client. Put directors in touch with directors, managers with managers, and engineers with engineers, etc.
- *Establish informal relationships with key client personnel.* Informal relationships develop a better understanding and interpersonal relationship. Use encounters at lunches, dinners, social and sporting events to improve relationships with key personnel of the client organization.
- *Conduct regular project status meetings.* Summarize progress and include forecasts to completion, future problems and needs. Meetings should be both informative and problem-solving in nature.

The above techniques should help project managers prevent project conflicts. Table 4.2 shows a summary of these ideas for proactively managing conflicts with senior management, project team members, peers (other project managers, functional managers and support staff), and above all, with clients and users.[21] Project managers must develop better interpersonal relationships with major project stakeholders and try to create an environment that encourages cooperative and collaborative behavior. Trust and effective communications reduce the destructive effects of conflict and increase the project manager's ability to positively influence other project participants.

Wilemon and Thamhain[13] conducted research to study the effects of using various conflict resolution styles on the project. They ranked the five main styles of resolving conflict from the most effective to least effective, as follows:[13]

1. Problem-solving (confronting, negotiating)
2. Compromising
3. Smoothing
4. Forcing
5. Withdrawal.

Confrontation (problem-solving), compromising and *smoothing* are most effective in dealing with project team members. *Confrontation* may increase the incidence of conflict, but it tends to resolve the conflict by finding a mutually acceptable solution.[13] Project managers can effectively use compromising styles to resolve conflicts with their superiors because it promotes both a free exchange of ideas and improved communications.[13] Project managers can also use this mode effectively in formal contract negotiations, negotiations about resources with functional managers, and informal negotiations with project participants about day-to-day issues of managing the project. These three styles are particularly important for project managers in dealing with their peers, functional managers and other support personnel.

Forcing is detrimental because it leads to win-lose outcomes and creates hard feelings. It increases the *negative* results of conflict. *Withdrawing* may tend to minimize conflict but it fails to resolve the conflict and may rather come back and haunt the project with increased intensity.

From this research, it appears that there is no single best method for dealing with conflict. Conflict resolution style is mainly dependent upon the situation and the players involved in the conflict. Depending upon the situation, the project manager should be able to use all the conflict management styles as necessary.

Use planning to resolve conflict. One option for managing conflict is to wait for it to happen and then resolve it by using appropriate conflict management techniques and skills. For this approach to be successful project participants must be able to identify conflict in its early stages and be aware of effective conflict resolution techniques.

Another approach to managing conflict is to formulate a proactive conflict management strategy (as outlined in the previous section). Sometimes, along with the proactive approach, project participants may be able to manage conflicts by using a "preventive planning approach." This involves setting the stage for beneficial conflict while avoiding negative conflict. Project participants must prepare sound plans and take timely actions to prevent crisis situations. Although it is necessary to use both preventive and corrective measures, planning is the key to keeping conflict at manageable levels. Here are some ways planning can assist in preventing conflict:[21]

Project planning. Wilemon and Thamhain[13] suggested that schedule, priorities and human resources (staffing and allocation) are primary sources of conflict followed by administrative procedures, technical issues, cost and personality. Therefore, sound project planning and carefully developed schedules can increase the probability of meeting project objectives and reduce the chances of conflicts in a project.

Integrative planning. In addition to "hard" factors—schedule, cost, manpower and quality, there are also some "softer," less tangible reasons for conflict in a project. Human factors and behavioral characteristics can also contribute a great deal to project conflicts. Both hard and soft factors are interrelated. Hard factors focus on the tangible issues of project conflict, whereas the soft factors are more subjective in nature. The hard factors and soft factors deal with the following questions:

- *What topics are the focus of conflict?* (hard factors)
- *What is the behavioral cause of the conflict?* (soft factors)

Because of the dynamic nature of human behavior, soft factors pose a real challenge in managing conflicts. Some of the main soft factors that can contribute to conflicts in a project include communication barriers; conflict of interest; lack of trust, respect and rapport; poor interpersonal relations; and differences in managerial philosophy. These sources of conflict can also be managed effectively through planning.

Project plans should be blended properly to prepare an integrative plan that should help prepare project team members and other participants to deal with conflict on a routine basis. Some guidelines that can be used to integrate project planning at different levels and blend the talents of key personnel in a project are:[21]

Setting an example has a multiplier effect in increasing productivity by fostering personal traits (charisma, leadership characteristics) and human skills (communication, conflict management, motivation and negotiation).

Coaching (usually done by the project manager) is aimed at aligning human behavior patterns in harmony with the project structure. Coaching can be done with team members, other functional and project managers (peers), and top management. Coaching techniques include:[1]

- The informal chat (with some preparation)
- In-depth coaching (working out a strategy on paper)
- Reviewing the position description to clarify roles, relationships, and responsibilities.

A combination of these techniques provides a binding "psychological contract" that helps adjust individual managerial philosophies prior to the implementation stage.

Training should aim to cover various aspects of project management, for example:

- *Behavioral topics* include effective communications, interpersonal skills, team building, motivation, group dynamics, conflict management and negotiating skills.
- *Management subjects* include time management, delegation, conducting meetings effectively, organization development, organization structures, and problem solving.
- *Project topics* tie management and behavioral themes into a harmonious form. These may include the project plan, planning and scheduling, project reviews (effective reporting and control), costing systems, project engineering, kick-off meetings and project start-up procedures, design freezing, fast tracking, and interface management and integration as well as project wrap-up meetings and shut-down procedures.

A correct combination of training approaches using behavioral, management, and project topics will boost overall productivity. This combination can be achieved through:

- *Round table discussions* that give the project team a motivational shot in the arm
- *Lectures* by experts on different topics from organizations such as the National Association of Speakers, the Project Management Institute, the International Project Management Association, and Toastmaster Clubs
- *Seminars or workshops* conducted by professional associations such as PMI, IPMA, American Management Association, American Association of Cost Engineers (AACE).

The planning *process* may be more important than the project plan itself. Gaining the commitment of project participants is a key to project success. Personal commitment of project participants can only be gained by encouraging their active involvement and participation in planning and decision making.

Project managers should empower their project teams to transform them into self-directed work teams. This approach builds mutual trust and helps reach consensus on key project issues. The consensus approach may appear to be slow and awkward at times, but it does help to work out a unified plan that can be implemented with a minimum of conflict. The intensity and frequency of conflicts are reduced because potential disagreements are thrashed out during the planning process when project resources are not yet fully committed.

CONFLICT CAN BE HEALTHY if managed effectively. Conflict management requires a combination of analytical and human skills. Every project participant should learn to resolve project conflicts effectively. Good conflict managers work at the *source* of conflict. To resolve it permanently, they must resolve the cause of the conflict and not just the symptoms of the conflict. They size up possible clashes before "contact" is actually made and then prepare their action plans to handle potential trouble. They should concentrate on building an atmosphere designed to reduce destructive conflict and deal with routine frictions and minor differences before they become unmanageable. The key to resolving conflict with a positive outcome includes looking for a win-win situation, cutting losses when necessary, formulating proactive conflict management strategies, and planning as a solution for preventing and handling conflict.

Summary

The essence of conflict is disagreement or incompatibility in goals, ideas, or emotions within or between project team members or between various project teams in an organization. Because of the dynamic nature of human behavior, team dynamics, and complex personal interactions in a project environment, conflict is inevitable. However, the negative effects of conflict can be minimized and positive results achieved by managing the conflict effectively. Effective conflict management is based, in part, on a thorough understanding of the different ways conflict emerges and how it can be resolved. A substantial portion of project management effort is spent in resolving conflict. Therefore, project managers and all project participants must develop effective conflict management skills.

There are several conflict resolution techniques. In some situations, stimulating conflict can increase project performance. Structural conflict resolution techniques can be used, including changes in procedures, personnel, authority or resources. Primary interpersonal resolution techniques include:

- Withdrawing/avoiding (retreating from an actual or potential conflict situation), which does not solve the problem
- Smoothing/accommodating (emphasizing the use of agreements rather than disagreements), which provides only short-term solutions
- Forcing (win-lose outcome), which may solve conflict temporarily at the surface but hard feelings may resurface later in other forms
- Compromising (searching and bargaining for solutions that bring some degree of satisfaction to both parties), which provides definite solution
- Collaborating (seeking consensus and commitment), which provides long term solutions
- Confronting, also called problem solving or negotiating (treating conflict as a problem to be solved; aiming for a win-win solution), which provides an ultimate resolution.

Project managers must evaluate the situation carefully and then use an appropriate conflict management technique. Five additional techniques—majority rule, consensus, mediation, arbitration, and superordinate goal—may also be used.

The choice of an appropriate style for resolving conflict depends upon factors such as the situation, relative importance and intensity of conflict, time pressures, position of the players involved and relative emphasis on achieving goals versus maintaining relationship. Individuals may have a preference for one or two of the styles but they are more likely to use all of them over time when dealing with different conflict situations. These styles can be compared by using the Thomas-Kilmann model, which compares the desire to satisfy oneself and the desire to satisfy others, and Filley's model, which deals with concerns for personal goals versus relationships.

Practically, confrontation (negotiating and problem solving) has been found to be the best approach because it aims at finding a win-win alternative. Both parties work sincerely to reach a mutually acceptable result that is also beneficial to the parties involved.

There are practical guidelines consisting of three main steps for managing conflicts in a project:

- *Preparing for the conflict* by assuming it is inevitable, planning for it and then being prepared with stress coping techniques
- *Facing the conflict*, which suggests that project managers should serve as a lightning rod by taking the heat themselves and then responding to both the emotions and the facts), then "surface" the issues, analyze the situation thoroughly and find the real cause of conflict
- *Resolving the conflict* with a positive outcome by looking for win-win alternatives, cutting losses when necessary (before it becomes too costly), formulating proactive conflict management strategies, and planning a proactive method for preventing and handling conflict.

Outline

5

When two men in business always agree, one of them is unnecessary.

— *William Wrigley, Jr.*

Negotiation

NEGOTIATION IS A fact of life. Everyone negotiates something every day; it seems that more and more situations require negotiation. People negotiate salaries and benefits with their employers, purchase prices with vendors, schedules with clients, priorities in the household with their spouses, and television time with their children. Negotiation is a basic means of getting what you want from others. It is a two-way communication to reach an agreement when both parties have a combination of shared and opposed interests.[1]

Most projects are organized in a matrix structure where the responsibility, authority and accountability are usually shared. Project participants are brought together from different functional areas and business sectors. They may have different perceptions and outlooks about the project, project management techniques or the resources, time and effort to be spent on the project. To achieve project success, project managers must be able to negotiate with technical specialists, work package managers, functional managers, other project managers, and upper management about the resources, project priorities and responsibilities. They must negotiate with clients regarding changes in scope, schedule, budget and performance standards; and with team members about various project management issues throughout the project life cycle.

This chapter deals with basic principles of negotiation, the impact of culture on negotiation, types of negotiations, a basic negotiation model and some negotiation strategies. This chapter highlights how to negotiate to resolve conflicts for increased performance. Fisher and Ury have done extensive research on negotiation strategies and have developed a very practical method of negotiation (Principled Negotiation) to reach agreements efficiently and amicably.[1] Most of these methods are basic and are equally applicable in a project environment. Some practical guidelines for negotiation in a project environment are also described in this chapter. ∎

About Negotiation

We must learn to explore all the options and possibilities that confront us in a complex and rapidly changing world. We must learn to welcome and not fear the voices of dissent.

— J.W. Fulbright

More and more situations in our lives require negotiation. Negotiation, a persuasive process,[2] is an important part, not only of business and industrial transactions, but of everyday life. In a project environment, negotiation may involve both tangible (budget, schedule, resources and project management system) and intangible issues (recognition, building trust, confidence and good working relationships, inspiring team performance, a sense of accomplishment and shared ownership of the product or service).[2] A successful negotiator must be able to analyze and evaluate the situations and then formulate an appropriate negotiation strategy and adapt a flexible negotiation style to suit specific situations and negotiators involved in the negotiation process.[3]

Principles of negotiation

Use soft words and hard arguments.

— English Proverb

In a project environment, negotiation involves bargaining with individuals concerning the transfer of resources, the generation of information, and the accomplishment of activities.[4] It is also a process through which parties with differing interests reach agreement through communication and compromise.[5] Negotiation is one of the most important skills a project manager must have in order to deal with customers, functional managers, project team members, and other stakeholders. Negotiating agreement among parties with conflicting interests involves four principles.

Separate the people from the problem. People and problems should be separated to avoid misunderstandings and the endless cycle of actions and reactions. Put yourself in the other party's shoes and separate the substance of the negotiation from the relationships and personalities involved. Give credit for the good advice and ideas of others and develop a proposal consistent with their values and fair to both parties.

Focus on common interests. It is more effective to focus on common interests rather than on the opposing positions of the parties. Acknowledge the interests of the other party, be flexible in the ideas offered as solutions, and be firm in dealing with the problem, yet open and supportive to the human beings on the other side. In this way, both parties attack the problem and not each other, improving the relationship between them and increasing the chances of reaching an acceptable agreement.

Generate options that advance shared interests. Generate a number of options and possible solutions that reflect shared interests and help reconcile opposing interests before starting the negotiation. Then these options can be evaluated and the best one chosen and adjusted to reach an agreement acceptable to both parties.

Results based on standard criteria. Results must be based primarily on the project objectives and success criteria. However, other criteria such as market value replacement cost, allocation of risk and a long-term cost/benefit analysis should also be considered. These criteria should be developed and agreed upon by all parties involved in the negotiation process.

The above four points help to develop an agreement based on the merits of the final result, as opposed to one based on an "I win-you lose" philosophy. This builds mutual trust, confidence, and respect for each other's ideas. Negotiations about scope definition and overall project goals, budgets and constraints should be done right at the front-end in order to avoid disputes and misunderstandings later in the project. Suppliers, contractors and project managers can thus work *with* each other rather than *against* each other. In such a cooperative environment, credit is given to both project teams and functional departments, and project managers will easily be able to negotiate the quality and timing of resources with functional managers. This kind of relationship frequently leads to additional contracts and a continuing, profitable relationship between satisfied clients, project mana gers and contractors.

Project managers are required to meet project goals and objectives with very little authority, especially over functional managers and staff personnel. This lack of authority forces them to negotiate company resources with functional managers and top management. Figure 5.1 shows the negotiation activities of a project manager.

Common methods of negotiating

Although everyone is involved in some sort of negotiation every day, it is not easy to do it successfully. After negotiating, people often feel dissatisfied, worn out, or alienated. In negotiation, process is as important as outcome. Therefore, project managers must be sensitive to human feelings and dynamics while negotiating in order to achieve the desired outcome, as well as to prevent being exhausted by the process.

The negotiation process (shown in Figure 5.2) consists of three main steps:
1. Pre-negotiation planning (planning how to conduct negotiations)
2. Actual negotiations or agreements (working out the details and reaching an agreement)
3. Post-negotiation critique (evaluating how successful the negotiation process and outcome was).

Most people view negotiation as a dilemma, requiring them to choose between two extremes of negotiation style: soft or hard. However, there are actually three common methods of negotiating:[1]

Soft negotiation. In "soft" negotiations, the negotiators are friendly, with a special emphasis on avoiding personal conflict. The sensitivity to personal feelings is high. A soft negotiator makes concessions readily in order to reach an amicable resolution. There is more emphasis on relationships.

Figure 5.1 The Negotiation Activities in Project Management

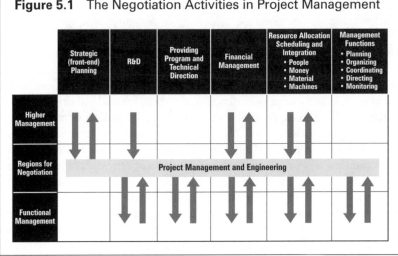

Source: Harold Kerzner. 1989. *Project Management: A Systems Approach to Planning, Scheduling and Controlling, Third Edition.* New York: Van Nostrand Reinhold, p11. Reprinted by permission of the publisher.

However, he or she may feel exploited or bitter about the negotiation process and its outcome.

Hard negotiation. In "hard" negotiations, the negotiators consider the situation a contest in which both parties take strong positions and are seen as adversaries. The side that takes the extreme position and holds out longer gains more. The goal of hard negotiators is to win, even at the cost of relationship with or well-being of another party.

"Principled Negotiation." This method, developed at the Harvard Negotiation Project, is neither soft nor hard but rather both soft *and* hard. It emphasizes resolving the issues based on merits rather than through a haggling process focused on what each side says it will and won't do. It suggests looking for mutual gains whenever possible and, in case of conflict, basing the results on fair standards rather than the will of either side. This method is also known as the *yes approach* and is "hard on merits and soft on people." The objective of this method is to achieve what one is entitled to and still be decent in the negotiation process. Both parties can be fair while protecting themselves against those who would take advantage of their fairness. It is based on following points:[1]

- Separate the people from the problem
- Focus on interests, not positions
- Generate options/alternatives for mutual gain
- Insist that results are based on some objective criteria or standard.

In principled negotiations, both parties ought to be problem solvers with the aim of reaching a fair, wise and amicable outcome by using a

148

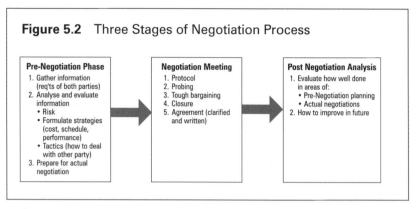

Figure 5.2 Three Stages of Negotiation Process

Pre-Negotiation Phase	Negotiation Meeting	Post Negotiation Analysis
1. Gather information (req'ts of both parties) 2. Analyse and evaluate information • Risk • Formulate strategies (cost, schedule, performance) • Tactics (how to deal with other party) 3. Prepare for actual negotiation	1. Protocol 2. Probing 3. Tough bargaining 4. Closure 5. Agreement (clarified and written)	1. Evaluate how well done in areas of: • Pre-Negotiation planning • Actual negotiations 2. How to improve in future

Source: M. Dean Martin. 1981. The Negotiation Differential for International Project Management. In *Proceedings of the 1981 Project Managment Institute Seminar/Symposium*. Drexel Hill, PA: Project Management Institute.

win-win strategy. It can be used in many situations, including when one or several issues are involved; whether negotiations involve two parties or many; whether the parties are experienced negotiators or novices; whether their level of experience is less or more, and whether the other party is a hard bargainer or a friendly one.[1]

Impact of culture on negotiation

It is critical that one seek to understand [people's] perceptions if one is to understand the circumstances under which their behavior might change.
— *Harold J. Leavitt*

Cultural differences influence the process and methods of negotiating. Therefore, it is important to understand what culture is and how it impacts negotiation in a project.

Culture is the distinctive way in which a group of people connected by geographical location, religion and/or ethnicity lead their lives.[6] It refers to a commonly shared set of values, beliefs, attitudes and knowledge. It can be created both by people and environment and can be transmitted from one generation to the next through family, school, social environment, and other agencies.[7] Though difficult to define precisely because of its complexity, culture has been described by Hofstede as a kind of "mental software ... the collective programming of the mind that distinguishes the members of one group ... from another."[8] Also, culture can be defined as an acquired knowledge used to interpret the experiences of a group and which forms the basis of its behavior.[9]

As we move into the 21st century, cultural differences are the reality of life in project environment. Project managers must develop skills in negotiating in a multicultural environment. They must identify and analyze major elements of culture. Martin identified seven major elements of culture (see Figure 5.3), which are briefly described below.[7]

Figure 5.3 Major Cultural Elements Affecting Projects

Cultural Element	What It Means or Implies	Impact on Project	Recommendations/ Comments
Material Culture	• Refers to tools, skills, work habits and work attitudes	• Determines technical and manpower constraints	• This information is needed for planning and negotiations
Language	• Medium of communication • Words and experiences may differ	• Affects communications • Influences understanding of beliefs and values	• Learning foreign language develops better understanding and rapport
Aesthetics	• Arts, music, dance, traditions and customs	• Encourages informal and open communication • Influences success directly	• Relationships are enriched by encouraging informal communication
Education	• Transmission of knowledge through learning process • Approach to problems and people	• Affects project planning and negotiations	• Knowledge of education system helps in determining level of skills and expertise (helpful in project planning and negotiations)
Religion, Beliefs and Attitudes	• Mainspring of culture • Affects dress, eating habits, attitudes of workers towards work, punctuality and work site	• Emphasizes on promptness and punctuality	• Appreciation of religion, beliefs and values develops mutual trust, respect and improves cooperation and team spirit
Social Organization	• Organizations/groups (labor unions, social clubs) • Relates to social classes	• Influences formal/informal communication • Affects business contacts for negotiating	• Social skills can lead to better results than formal meetings
Political Life	• Government involvement in joint ventures with foreign companies • Concerned about treatment of people, jobs, financial, economic and safety factors	• Affects delivery of materials, supplies and equipment • Influences permits and licenses	• Staying in tune with political life helps identify strengths, constraints and business contacts

Source: M. Dean Martin. 1981. The Negotiation Differential for International Project Management. In *Proceedings of the 1981 Project Managment Institute Seminar/Symposium.* Drexel Hill, PA: Project Management Institute.

1. *Material culture* refers to the physical objects or technologies created by people.[10] It includes the tools and skills of workers, their work habits and attitudes towards work and time. Project managers need this information to plan for negotiations with international partners.
2. *Language* is a mirror of any culture,[11] as well as the primary medium of communication (which is vital in managing projects). It also includes phrases, gestures and expressions that may be interpreted differently by ethnic or regional cultural groups, even within the same language. To learn the language of a culture is to know its people, which helps in understanding their beliefs, values, way of life, and point of view.[12] Project participants from other countries appreciate the efforts people make to learn their language and it helps in negotiating and developing better understanding and rapport among all project participants.
3. *Aesthetics* refers to art, music, dance, literary traditions and other related customs and artifacts. Aesthetics may not directly influence project activities but an appreciation of the aesthetics of different countries enriches relationships and hence encourages principled negotiation, which may influence project success.

Human Resource Skills for the Project Manager

4. *Education* deals with the transmission of knowledge.[7] It includes how people from different cultures approach problems and relate to others. Knowledge of the educational system can lead to better understanding of a culture and help in project planning and negotiations.

5. *Beliefs and attitudes (including religions)* form a vital component of culture. Religion is often called the "mainspring" of a culture, as it significantly influences each of the other elements of the culture. Beliefs and attitudes affect dress, eating habits, and the attitudes of workers towards work, punctuality and the work site. Hall indicated that different cultures have different attitudes towards time.[13] For example, in the United States and Germany, promptness and punctuality are valued, whereas in some other cultures, appointments cover a general time interval rather than a precise time. In Arabian countries, the concept of saving face is important because it involves the negotiator's perception of his self-worth.[14] The project manager must recognize that these critical cultural variables may influence the negotiation process and its outcome.

6. *Social organization* deals with the organization of negotiators into groups and the way they structure their activities to accomplish goals. It includes family relationships, labor unions, social clubs and other social groups that influence attitudes and values.[7] Social organization also refers to the classes in a society. A better understanding of a culture's social organization helps the project manager in terms of business contacts, time scheduling and formal/informal communication, networking and win-win negotiations. For example, with some people, a project manager may achieve more successful negotiations at informal cocktail or dinner meetings than at formal daytime meetings in an office environment.

7. *Political life* plays an important role when governments are involved in joint ventures between home companies and foreign companies entering their market. This is increasing with the growth of multinational corporations and the need to compete globally through partnering and collaborations with other countries.[15] A government's concerns relate to the amount of profit, the legality of economic and financial transactions, the number of jobs created, the treatment of its people, safety, and environmental factors. In some cases, foreign governments may demand that their representative be involved actively in front-end project planning and decision making if the amount of money, level of technology, and the amount of government support needed for the project are high. A government can approve or disapprove issuance of licenses and permits and the import and export of equipment, supplies and materials and can in various other ways make the job of a project manager easy or difficult.

While negotiating, project managers should be familiar with the following conditions within themselves when approaching people from another culture:[7]

Self-reference criterion. According to this criterion, the negotiator evaluates others in terms of his or her own value system. Project managers with such an attitude set up barriers that may cause conflicts and breakdowns in communication. For example, a project manager who criticizes the language, food and religion of a foreign country may offend people, reducing mutual understanding, open communication, and the chance of achieving win-win negotiations.

Culture shock. When a negotiator is away from the known and familiar and is faced with differing customs and ways of doing things, this can be the result. Project managers should focus on getting things done, rather than trying to teach people their own values or work styles. There is always more than one way to do a job.

The impact of culture can be evaluated by looking at all three phases of negotiation process (as shown in Figure 5.2).[7]

The pre-negotiation planning phase involves a problem-solving mode. In this phase, project managers develop a plan or an approach to the negotiations. They must understand the other parties and their environment in order to:

- Develop a contingency plan
- Decide whether to take individual or team approach
- Develop cost, schedule and performance objectives (both minimum and optimum)
- Designate a team leader
- Identify pros and cons (give and take points).

To problem-solve effectively, project managers must be aware of the extent to which they are influenced by the self-reference criterion and culture shock and make an effort to appreciate the cultural differences of the participants involved in international or multicultural projects.

For international projects, project managers should perform a cultural analysis of the country where the project is to take place. They may gather information for the cultural analysis by visiting the country, studying about the country (economic, political and social life), and above all, by keeping an open mind. After gathering the information, they must analyze and evaluate it to form the basis for preparing a pre-negotiation plan. This plan includes:[7]

- Formulation of detailed strategies and tactics.[16] Strategies relate to cost, schedule and performance, whereas tactics relate to the actual negotiation meeting
- Analysis and assessment of project risks
- Deciding how the negotiator should react to and deal with the other party.

The negotiation meeting phase. All this planning, analysis and evaluation leads to the negotiation meeting itself, which has five distinct stages:[7]

1. *Protocol.* In this stage, the participants get acquainted and set some ground rules for the negotiation meeting. The cultural analysis done in the pre-negotiation planning stage plays a very helpful role. It is often more useful to create a collaborative atmosphere and let the meeting evolve, rather than trying to rush things.
2. *Probing.* During this stage, the parties actually start communicating with each other. Verbal communication plays a significant role,[17] so participants need to feel comfortable and speak fluidly. But non-verbal components such as eye contact, gestures, vocal tones, postures, etc., also become meaningful, as discussed in Chapter One. Through language, gestures and body language, the parties start to feel each other out. They try to identify weaknesses and areas of shared interest. During this stage, negotiators try to verify the adequacy of their strategies or fall back on contingency plans developed during their pre-negotiation planning.
3. *Rough bargaining.* This involves knowing your points and issues and going after them with confidence and assertiveness, which is very important for successful negotiations.[18]
4. *Closure.* The issues of cost, schedule and performance are settled during this stage. The agreements reached on individual bases are summarized and, if no objections are raised, last stage follows—agreement.
5. *Agreement.* Reaching an agreement is the final goal of negotiation. During this stage, discussions take place about where and when the work should start, when to meet again, how the progress will be monitored, and other side issues. This is a good time to review key phrases to be included in the contract because different words have different meanings for different people.[19] Project managers must recognize that sometimes negotiations reopen at this stage. If one party feels like the "loser" in the process, this final round of negotiation can permit that party to "save face" by regaining some ground. In successful negotiations, both sides must feel like "winners"—even though one side may actually have gained more.

   The post-negotiation analysis, also known as a post-mortem analysis, provides feedback about how well the planning and negotiating was carried out.[20] It often reveals that a lack of facts has hampered certain aspects of the process. During this stage, the agreement is written up in the form of a contract or memo of understanding.[21] The mode of recording depends upon the country. However, the project manager must ensure that a jurisdiction clause is included in order to fix the country whose laws will govern the terms of contract.[7]

   TODAY MORE PROJECT MANAGERS operate in an environment characterized by cultural diversity. Cultural differences may significantly influence success in project management, especially in negotiations for international projects.[7] More business organizations are now investing in educating managers to develop their cultural sensitivity and increase their intercultural communicating and negotiation skills. To achieve this, it is important to understand and analyze the major elements of culture.

Negotiation Strategies

If there is any secret to success, it lies in the ability to get the other person's point of view and see things from his angle as well as from your own.
— Henry Ford

Resolving conflicts of interest requires negotiation, a process by which persons who have shared and opposed interests try to work out a settlement and come to an agreement.[22] Negotiations take place when both parties want to resolve their different interests and continue their relationships in productive and fulfilling ways. Project stakeholders (client, contractors, project manager, vendors/suppliers) may have different needs and wants in terms of cost, schedule, quality and rate of return. To get their needs met, one party makes proposals to the other(s), which are then evaluated in terms of how well they meet the needs, wants, and interests of all parties. On the basis of this evaluation and analysis, they either agree or make a counter-proposal. The parties involved, having both common and conflicting goals and interests, discuss the specific terms of a possible agreement.[23]

Negotiation is thus the key to resolving conflicts. It usually includes a combination of compromise, collaboration and, perhaps, some forcing on particular issues that are important for project success or to one or more of the participants. A negotiated agreement that is reached through proper participation of the parties involved throughout the process often leads to a result acceptable to all parties.

Types of negotiations

Before formulating a negotiation strategy, it is important to understand the various types of negotiations. Negotiations can be classified on the basis of:
- Results or outcomes achieved (win-lose, win-win, and lose-lose)
- Process or environment (related to relationship and negotiation for groups).[23,24]

Distributive negotiations (win-lose). In a traditional "win-lose" situation, one party's gain is another party's loss. This often occurs during intense conflicts over economic issues such as negotiating cost overruns or schedule delays. Under such circumstances, interaction patterns include limited trust, guarded communication, use of threats, disguised statements, and demands. Project managers must try to find the true boundaries of the other party, as well as of their own organizations; in other words, how far are the parties willing to bend?

Integrative negotiations (win-win). The focus of integrative negotiations is to seek solutions in which both parties gain. The final resolution may not always be what each party wanted, but because it is beneficial to both sides, it is mutually acceptable. The integrative approach can be used

154

when both parties show flexibility and trust and are strongly motivated to solve problems and explore new ideas. In these negotiations, the parties identify mutual problems, explore, analyze, and evaluate alternatives and jointly reach an acceptable solution. Team members in a matured project team strive for win-win outcomes.

In project environments, integrative negotiation is the most effective approach and should be used by the project manager to resolve any conflicts with the client regarding the impact of scope changes. Unexpected impacts may include labor problems, adverse effects on final budget, technical failures, schedule, and quality.

Lose-lose negotiations. Negotiations lead to "lose-lose" outcomes when both parties take an extreme position and consequently no satisfactory agreement can be reached. Badly managed win-lose situations may sometimes lead to lose-lose outcomes. For example, a fixed-price contract that takes advantage of a financially pressed contractor may prove to be a lose-lose situation because the contractor may quit when he or she is unable to perform contract obligations. Thus, a hard-nosed negotiation approach may lead to tangible losses for both parties and poor working relationships in the future.

Attitudinal structuring. Throughout negotiations, the pattern of relationships exhibited by the parties involved, such as hostility/friendliness and competitive/cooperativeness, influence their interactions. Attitudinal structuring is the process by which the parties seek to establish desired attitudes and relationships. The aim should be to curtail hostile and competitive attitudes and encourage friendly and cooperative relationships. Project managers must recognize that conflicts among project team members and project team support groups may occur due to undesirable attitudes and relationships that must be resolved by using an integrative and problem-solving approach.

Intra-organizational negotiations. These negotiations are carried out by the representatives of each group by obtaining the agreements of their respective groups. The key players on each side seek to build a consensus for agreement within their side with the aim of resolving intragroup conflicts. Labor-management issues are normally resolved using this approach.

Negotiations between parties from different cultures or legal and political systems can be quite complex. Therefore, project management strategies in the next century will require more collaboration than competition. Project managers must analyze and evaluate circumstances and then negotiate to achieve a win-win situation. Such an outcome is not only beneficial to both parties in tangible terms, but also leads to improved future working relationships, which often increases project success.

Basic negotiation model

Savage, Blair, and Sorenson developed the SBS model of negotiation by combining various concepts of negotiation and various interpersonal styles of conflict resolution. The SBS model integrates the priorities of individuals (or groups) with those of other individuals (or groups) under different negotiation situations (contacts).[25]

The SBS model is based upon the assumption that the negotiation approach varies from situation to situation. According to this model the best negotiation strategy depends upon desired substantive and relationship outcomes. A crucial context for any negotiation is the current and desired relationship outcomes (feelings and attitudes) between two parties.

Sometimes negotiators may give a higher priority to securing the best possible substantive outcome (issues and goals at stake) than to relationships. This oversight can damage the relationships between two parties or limit one party's ability to achieve desired substantive outcomes now or in the future.[26]

Interaction in the negotiation process is influenced by current relationships and affects future relationships and substantive outcomes. Sometimes negotiators may be keen in maintaining positive relationships and willingly share the "pie" through mutually beneficial collaboration. Other negotiators may go after substantive outcomes that will benefit only one negotiator at the cost of another. These negotiators view the possible outcomes as a "fixed pie"—whatever is given to one party diminishes the share available for the others. These negotiators discount the relationship and try to get as much "pie" as possible for themselves.

Many negotiations in a project are not straight win-win or win-lose but a combination of both. Both collaboration and competition may occur in such situations. The relationship that exists before the negotiation, the relationship that develops during the negotiation, and the desired relationship after the negotiation often influence whether each party will be motivated to share the pie, grab it, give it away or recreate it.[27]

The SBS model can be explained in more detail by looking at four important aspects of negotiation.

1. *Unilateral strategies* based on interpersonal styles of conflict management
2. *Interactive strategies* that consider the other party's substantive and relationship priorities
3. *Framework of negotiation strategies* that combine both unilateral and interactive strategies
4. *Negotiation tactics* proposed by the SBS model in each negotiation phase.

Unilateral negotiation strategies. Before selecting a negotiation strategy in the SBS model, negotiators should consider their own interests or managers should consider the interests of their organizations. These interests can be identified by answering the following basic questions:[28]

- Is the substantive outcome (goals and issues at stake) very important?
- Is the relationship outcome (feelings and attitudes between the parties) very important?

In unilateral strategies, negotiators consider only their own interests or the interests of their organizations without any concern for the interests

Human Resource Skills for the Project Manager

of the other party. Four unilateral strategies emerge from the answers to the above questions:[23]

1. Trusting collaboration. Negotiators should consider this strategy when both relationships and substantive outcomes are important. The negotiator seeks a win-win outcome in terms of both substantive goals and positive relationships. Trusting collaboration is most effective when both parties are open, interdependent, and support each other. It increases mutual trust and leads to effective problem solving and a win-win settlement.[29] Project managers should use this strategy when negotiating important issues with the client, project team members, and functional managers.

2. Open subordination. This corresponds to an accommodating style of conflict management in which negotiators are more concerned about positive relationships than about substantive outcomes. Open subordination can dampen hostility, increase support and cooperation, and foster more interdependent relationships. Project managers should use this strategy with support staff.

3. Firm competition. This is used when substantive outcomes are important and relationships are not. Similar to the forcing style, this is used when a negotiator has little trust in the other party or the relationship is not good from the beginning. The negotiator exerts status or position power to gain substantive outcomes for himself or herself. In this strategy, people may become very aggressive, bluff, threaten the other party or misrepresent their intentions. In competitive strategy, negotiators seek a win-lose outcome and are willing to risk their relationships. This is not a very effective strategy in project management and should be used cautiously.

4. Active avoidance. People consider this strategy when neither the substantive outcomes nor the relationship are important to them or to their organizations. Refusing to negotiate is the most direct and active form of avoidance. Generally, such an action affects relationships negatively. Moreover, negotiators must decide which issues are a waste of time to negotiate. This strategy does not lead to successful negotiations in a project environment and therefore should be used only as a last resort.

The SBS model assumes that these strategies are successful only in certain situations. In the next section, some modifications are suggested to the above strategies so that they can be applied to a wider set of negotiation situations for project managers and project team members.

Interactive negotiation strategies.[23] Before using any unilateral strategy, the SBS model suggests that it is important to examine the negotiation from the other party's perspective. The choice of negotiation strategy should be based upon the interests and priorities (associated with both substantive outcomes and relationships) of both parties. Unilateral strategies can lead to problems especially if the priorities of the parties are different. When anticipating the other party's priorities, negotiators should consider the kinds of actions the other party might take.

- Are those actions likely to be supportive or hostile?
- Do those actions represent short-term reaction or long-term approaches to the substantive issues?
- Are those actions likely to change the party's degree of cooperation and interdependence with the negotiator or the organization?

The answers to the above questions will depend upon the history of the relationship between the negotiator and the other party and the influence of key negotiators and groups upon both parties.[30]

Incorporation of these answers in the negotiation strategy leads to better interactive negotiations. Following are five types of interactive negotiation strategies.[23]

1. Principled collaboration.[25] The trusting collaboration strategy assumes that both parties discuss the issues openly. However, if a negotiator negotiates openly but the other party is not open or is competitive, the negotiator could be in trouble. Under these circumstances, the negotiator should use the modified strategy of principled collaboration. Instead of relying upon only trust and reciprocity, the negotiator should persuade the other party to negotiate based upon a set of mutually agreed principles that will benefit both parties. For example, in a large research and development program, the organization may share certain documents (such as national science strategy) with funding agencies to prepare a strategy to get funding or a project sponsor and urban planning authorities may negotiate on some building issues so that long-term goals of both parties are met.

2. Focused subordination. In this strategy, open subordination can be modified by discovering and then agreeing to those key needs that are of interest to the other party. Thus the parties can gain substantive outcomes for themselves or the organization while assuring a relatively positive relationship outcome. For example, a project manager can use this strategy when negotiating with regulatory agencies by acquiescing to some of their demands regarding gray areas in the bylaws.

3. Soft competition. The SBS model suggests that the directness of firm competition strategy should be softened because good relationships may be important for the future of the project, especially if the other party is powerful and potentially threatening. For example, the project manager should soften the competition strategy while negotiating with support groups and functional managers, even if the project manager can get his or her way by going through top management. The project manager must be tactful and avoid overly aggressive behavior because he or she may need support from functional managers and support staff in the future.

4. Passive avoidance. Instead of a direct refusal to negotiate, negotiators can passively avoid negotiation by delegating someone else to explore possible outcomes. This prevents the relationship from becoming too hostile and frees the negotiator from low-priority negotiations. For example, a functional manager may not consider either the relationship with the project manager or the

158

substantive outcome important, but instead of showing direct avoidance, he or she may delegate someone else to work with the project manager on the controversial issues and thus maintain a positive relationship with the project manager, which is helpful for both of them and the organization as a whole.

5. **Responsive avoidance.** If both the substantive outcome and the relationship are unimportant to one party, but the other party considers the outcome important and the relationship unimportant, the negotiator can be responsive but still avoid negotiating either by applying standard operating procedures or by developing new policies that address the other party's concern. This strategy is practical only for project managers or project leaders.

Combining unilateral and interactive strategies. Although the modifications suggested in interactive strategies may increase the effectiveness of negotiations, project managers should establish a sound framework of negotiation strategies that connects both unilateral and interactive strategies. The SBS model suggests that a decision to modify or replace a unilateral strategy depends almost exclusively on the priorities of the negotiator and the other party. Three core outcome conditions that influence the choice of interactive strategies are:[23]

1. **One party values the relationship but the other party does not.** For example, a negotiator using trust and collaboration may be victimized by another party who is concerned with substantive outcomes. In such situations, principled collaboration or soft competition should be used to ensure that the other party does not take advantage of the negotiator.

2. **One party does not value the relationship but the other party does.** In such situations, negotiators should firmly compete or actively avoid negotiations. However, if the other party is interested in the relationship the negotiator may not have to compete firmly to get the desired outcome. The negotiator may collaborate or softly compete and still gain substantive goals without alienating the other party. Such strategies foster a long-term relationship with substantive gains for the negotiator.

3. **Both parties value the relationship, but one party does not value substantive outcomes.** In such situations, whether or not the other party is interested in substantive outcomes, the negotiator may choose a trustingly collaborative strategy to maintain positive ties with the other party.[31]

Third-party facilitator. Most conflicts and negotiations occur between two parties. However, if both parties are in a deadlock and are involved in a strong win-lose conflict, a third-party facilitator, acting as a neutral party, may help them resolve their conflicts.[32] A third-party facilitator must acquire appropriate skills and use intergroup confrontation techniques to resolve conflicts effectively and to negotiate outcomes agreeable to both parties.

Skills and functions. Third-party facilitators play some key roles and therefore must have special skills in the following areas:[23]
- *Diagnosing* the conflict
- *Breaking deadlocks*

- *Facilitating discussions* at the right time
- *Ensuring mutual acceptance* of the outcome
- *Providing emotional support and reassurances* after negotiations are completed.

A third-party facilitator must win the trust, confidence, and acceptance of the parties involved in the conflict. The key functions of a third-party facilitator are to:[23,33]

- *Ensure mutual motivation* by providing incentives for resolving conflict
- *Achieve a balance in situational power,* which is necessary to establish trust and maintain open lines of communication
- *Coordinate confrontation efforts.* Failure to coordinate one party's positive initiatives with the other party's readiness to respond can undermine future efforts in resolving conflict
- *Promote openness in dialogue,* which increases the probability of a mutually acceptable outcome
- *Limit the level of tension,* because too much tension leads to failure; encourage both parties to cool down and communicate to understand each other's point of view.

Third-party facilitators should ensure that the level of threat and tension do not become too high or too low. Too low a level provides no motivation to find a solution while, if tension and threat are too high, the parties get nervous and become unable to process information and think of creative solutions. Consequently, they may start to polarize and take rigid positions.[33]

Intergroup confrontation technique. Due to the high levels of emotion and tension associated with confrontive situations, a third-party facilitator may be able to resolve the conflicts and negotiate effectively by using a structured approach. This ensures that both parties concentrate on the appropriate issues and direct their efforts objectively toward resolving them. Intergroup confrontation technique is one such approach that includes the following steps:[23,34]

1. *Each group meets separately and prepares two lists,* one list indicating how they perceive their own issues as a group, and the second list indicating how they view those of the other group.
2. *The two groups come together and share their perceptions* with the third-party facilitator helping them clarify their views and develop a better understanding of themselves and the other group.
3. *The groups separately look deeper into the issues.* This helps diagnose the current problem and source of conflict and determine what and how each group can contribute to conflict resolution.
4. *The groups meet together to share their new insights.*

This becomes a real collaborating and problem-solving session. The third-party facilitator urges them to define common goals and issues and to plan the next stages for seeking solutions with a timeline.

160

Although the intergroup confrontation technique seems quite logical, it may not always lead to successful conflict resolution. However, it provides a useful process for both parties involved in conflict to explore and work together through their differences. The third-party facilitator with proper skills and experience, can use this technique quite effectively in moving both parties towards an acceptable solution.

Practical Guidelines for Negotiation

To be persuasive, we must be believable; to be believable, we must be credible; to be credible, we must be truthful.

— *Edward R. Murrow*

Although negotiation takes place every day, it is not easy to do it effectively. Standard strategies for negotiation often leave people dissatisfied, worn out, or alienated—and quite often all three.[1] There are seven main practical guidelines for negotiating effectively which are based on the principled negotiation method, suggested by Fisher and Ury.[35] These are summarized in Figure 5.4 and are briefly described below.

Commit to negotiate for mutual gain

In order to negotiate successfully, both parties must be committed to negotiate in good faith and for mutual gain. Often, people see only two ways to negotiate: soft or hard. Both these methods have their limitations. The third way to negotiate, principled negotiation, has all the advantages of both methods and minimizes their disadvantages. It is based upon the premise that both parties must make a strong commitment to achieve win-win outcomes. If committed to achieve mutual gain, both parties focus on positive aspects and agreements rather than on negative aspects and differences. They view mutual gains as attainable and emphasize building trust, improving understanding, and the need to look at things from the other person's perspective. This approach not only makes the negotiating process easier, but also ensures positive outcomes.

Avoid bargaining over positions

When the parties in a negotiation take inflexible positions on an issue and refuse to bend from them, they cannot really negotiate—they can only argue. Arguments over positions lead to polarization and entrenchment, and often take both parties away from the real issues under negotiation. Such situations may happen in political projects, larger mergers, or issues with strong historical traditions. The disadvantages of bargaining over positions are many.[35]

It produces unwise agreements. When bargaining over positions, negotiators tend to lock themselves into those positions. The more you clarify and define your positions, the more you become committed to them. It becomes hard to change your position because your ego becomes identified with that position. You now have a new interest in "saving face." The

Figure 5.4 Summary of Guidelines for Successful
Negotiations

Guideline	Main Features and Why It Works
1. Commitment to negotiate for mutual gain	• Commitment leads to results
2. Don't bargain over positions	• It produces unwise agreements • It is inefficient • It endangers ongoing relationships • It is ineffective when many parties are involved and form a coalition • Makes you vulnerable with hard negotiators
3. Separate the people from the problem	• People have emotions, beliefs and perceptions; they must be dealt with sensitively. • Negotiators are interested both in substance and relationship
4. Separate the relationship from the substance; deal directly with people problem	• Negotiations are highly influenced by people problems, which include perceptions, emotions and communications. • People problems (if not prevented or resolved at early stages) leads to failure
5. Focus on interests, not positions	• Interests define the problem. Therefore clarify and communicate interests effectively • Reconciling interests leads to a wise solution • There are many shared and compatible interests behind opposed positions
6. Generate options for mutual gain	• Separates inventing from deciding • Options are broadened to achieve mutual gains and making decisions easy to live with
7. Use objective criteria or standard	• Neither party can complain against objective criteria • Objective criteria produces wise agreements

Source: Data based on information from the work of Roger Fisher, William Ury and Bruce Patton in *Getting to Yes: Negotiating Agreement Without Giving In, Second Edition,* 1991, Penguin Books, pp. 4–94.

need to reconcile future actions with past positions makes it less and less likely that any agreement will achieve mutual gains.

It is inefficient. Bargaining over positions takes time and creates incentives that stall settlements. Both parties start with an extreme opening position and tend to stubbornly hold to it by making only small concessions to continue negotiations. The more extreme the opening positions and smaller the concessions, the more time and effort is needed to discover whether or not agreement is possible. Each party feels pressured to yield to the other side and therefore is less motivated to move quickly. Both

Human Resource Skills for the Project Manager

parties tend to drag their feet or walk out, increasing the time and cost of negotiating as well as the risk of reaching no agreement at all.

It endangers an ongoing relationship. Bargaining over positions becomes a contest of will. Both parties declare strongly what they will and won't do. Each party tends to force the other party to change its position. For example, project managers may try to take advantage of the situation when negotiating prices with some contractors. In such cases, positional bargaining strains and sometimes shatters the relationship. Hard feelings and resentment may occur when one party is forced to accept the terms of another party without appropriate returns.

Being nice is not the answer. Many people recognize the risk of spoiling their business relationships by using hard positional bargaining. For example, a project management consultant may not be too hard while negotiating with a client who may offer good business opportunities in the future. Consequently, they may tend to use a soft negotiation approach that emphasizes the importance of building and maintaining a relationship. However, this may make the negotiator vulnerable to someone who uses hard positional bargaining because in positional bargaining, a hard negotiation approach dominates a soft one.

Positional bargaining is worse when many parties are involved. Negotiations may involve more than two parties. Positional bargaining becomes worse when many parties are involved because parties may form a coalition even when their shared interests are more symbolic than substantive.

Separate the people from the problem

Project participants recognize that it is hard to deal with a problem without people getting emotional, angry, upset, pointing fingers, and misunderstanding each other. Successful negotiators must separate the people from the problem because it helps them focus on the real issues and avoid personalities and behavioral biases. Some important points that reinforce the benefits of separating the people from the problem are:[35]

Negotiators are people first. While negotiating in project environments, industrial sectors, corporate or business transactions, it must be remembered that we are dealing not with abstract and imaginary parties, but with real human beings. They have emotions, values, beliefs, perceptions, different backgrounds (social, cultural and educational), and opinions. Human behavior is often unpredictable. If not dealt with properly, people get offended, angry and hostile. Misunderstanding can lead to actions and reactions that make it impossible to reach a viable solution.

Failing to deal with others sensitively can be disastrous for successful negotiations. Negotiators must pay attention to relationships and the people problem from pre-negotiation/planning to the post-negotiation phases of the negotiation process.

Negotiator's interest both in the substance and relationship. Every negotiator wants to achieve his or her substantive interests. However, a successful and effective negotiator is also equally interested in maintaining an ongoing relationship. In fact, with many long-term clients, project partners in joint ventures, or project team members, ongoing relationships are far more important than the outcome of any particular negotiation. Negotiators must remember these two points while looking after both substantive and relationship interests:[35]

- The relationship tends to become entangled with the problem.
- Positional bargaining puts relationship and substance in conflict.

Successful negotiators assess the situation carefully and plan the negotiation process to achieve a balance between their substantive and relationship interests.

Separate the relationship from the substance

One does not have to choose between meeting the goal of dealing successfully with substantive problems and maintaining good working relationships. To negotiate successfully, both parties must be committed to reaching win-win outcomes and be prepared to deal objectively with both goals and relationships on their own legitimate merits.

Successful negotiators must deal with "people problems" directly rather than trying to solve them with substantive concessions. They must deal with their own people problems as well as those of the other party. Following are some important factors that should be considered at early stages of the negotiation process to solve the people problems of both parties involved in negotiation.[35]

Perceptions. Successful negotiations involve understanding things from the other party's point of view. Project participants may have different perceptions of the issues under negotiation. Perceptual differences, if not overcome, can lead to failure in reaching agreements. Often conflict lies not in objective reality but in people's heads.

Irrespective of whether perceptions are logical or ill-founded, perceptual differences must be dealt with at early stages of the negotiation process. Some suggestions to overcome perceptual differences are:[35]

- Put yourself in their shoes.
- Don't deduce their intentions from your fears.
- Don't blame them for your problems.
- Discuss, clarify and verify each other's perceptions.
- Explore ways to act inconsistently with their perceptions.
- Ensure that they participate in the process by giving them a stake in the outcome.
- Help in saving face (if the other party requires it) by making your proposals compatible with his or her values.

Human Resource Skills for the Project Manager

Emotions. In bitter disputes, emotions can flare leading to head on collisions and non-cooperation. The following ideas can be used to dampen the negative impact of emotions on successful negotiation.[35]

- Recognize and understand emotions, theirs and yours.
- Make emotions explicit and acknowledge them as legitimate
- Allow the other side to vent.
- Allow a cool-down period: don't react to emotional outbursts.
- Use symbolic gestures that produce constructive emotional impact—offer praise, admit mistakes.

Communication. Effective communication is the key to successful negotiation. Negotiation is the process of communicating back and forth to reach a joint decision or satisfactory outcome. While negotiating, both parties must recognize the important role of communication in terms of not only *what* is said but *how* it is said. Some big problems in communication in context of negotiation are:[35]

- Negotiators may not be talking to each other; they may avoid the negotiation process.
- Negotiators may be talking, but may not listen to each other effectively.
- There may be a misunderstanding due to cultural differences, misinterpretations or lack of shared values and experiences.

These are only representative of the many possible problems in negotiations. Some practical suggestions to solve communication problems include:[35]

- Listen actively and acknowledge what is being said.
- Speak to be understood. Use language that they are familiar with and address their interests, not just your own.
- Speak about yourself, not about them (use "I" messages, as covered in Chapter One). Don't assume you understand their intentions.
- Speak to achieve the final purpose, and weigh the impact of your words on that purpose before you speak.

Prevention. The best time to handle people problems is before they become serious. Project managers should build good personal and organizational relationships to soften the blow of undesirable agreements. They should try to separate the substantive problem from the relationship and protect personal egos from getting involved in substantive discussions. People problems can be prevented by:[35]

- *Building good working relationships before the negotiation begin.* Use informal meetings to build a good rapport with team members and the client.
- *Facing the problem, not the people.* Think of the other party as a partner and search for a fair, win-win outcome.

Separating the people from the problem should be an ongoing practice. It basically involves dealing with people as human beings, communicating effectively, overcoming perceptual differences and negative impacts of emotions, and preventing people problems by continually working on building trust, mutual understanding and better working relationships.

Focus on interests, not positions

Often negotiations fail because people focus on positions instead of interests. For example, in a project requiring public opinion and regulatory approvals, regulating agencies may take the position of stalling the project rather than addressing the interests of the public as well as those of the project owner and manager. Understanding the difference between interests and positions is crucial.[35]

Reconciling interests leads to a wise solution. Successful negotiations are accomplished by reconciling interests rather than positions. It is important to understand the difference between interests and positions and the roles that interests play in the negotiation process.[35]

Interests define the problem. It is conflicting interests, not conflicting positions, that make negotiations difficult. Interests are generated by needs, desires, concerns and fears. Positions are built upon interests. Interests motivate people to decide upon a position. In order to develop a solution, it is better to look at interests instead of positions because:

- There are several satisfactory positions corresponding to every interest.
- Even behind opposing positions, there are many more interests than just the conflicting ones.

Shared and compatible interests lie behind opposing positions. There is a tendency to assume that the interests of opposing parties involved in negotiation must also be opposed. However, a deeper analysis of many negotiations suggests that there are many more shared and compatible interests than opposing ones. For example, sometimes contractors working on projects may be perceived to be interested in making quick financial gains rather than being concerned about quality. In reality, this is not usually true, especially in the case of smart contractors who are interested in working collaboratively with the project manager and the project team to improve the quality in order to build and maintain their professional reputation. It helps them build trust and better future working relationships and eventually leads to much higher financial gains for both parties. Shared interests and differing but complementary interests can lead to a wise agreement.

Identifying interests. Project participants often have interests that may be abstract, unexpressed, intangible and inconsistent, even though their positions are relatively concrete and clear. Looking after these *interests* and not *positions* leads to successful negotiation. Identifying these interests is a first step in understanding their interests as well as yours. Some suggestions that can be used in identifying interests are:[35]

- Ask for reasons behind their interests in order to understand the needs, hopes, fears or desires served by those interests.
- Ask "why not?" Think about their choices.

- Realize that each side has multiple interests.
- Recognize that the most powerful interests come from basic human needs, such as safety, security, social affiliation, recognition and desired autonomy.[35]
- Make a list to help you sort and assess your interests.

Communicating interests. The goal of negotiation is to serve your interests. This can be effectively done only when both parties communicate their interests to each other. Failing this, they may be acting based on perceptions and personal biases and focusing on past grievances instead of future concerns.[35] Consequently, the parties may not be listening to each other. The main issue is how to discuss interests constructively without becoming stuck in rigid positions.

You must be able to communicate your interests clearly if you want the other side to take them into account. For example, special interest groups opposing a particular highway construction project or a nuclear power plant must emphasize explicitly the risks and issues of pollution, safety, increased traffic, etc. Some ideas that can be helpful in communicating interests effectively include:[35]

- Make your interests come alive. Be specific, verify and establish the legitimacy of your interests.
- Acknowledge that their interests are related to the problem at hand. Appreciate their interests and they will appreciate yours.
- Put the problem before your answer. Outline interests and reasoning first and conclusions and proposals later. This helps others understand your logic and point of view.
- Focus on the future, not the past. Emphasize what a project team could do better to meet project objectives rather than past mistakes.
- Be concrete but flexible. Know your goals, yet be open to fresh ideas. Find out what the other party has to offer or demand.
- Be hard on the problem, soft on the people. Be committed to your interests, not to your positions.

People become defensive and stop listening when they feel personally threatened. Therefore, it is wise to separate the people from the problem. Attack the problem without blaming the people. Be supportive and courteous, listen to them with respect, and appreciate their time and effort. Give positive support and emphasize the problem with equal vigor and persistency.

Fighting hard on the substantive issues increases pressure for an effective solution; giving support improves working relationships and chances of reaching an agreement. It is this combination of supporting the people and attacking the problem that leads to successful negotiations. This combination of support and attack may seem inconsistent, but it creates an environment where compromise can take place.

Negotiating hard for your interests does not imply having no concern for the other party. Actually, in negotiating successfully, you cannot expect the other party to listen to your interests and discuss your proposal favorably if you don't consider their interest and be open to their suggestions. It is important to focus on interests rather than on positions. Successful negotiations require both being firm and open.

Generate options for mutual gain

One completely overcomes only what one assimilates.

— Andre Gide

A common problem in negotiations is the lack of options for mutual gain. Successful project managers are able to see the advantages of generating options for contractors, team members, vendors and clients that are likely to lead to win-win situations. All stakeholders must be encouraged to work together for mutual gains rather than feeling that gain for one must mean loss for the other. This can be done by diagnosing the situation carefully and then prescribing by generating options for mutual gain, as described below.

Diagnosis. Parties involved in a dispute are sometimes not able to see the merits of inventing options for mutual gain. In a contract negotiation, both parties believe that their offer is reasonable and should be accepted perhaps with minor adjustments. In most negotiations, there are four major obstacles that limit the generation of creative options:[35]

1. Premature judgment
2. Searching for the single answer
3. The assumption of a fixed pie (gain for one is loss for another)
4. Believing that "solving their problem is their problem"; the inability to address the other party's interests.

In a project environment, project managers involved in negotiations must understand these obstacles and then formulate a strategy to overcome them.

Prescription. Fisher and Ury suggested some ideas to invent creative options:[35]

Separate inventing from deciding. This involves brainstorming, which should be carefully planned and conducted. Promising ideas should be evaluated and implemented. If possible, consider brainstorming with the other side to create a climate for collaborative problem solving and educating each side about the interests and concerns of the other.

Broaden your options. Negotiating parties should not assume that they must look for the one best answer at the prescription stage. The purpose of inventing creative options is to develop a framework within which negotiation can take place. A brainstorming session frees people to think creatively. Once freed, they must think of their problems and generate creative solutions. The following ideas can be used to broaden your options:[35]

Multiply options by shuttling between the specific and the general. The task of inventing options involves four basic steps as shown in Figure 5.5.[35]

Human Resource Skills for the Project Manager

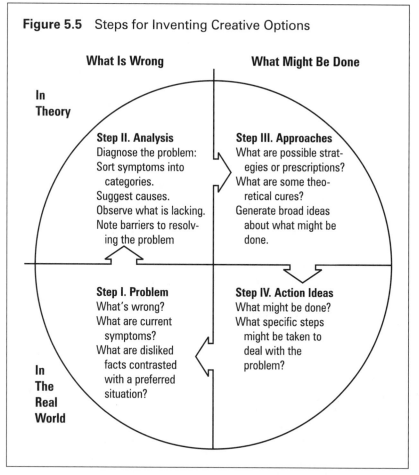

Figure 5.5 Steps for Inventing Creative Options

What Is Wrong   **What Might Be Done**

In Theory

Step II. Analysis
Diagnose the problem:
Sort symptoms into
categories.
Suggest causes.
Observe what is lacking.
Note barriers to resolv-
ing the problem

Step III. Approaches
What are possible strat-
egies or prescriptions?
What are some theo-
retical cures?
Generate broad ideas
about what might be
done.

Step I. Problem
What's wrong?
What are current
symptoms?
What are disliked
facts contrasted
with a preferred
situation?

Step IV. Action Ideas
What might be done?
What specific steps
might be taken to
deal with the
problem?

In The Real World

- Define the problem: describe the factual situation that you dislike in general terms.
- Analyze the problem to identify causes and effects.
- Generate alternatives and options.
- Analyze alternatives and select appropriate action points.

For example, an organization may be losing money on international projects (problem definition). This problem may be caused by a lack of education and awareness of different cultures, leading to failure in contract negotiations (diagnosis). Several options may be generated to resolve this problem, such as encouraging the project manager and key team members to learn about the culture where the project is taking place (generating approaches), and top management may actually send them for such training (action ideas). More creative options can be generated by:

- *Looking through the eyes of experts.* Examine the problem from the perspective of different professionals and disciplines.
- *Inventing agreements of different strengths.* This keeps the negotiation process going. Sometimes the naming of an agreement can have an influence on the parties willingness to commit themselves to it. For example, an agreement can be: substantive, permanent, final, comprehensive, unconditional; or it can be procedural, provisional, in principle, partial, contingent.[35]
- *Changing the scope of a proposed agreement.* Try to vary not only the strength but also the scope of the agreement by "sweetening the pot."

Look for mutual gain. The assumption of a fixed pie is a major barrier to creative problem solving and successful negotiations. In addition to minimizing joint losses, emphasizing shared interests can often lead to joint gain. This can be done by:[35]

- Identifying shared interests
- Dovetailing differing interests by identifying differences in interests, beliefs, values placed on time, forecasts and aversion to risk, and then asking for their preferences in order to reach an acceptable agreement.

Make their decisions easy. You can reach a successful negotiation only if the other party makes a decision you want. Therefore, you should do everything possible to make that decision an easy one. You must make the choices less painful for the other side. For example, in project litigation, the winning party must protect the ego of the losing party and offer them an opportunity to reach a settlement and help them to save face. They can help make a decision easy by using the following ideas:[35]

- Try to identify a person and then see the problem from his or her point of view. Knowing about the person will help in developing suitable strategy.
- Identify what decisions are required, then provide an answer, not just a problem. This facilitates easy decision making.
- Evaluate the consequences of making threatening statements—they are usually counterproductive.

Inventing options for mutual gain is a part of successful negotiation strategy. In a complex international project negotiation, it is necessary to be creative in inventing options. It opens doors and may produce a range of mutually satisfactory agreements. So generate options before deciding. Look for shared interests and dovetail differing interests. Protect their egos and make their decisions easy to make and implement.

Insist on using objective criteria

In negotiations, you will always face the harsh reality of conflicting interests regardless of how well you understand their interests, how creatively you reconcile interests and how highly you value an ongoing relationship. Insist

Human Resource Skills for the Project Manager

on using objective criteria rather than reconciling conflicts by positional bargaining. No negotiation is likely to be efficient if it becomes a contest of wills. Successful negotiators are committed to reaching a solution based on objective criteria, not pressure. Fisher and Ury have suggested some ideas about developing objective criteria and negotiating with objective criteria.[35]

Negotiations reached by using objective criteria are principled negotiations that produce wise agreements efficiently and amicably. They are based upon using standards of fairness, efficiency and merits of interests. Principled negotiation protects participants from a constant battle for dominance that threatens a relationship. It involves discussing objective standards rather than taking positions and forcing others to back down. Negotiations based on objective criteria reduces the probability of flip-flopping and thus both parties use their time efficiently by focusing on interests and solutions, not positions.

Developing objective criteria. Conducting a principled negotiation involves determining how to develop objective criteria, and how to use them in negotiation. Objective criteria should be based on fair standards and should be developed by using fair procedures. They should be independent of each side's will and should also be legitimate and practical. An old way of sharing a piece of cake between two children, where one divides and the other chooses first, provides a simple illustration. Neither can complain about an unfair division.

Negotiating with objective criteria. After identifying some objective criteria and procedures, the question is how to discuss them with the other side. There are three basic points to remember:[35]
- Frame each issue as a joint search for objective criteria.
- Reason and be open to reason to determine which standards are most appropriate and how they should be applied. The reasons should be based on merits.
- Never yield to pressure.

Pressure can take many forms: a bribe, a threat, a manipulation to trust, or a simple refusal to budge. In principled negotiation, the emphasis is on logical reasoning and convincing based on merits rather than yielding to pressures.

NEGOTIATION IS A FACT OF LIFE in project management. Project managers must negotiate about different issues with clients, functional managers, project team members, vendors, contractors and regulatory agencies. They must recognize that bargaining over position is inefficient and produces unwise agreements. To negotiate successfully, it is necessary to separate the people from the problem. Project participants should separate the relationships from the substance and deal directly with people by overcoming perceptual differences, emotions and communicating interests. Practically, it is beneficial to focus on interests, invent options for mutual gain and insist on using objective criteria to conduct a principled negotiation that leads to wise agreements.

Summary

Negotiation is a fact of life in project environments that are characterized by matrix structures in which responsibility and authority are shared. Negotiation is the process of bargaining and reaching an agreement with project stakeholders concerning the transfer of resources, the generation of information and the accomplishment of tasks. It is a persuasive process and is one of the most important skills needed to manage projects successfully.

The negotiation process consists of three stages: pre-negotiation planning, actual negotiations, and post-negotiation analysis/critique. The negotiation process is as important as its outcome. Project managers should be sensitive to human feelings and to the importance of maintaining good working relationships. Successful negotiations are based on basic principles that involve focusing on real issues, problems and common interests rather than on people; generating options that advance shared interests; and then negotiating based on objective criteria.

There are two commonly used methods of negotiation: soft or hard. Soft negotiators are friendly and make concessions readily to avoid conflict and the risk of spoiling future relationships. On the other hand, hard negotiators take strong positions and try to win, even at the cost of relationships.

Fisher and Ury developed a third negotiation method, called "Principled Negotiation," which is neither soft nor hard but is rather both soft *and* hard. It emphasizes deciding and resolving the issues based on merits rather than on positions and it often leads to a win-win situation. This method is based upon four points: separate the people from the problem; focus on interests, not positions; generate options for mutual gain; and base results on objective criteria.

Culture has a significant impact on negotiation strategies. Cultural differences may exist (especially in international projects) that influence methods of negotiating, the negotiation process and its outcome. Project managers must develop skills in negotiation in a multicultural environment. They must identify and analyze seven major elements of culture: material culture, language, aesthetics, education, religion/beliefs and attitudes, social organizations, and political life. They must evaluate the impact of cultural differences during all three stages of negotiation. During pre-negotiation planning, they must formulate appropriate strategies (which relate to cost, schedule, and performance) and tactics (which relate to the actual negotiation meeting) and analyze and assess project risks and determine how one should act and deal with the other party.

The actual negotiation meeting involves five distinct stages: protocol, probing (using verbal and non-verbal components which include vocal tones and body language), rough bargaining, closure, and agreement. Post-negotiation analysis is done to provide feedback about how well planning and conducting the negotiations actually went. Project managers must be cautious of cultural aspects when progressing through all three stages of the negotiation process.

Negotiation is a process by which persons who have shared and opposed interests try to work out a settlement and come to an agreement. Negotiations take place when both parties want to resolve their different interests and continue their relationships in productive and fulfilling ways. There are various types of negotiations that can be classified based on outcomes achieved (win-lose, win-win, and lose-lose) and on the negotiation process or environment (attitudinal structuring and intra-organizational negotiations). Savage, Blair and Sorenson developed a negotiation model called the SBS Model. It is based upon various styles of conflict resolution and the fact that negotiation approach varies from situation to situation.

There are two main types of negotiation strategies: unilateral or interactive, depending upon whether the negotiations consider only one party's perspective or both parties' perspectives, respectively. Successful negotiation strategies combine positive features of both unilateral and interactive strategies with an aim to achieve a win-win outcome while maintaining good working relationships. Negotiating successfully is not easy. After negotiation, people often feel dissatisfied, worn out, alienated, or all three. Project managers must negotiate with clients, contractors, vendors, technical specialists, functional managers and project team members about budget, schedule, design constraints, priorities, resources, responsibilities and performance requirements.

To negotiate successfully, project managers must be strongly committed to mutual gain and must not bargain over position because it is inefficient, produces unwise agreements, and endangers an ongoing relationship. Other practical guidelines, suggested by Fisher and Ury, include: separating the people from the problem; dealing directly with people by overcoming perceptual differences and emotions; enhancing communication and preventing people problems at early stages. Also, project managers must focus on interests, not positions, because reconciling interests leads to a wise solution and there may be shared and compatible interests behind opposed positions. They must identify and communicate interests clearly. It is essential to generate options for mutual gain by diagnosing the issues carefully and then inventing creative options that separate inventing from deciding, broaden the options, emphasize mutual gain, and make the decisions easy to live with. To negotiate successfully, project managers must insist on using objective criteria because working together in developing objective criteria and then negotiating on those criteria often leads to wise agreements.

Outline

6

Human Resource Skills for the Project Manager

*The reason more people die from worry than from work is that
more people worry than work.*

— *Anonymous*

Managing Stress

A LL OCCUPATIONS HAVE a certain amount of stress associated with them, and project management is no exception. Stress is one of the outcomes of change and conflict, which are inevitable in a project environment and are sometimes even necessary to increase project performance. Therefore, stress becomes a necessary part of life in a project, and stress management must be considered an important element of project management.

Recently, there has been an increased interest in stress management in the project environment. This is due not only to the obligation to improve the organizational life of company employees, but also to the tremendous economic consequences. According to a study conducted by the Research Triangle Institute, stress-related disorders cost the U.S. economy approximately $187 billion in 1990 alone.[1] U.S. industries also lose an estimated $75–$100 billion each year in absenteeism and reduced productivity attributable to stress-related illnesses, ranging from migraine headaches to hypertension and ulcers.[2,3] Stress has also been related to heart disease and heart attacks, which cost more than $26 billion annually in disability payments and medical bills in the U.S. alone.[4] Research has suggested that stress may also lead to alcoholism, drug abuse, marital problems, absenteeism, and child abuse.

Stress-related problems are common in all types of organizations throughout the world. For example, the average Japanese worker, who works 200 hours more per year than his or her North American and British counterparts, suffers higher stress and even more dramatically, "karoshi" (death from overwork).[5] ■

About Stress and Stress Management

All occupations have a certain degree of stress associated with them. But the project manager experiences a significant level of stress because of an endless list of demands, deadlines, and problems throughout the project life cycle. Project managers must learn how to cope with and manage stress in order to avoid headaches, ulcers, anxiety or other stress-related ailments. For effective stress management, they must understand what stress is, how and why it is created, and then how to manage it. This section highlights the definition of stress, the three-stage stress reaction, and types of stress.

What is stress?

According to Selye, stress is the nonspecific or psychological response of the body to any demand made upon it.[6] Stress is a perception of threat or an expectation of future discomfort that excites, alerts, or otherwise activates the organism. More generally, stress is a response to pressures, responsibilities, and real or imaginary threats from the environment.[7,8] Stress is a response, not the elements that cause it. The factors that generate stress are called *stressors*.

According to Schuler,[2] stress is a dynamic condition in which an individual is confronted with an opportunity, constraint or demand related to what he or she desires and for which the outcome is perceived to be both uncertain and important.[5] In other words, stress is composed of three elements: *Total stress = f (opportunity, constraint and demand)*.

Though stress is typically discussed in a negative context, it also has positive value. Stress implies an opportunity when it offers potential gain. For example, an athlete, stage performer or a project manager may use stress positively to perform at or near their maximum at crucial periods.

More typically, in a project environment, stress is associated with constraints and demands. *Constraints* (time, financial and others) prevent individuals from doing what they desire; whereas *demands* refer to the loss of something desired.

For example, when individuals undergo performance reviews, they may feel stress because they confront opportunity, constraints, and demands. A good performance review may provide an opportunity for promotion, greater responsibilities, and financial rewards. However, a poor review may block advancement (constraints), and an extremely poor review may lead to removal from the project or even being fired (demands).

Potential stress can become actual stress only under two conditions: if there is uncertainty over the outcome and if the outcome is important.[2] In other words, a stressful condition only exists when there is doubt or uncertainty whether an opportunity will be lost (a contract will be won or not), whether the constraints will be removed, or whether a loss will be avoided (penalties will be waived or not). Also the importance of the outcome is critical. For example, a project manager may feel more stress if winning the next project depends upon the performance of the present project. By contrast, project team members feel hardly any stress when working on tasks they hold to be unimportant for that project.

Since stress represents a response to a situation, it is accompanied by a response/reaction, as discussed in the next section.

Three-stage stress reaction

Individuals react to stressful situations in different ways. When the body encounters a stressor, it goes through a pattern of reaction that Selye called the General Adaptation Syndrome.[6] There are three stages of this reaction pattern.

Alarm reaction. This reaction begins as soon as the body perceives a stressor. In this stage, individuals feel a sensation of "fight or flight." They want to either confront the stressor or avoid it. A person may feel this reaction, for example, on a construction site, when he or she discovers some aspect of the work that is not right or that is likely to fail. A biochemical reaction releases hormones from the endocrine glands to help the body fight stress. These hormones either try to return the body to its previous steady state or provide energy to fight the stressor. During the alarm reaction, the body goes through some physiological changes, such as rising heartbeat, blood pressure, blood flow, demand for oxygen, and blood sugar level, tensing muscles, dilating pupils, and slower digestion.[9]

Resistance stage. During the resistance stage, the body adapts to the stressor or tries to resist it. If the body is able to overcome the stressor, it then recovers from the damage caused during the alarm stage. The physiological symptoms of stress disappear and the body becomes more resistant to the stressor. However, although the body is more resistant to stress, it is still less resistant to invading pathogens.

Exhaustion stage. This is the final stage of the General Adaptation Syndrome, which occurs when stress persists longer than the body's ability to cope with it. During exhaustion, the symptoms of the alarm reaction reappear but the body is unable to do anything about it. Thus the individual feels helpless and may succumb to headaches, ulcers, high blood pressure, and heart attacks. An individual's capacity to maintain the resistance stage is highly variable and depends upon numerous factors, including personality and the gravity of the stressor.

Types of stress

Stress is unavoidable in life: Selye commented that only dead people are completely free of stress.[10] However, not all stress is bad. Stress can be either positive or negative depending upon how people perceive it. Their reaction to and capacity to cope with stress depends upon their personality and their perception of the stressor.

The two major types of stress are *eustress* and *distress.*

Eustress is constructive stress. For example, when a student considers final examinations as a challenge to be met, he or she experiences eustress. Eustress can be viewed as a motivator that contributes to an increase in performance. In project environments, when project teams face deadlines or challenges to cut costs, they often put forward their best efforts to overcome problems. Typically, individuals experiencing eustress feel that they have control over the situation (e.g., a confident project manager presenting a project plan). Generally, these individuals use their conceptual skills to develop a sound plan and their interpersonal and communications skills to carry it out.

Distress is destructive stress. A student who views a final examination as an insurmountable crisis experiences distress. Distress is a demotivator that reduces the ability to perform. Its presence may cause physical and/or emotional suffering and disturbance. Individuals experiencing distress feel that they have little or no control over the situation. For example, a technical project manager lacking in human skills may be nervous about leading the project team and managing the project. Because of this fear, he or she may lose self-confidence and self-esteem, consequently reducing the quantity and quality of performance.

Project managers must try to avoid distress situations and create an atmosphere that encourages eustress. They must be in close touch with their project team members and ensure that team members face mostly eustress situations that will lead to an overall increase in project performance.

Sometimes in large, bureaucratic organizations, management may deliberately introduce organizational change to shake up the organization. This temporarily increases stress but usually wakes everyone up, leading to increased productivity. In some organizations, an appropriate dose of occasional eustress may be helpful to stay competitive.

Stress and strain are usually coupled. Sress is a response to a situation whereas strain represents the psychological or physiological changes that take place in the individual. In short, stress is the cause and strain is the symptom. If the project managers fail to communicate openly with their project team members and overuse their positional/formal power and authority, their relationships with project personnel deteriorate. Consequently, both the project manager and team members feel the strain, which may create physical and psychological problems.

STRESS IS NORMALLY CAUSED by conditions or outcomes that are both uncertain and important to us. It can be caused by opportunities, constraints or demands. The effects of stress are additive in nature. Though stress is normally viewed in a negative manner, if managed properly it can lead to increased

Human Resource Skills for the Project Manager

productivity. Project managers are expected to fulfill a heavy load of responsibility with limited formal authority, which may lead to stress. Therefore, project managers must understand basics of stress and stress management.

Sources of Stress

Don't be stressed by problems. Problems often lead to opportunities.

— Anonymous

Many work-related stressors, such as fear of job loss, corporate politics or excessive demands on time, are quite common in a project environment and the project manager has limited control over them. Figure 6.1 lists come of the most common sources of stress, not in any order of importance.[11] Since each individual perceives stress differently, some may feel that not all sources listed are stressors, while others may think there are stressors missing from the list.

Different project managers perceive these stressors differently and may have their own style of managing stress. Once project managers realize the impact of these uncontrollable factors on their own lives and on overall project performance, they should develop their own stress management techniques to reduce the personal effect of stress.

The stressors listed in Figure 6.1 are discussed below, grouped into four main categories of stress-creating factors:

1. Factors related to roles and relationships
2. Factors related to job environment
3. Personal factors
4. Factors related to project environment/climate.[12]

Factors related to roles and relationships

These factors include the stress caused by the conflicting and ambiguous roles that project participants play and the relationships among them.

Role conflict. Role conflict occurs when an individual receives conflicting expectations from others. There are four major types of role conflicts:[13]

Intersender role conflict is caused when expectations from one source conflict with expectations from another source. For example, John's boss tells him to "crack down" on his project team members in order to increase their output and accelerate the project schedule. However, team members suggest that John will regret doing this because the desired schedule is totally unrealistic, and ask him to take their concerns back to the boss. In this situation, the project manager will experience intersender role conflict because two parties are asking him to play conflicting roles, as taskmaster and as team member/advocate.

Intrasender role conflict arises when an individual is given contradictory orders by another person. For example, Barbara will experience intrasender role conflict if her boss tells her to get a project completed on time as a high priority, and then later gives her another project that also

---

Figure 6.1 Common Sources of Stress

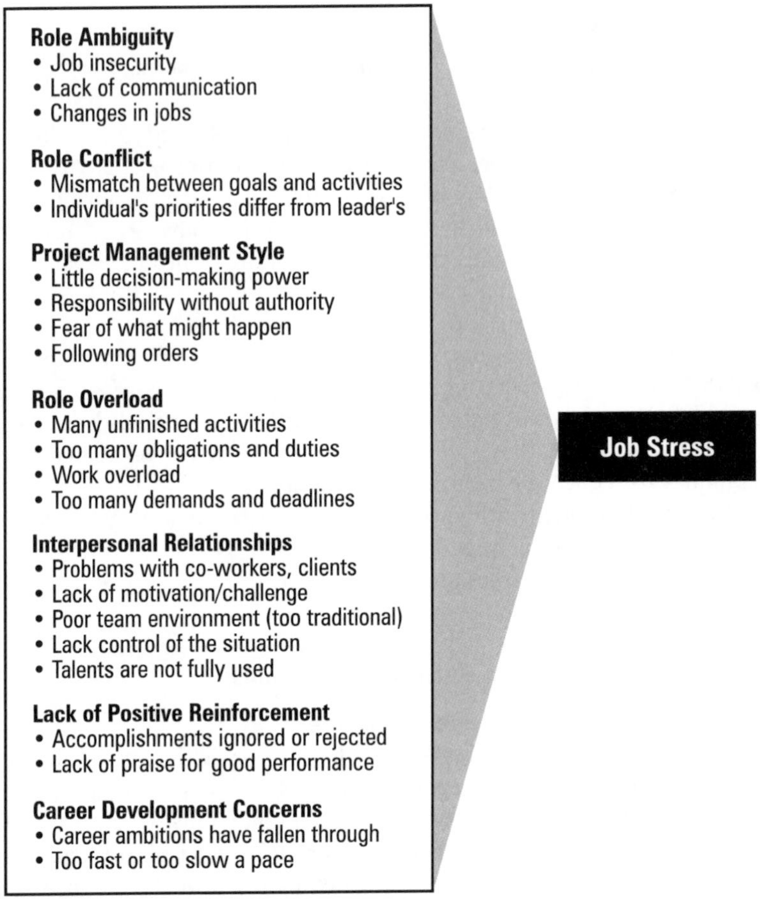

Role Ambiguity
- Job insecurity
- Lack of communication
- Changes in jobs

Role Conflict
- Mismatch between goals and activities
- Individual's priorities differ from leader's

Project Management Style
- Little decision-making power
- Responsibility without authority
- Fear of what might happen
- Following orders

Role Overload
- Many unfinished activities
- Too many obligations and duties
- Work overload
- Too many demands and deadlines

Interpersonal Relationships
- Problems with co-workers, clients
- Lack of motivation/challenge
- Poor team environment (too traditional)
- Lack control of the situation
- Talents are not fully used

Lack of Positive Reinforcement
- Accomplishments ignored or rejected
- Lack of praise for good performance

Career Development Concerns
- Career ambitions have fallen through
- Too fast or too slow a pace

Job Stress

Source: Data based on information from Paul C. Dinsmore, M. Dean Martin and Gary Huettel, 1985, *The Project Manager's Work Environment: Coping with Time and Stress,* Drexel Hill, PA: Project Management Institute, p. 34.

requires time and effort and may prevent her from completing the first task. This happens quite often in a project environment when experts working in a matrix style on several projects, even under the same project manager, are forced to switch back and forth.

Person role conflict is caused when people are asked to act in a manner that they think is wrong. For example, if Mary's job makes demands that are against her values or beliefs, she will experience "person role conflict." Such situations can arise in marketing, when an individual finds the prod-

Human Resource Skills for the Project Manager

ucts or the marketing styles required by management distasteful, unethical, or counter to his or her beliefs. Recently project personnel have experienced person role conflicts in situations associated with health care (approval of certain drugs and procedures) or the environment.

Inter-role conflict can occur when people play multiple roles. For example, if Alan is unexpectedly asked by his boss to work overtime (work role) but he has promised his son to come to the final game of his soccer league (father role), Alan will experience inter-role conflict. This type of conflict is quite common in a project environment where there is continuous pressure to meet project schedules and budgets.

Project managers may be expected to attend evening meetings or participate in other activities associated with the project that take time away from their families. This can lead to stress, tensions, and eventually to serious family problems. Project managers must learn to analyze their situation and avoid role conflicts by balancing their obligations among work, family and personal life through exercise and spiritual and professional growth.

Role ambiguity occurs when an individual is not clear about his or her job responsibilities. It is commonly experienced by new managers in an organization and is typical in projects structured as a matrix. Role ambiguity is evident if a person cannot answer the following questions:[12]
- Who is my boss?
- Who is authorized to give me orders?
- What is my responsibility?
- How much authority do I have?
- What determines satisfactory performance in my job?
- What are appropriate behaviors in my job?
- What kind of rewards or punishments are available, based upon my performance?

Factors related to job environment
These factors refer to characteristics of the job itself (boring, too difficult, lack of challenge) or to job insecurity, unsafe working conditions and the workload.

The workload. This is one of the most common sources of job related stress in a project environment. Overload occurs when a person is given more responsibilities than he or she is capable of fulfilling. Project personnel experience overload under the following conditions:
- When work quantity is too heavy to accomplish
- When the person responsible is not provided with sufficient resources
- When the person is not capable of completing the work for lack of training and skills.

People working in a project environment are usually self-motivated high achievers. Sometimes they self-impose overload situations because they are unable to gauge how much workload they have and how much more they can handle comfortably. Such people easily get overloaded because they don't know how to say "no" to additional responsibilities. Occasionally, project personnel deliberately accept work overload in order to keep themselves too busy, thus avoiding some other unpleasant situation (conflicts in their personal life, for example).

Underload can also create stress because the job does not provide enough challenge and does not require the person to use his or her full range of skills.

Unsafe working conditions create stress from the fear of being injured or killed on the job. Such circumstances occur in some heavy construction or risky development projects such as mining, offshore drilling, etc.

Overemphasis on deadlines. In a project environment, there is a continual, often unreasonable, pressure to finish tasks by certain times. There are always deadlines to be met, which keeps project personnel under constant stress. As a result, project personnel try to fit several activities into an overly optimistic schedule. Project managers must take care that stress caused by overemphasis on deadlines does not lower the quality of the work.

Personal factors

These factors include personal problems, personality conflicts and interpersonal relationships, and lack of recognition.

Interpersonal relationships are among the most common and important stressors. In a project environment, people must interact with each other. Project managers are expected to integrate the efforts of all project stakeholders and manage all interfaces effectively. To do this, they must acquire good, pleasant interpersonal skills to establish rapport and trust. In this way, they can establish mutual understanding and good working relationships with everyone in their relationship molecule: senior management (upward relationship), other project managers and functional managers (lateral relationship), and project team members (downward relationship). They must learn to listen effectively and respect the opinions of others. Empowerment should be encouraged on the project because it motivates team members and provides them with a sense of ownership, power and responsibility. All these interpersonal relationships and contacts create a myriad of opportunities for stressful situations to arise. Some of the elements included in interpersonal relationships that can reduce or increase stress are:

Human Resource Skills for the Project Manager

- Building relations with team members to create cohesive project teams
- Developing effective communication skills with special emphasis on listening skills
- Achieving a balance between authority, responsibility and accountability
- Delegating effectively
- Negotiating to achieve a win-win outcome
- Using motivational techniques that increase the individual's and team's output
- Counseling people when they need help
- Using power and influence effectively
- Emphasizing a problem-solving climate and style in the project structure
- Respecting each other's opinions
- Helping each other succeed
- Empowering project teams and developing self-directed work teams.

These principles are more easily described than implemented. Nevertheless, project managers should try to practice them, emphasize their importance and encourage everyone else to practice these principles, too. They will help develop better interpersonal relationships and avoid negative stress situations that can reduce project performance.

Lack of positive reinforcement. Everyone likes praise, rewards and positive feedback. Positive reinforcement facilitates future improvements in performance. At the same time, a lack of positive feedback and reinforcement discourages people and may even cause stress to some project personnel. Similarly, performance appraisals cause stress if they echo negative impacts, or if people expect negative feedback.

Conflicts and changes are not only inevitable in a project environment, they are sometimes necessary to increase project performance. As one of the outcomes of change and conflict, stress therefore becomes a necessary part of life in a project environment. Although change can open doors to new opportunities, it is overcast with the clouds of uncertainty, creating stress. Conflicts and disputes between individuals and teams about what changes are needed and how they will be introduced can cause stress. In addition, since projects are done by people with diverse backgrounds, experiences and norms, personality conflicts and clashes are a major source of stress.

Factors related to the project climate

These factors include project organizational problems that are normally caused by ambiguous responsibiliy, accountability and communication channels, lack of authority, ineffective delegation and corporate politics. Overall management style in terms of team building and decision making, policies for career development and recognition can also cause stress to project participants.

Project management style. Project personnel feel a high degree of stress if the project environment or climate and the project management style adopted by senior management and/or the project manager is too difficult to live with. Significant aspects include:
- Organizational structure (hierarchical, flat or matrix)
- Communications
- Importance of and emphasis on communication
- Management style of communication (open or closed)
- Communication channels versus chains of command
- How well the project manager listens to project personnel
- Training to improve communications
- Decision making
- Decision-making process (participation encouraged or not)
- Tolerance for failure
- Empowerment
- Decision-making styles (command, consultation or consensus)
- Selection of team members
- Selection process
- How much input was sought
- Was the process fair and equitable?

Career development. Stressors associated with future professional growth potential include concerns that poor economic conditions, corporate restructuring, or conflict with clients or with one's boss will result in job loss. Recently, due to tough economic times and global competition, fear of job loss has become a leading cause of stress. In contrast, Japanese workers do not suffer from this type of stress to the same degree because their jobs are relatively more secure and permanent.

Corporate politics. Project managers and project personnel can get quite fed up with corporate politics that take up an extensive amount of time and effort in order to attain any positive results. Competition for promotions, undercutting others with rumors, backstabbing, and jockeying for position are some of the examples of corporate politics that can lead to destructive stress. The situation becomes worse when these factors are not under the direct control of those most affected by them—which, unfortunately, is usually the case.

IN SUMMARY, THE PROJECT ORGANIZATIONAL ENVIRONMENT and project management style play the most significant roles in encouraging or discouraging project personnel. Together they produce a climate that can either give one an opportunity to produce one's best while having fun, or cause considerable stress to everyone working on the project, leading to lower morale and reduced productivity. Above all, it may have a negative impact on personal health and behavior. Since stress is not only a leading killer, but also a contributing factor in reduced productivity and increased medical costs, it is imperative that project managers understand the various stressors. With this knowledge and some background about the sources and effects of stress, they can learn to manage stress effectively.

Effects of Stress

Stress is what you let it be. It can act as a motivator or cost billions of dollars in lost productivity, job errors and medical costs.

— Fortune, *October 1990*

Though stress has both positive and negative effects, research on work-related stress has tended to focus on the negative. This is not surprising, since the negative effects are so costly, both in personal and financial terms.

Stress causes problems for individuals and their employers. One researcher has identified five areas where the effects of stress are evident. These five areas and some examples of the effects of stress are listed below.[14]

1. Subjective: aggression, fatigue, irritability, moodiness
2. Behavioral: emotional outbursts, increased drug use, accidents
3. Cognitive: indecision, forgetfulness, sensitivity to criticism
4. Physiological: indigestion, increased blood pressure, breathing difficulties, heart problems
5. Organizational: high turnover, increased absenteeism, job dissatisfaction, low productivity.

The effects of work stress can also be said to occur in three major areas:[15]

Physiological effects of stress include increased blood pressure, breathing difficulties, increased heart rate, muscular tension, increased gastrointestinal disorders, sweating, hot/cold spells.

Emotional effects of stress include lowered self-esteem, poorer intellectual functioning, anger, anxiety, depression, inability to make decisions, nervousness, aggression, moodiness, irritability, fatigue, resentment of supervision, job dissatisfaction.

Behavioral effects of stress include decreased performance, increased absenteeism, higher accident rates, higher turnover, impulsive behavior, emotional actions, difficulties in communication, abuse of alcohol and other drugs.

Health and stress (physiological effects)

More men are killed by overwork than the importance of the world justifies.

— Rudyard Kipling

The impact of stress on the productivity of project personnel is of great concern to project managers and organizations using the philosophy of "management by projects." Most projects are managed under severe constraints that may cause health-related stress. Therefore, the project manager must recognize that health is an important factor in determining the quantity and quality of output. Although it is difficult to determine the precise relationship between stress and health in all individual cases, it is becoming increasingly clear that many illnesses are related to or caused by stress. There is considerable evidence linking stress to coronary heart disease. And, possible links between stress and cancer have recently been discovered.[16]

Stress-related health problems place a significant burden on individuals and organizations. The costs to individuals are sometimes more obvious than the costs to organizations. Following are some of the major costs to the organization:[15]

- Increased premiums for health insurance
- Lost work days from illnesses ranging from headaches and back pain to heart disease. It has been estimated that, on average, employees suffering from stress-related health problems lose approximately 16 days of work per year.
- Over 75 percent of all industrial accidents are caused by emotional problems worsened by stress.
- Legal problems for employers, such as stress-related worker's compensation claims, are growing and becoming more complex. Some experts estimate that if the current rate of growth in worker's compensation claims continues, stress-related compensation claims will outnumber all other claims during the 1990s.[17]

Performance and stress

The trouble with the rat race is, even if you win, you're still a rat.

— *Lily Tomlin*

The impact of stress on productivity or performance is of great concern to most organizations. To deal with stress in a project environment, project managers must understand the relationship between stress and performance. Stress can have both positive and negative impact on performance, depending upon the stress level.

Figure 6.2 shows the curvilinear relationship between the amount of stress felt by workers and their level of performance.[18] It shows that both extremely low and high levels of stress tend to have a negative effect on performance. For projects or tasks that are too easy and of routine nature, project personnel feel a very low level of stress and therefore they may not feel challenged or involved to perform at their best. Increasing the stress by introducing more challenges, constraints and a need for creative solutions tends to increase worker's performance up to a certain point (as shown by point A in Figure 6.2), which corresponds to an optimum level of stress for optimum performance. If the level of stress increases beyond this point, performance will begin to deteriorate. This happens quite often when senior management has unreasonable expectations and imposes unrealistic budget and time constraints. At excessive levels of stress, pro-

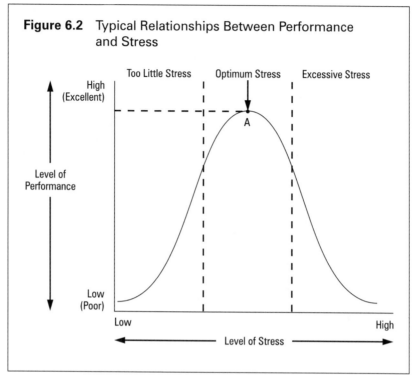

Figure 6.2 Typical Relationships Between Performance and Stress

ject participants may become agitated or emotionally upset, causing a significant reduction in their level of performance.

Due to this relationship between the level of stress felt by people and their level of performance, project managers must try to determine the optimum level of stress for both themselves and their project team members. This information is not readily available and can only be obtained by developing better communication, understanding and rapport with project participants. For example, a project team member may be frequently absent from work because of boredom and lack of challenge (too little stress) or because of overwork and inability to meet deadlines (too high stress).

Of course, the curve shown in Figure 6.2 varies for different people and for different tasks. Too little stress for one team member may be just appropriate for another. Also, the optimum stress for a specific team member for one task may be too much or too little for his or her optimum performance on other tasks.

Project managers must try to avoid a drop in performance and therefore must be more concerned about the "excessive stress" part of the curve than with how to add useful stress to project team members. Motivation to perform better is a critical issue in most projects. However, studies of relationships between stress and performance in organizations suggest that there is a strong negative correlation between the amount of stress in a group, project team, or department and its overall performance.[19] In other words, the greater the level of stress felt by people, the lower will be their productivity. Project managers and project team members in these situations need to find effective ways to reduce the number and magnitude of stressors. High levels of stress should be watched because they may lead to job burnout, resulting in significant costs to people, projects and organizations.

Job burnout. In general, burnout is physical and emotional exhaustion caused by excessive demands on emotions, energy and other personal resources. It occurs when a person works too hard for too long on a regular basis or when he or she undergoes too many stressors over a short period of time. Burnout is a common word in the project environment. It refers to the adverse effects of working under conditions in which stressors seem unavoidable, sources of job satisfaction and relief from stress seem unattainable, and people are subjected to high levels of stress for extended periods.[20] The burnout phenomenon typically contains three components:[21]

1. A state of emotional exhaustion
2. Depersonalization of individuals dealt with in the work setting
3. Feelings of low personal accomplishment.

People suffering from job burnout feel besieged, display a cynical attitude, are irritable, feel constantly fatigued, and become angry with those making demands on them.[22] Burnout is common in projects because it often occurs among high achievers. Project managers and team members are typically of such a nature because they set very high standards for themselves.

Depersonalization means treating people like objects. For example, a nurse might refer to the "broken leg in room 110," rather than using the patient's name. Most job burnout research has focused on the human services sector (sometimes called the "helping professions"). Generally, burnout is predominant in these occupations because they require continuous direct contact with people who need assistance. Professionals who are potential candidates for burnout include social workers, nurses, physicians, police officers, air traffic controllers, teachers, and lawyers.[23] However, burnout can occur among any individuals who must interact extensively with other people as a part of their jobs or who constantly face stressors with little relief—which includes project managers. It should also be noted that the human services field is one in which project

Human Resource Skills for the Project Manager

management is growing, so the stresses common to both fields of endeavor will apply to human services project managers.

Characteristics of people who experience job burnout. Individuals who experience job burnout seem to have certain common characteristics. Three major characteristics associated with a high probability of burnout are:[15,24]

1. They experience a high level of stress as a result of job-related stressors.
2. They are generally self-motivated, idealistic high achievers.
3. They set too high a standard for themselves and often seek unattainable goals.

The burnout syndrome represents a combination of characteristics of the individual and of the job environment. Individuals who suffer from burnout often have unrealistic expectations concerning their work and their capability to attain desired goals in the given work environment. They tend to have no outlets to relieve their stress from the hostile work environment, or lack the resources to enable them to achieve their best. Consequently, unrelieved stressful working conditions, combined with unrealistic expectations or ambitions of the individual, can lead to a condition of complete physical, mental, and emotional exhaustion. Once "burned out," the individual can no longer cope with the demands of the job and their self-confidence and willingness to try reduce significantly.

Symptoms of job burnout. The project managers should be on the lookout for symptoms of burnout in their team members and also in themselves. These symptoms include:[15]

Physiological symptoms: A noticeable decline in physical appearance; chronic fatigue and weakness; frequent infections, especially respiratory infections; health complaints such as headaches, back pains, or stomach problems; signs of depression such as a change in weight or eating habits.

Emotional (psychological) symptoms: Boredom or apathy; cynicism, resentfulness and short temper; depressed appearance such as a sad expression or slumped posture; expressions of anxiety, frustration, and hopelessness.

Behavioral symptoms: Absenteeism and tardiness; abuse of drugs, alcohol, or caffeine; increased smoking; excessive exercise to the point of injury; hostile behavior; easily irritated; reduced productivity; inability to concentrate or complete a task; withdrawal; restlessness.

The costs of job burnout in a project environment can be very high both to the project participants suffering from this syndrome and to their organizations. In order to minimize this cost, senior management and project managers should be aware of the typical symptoms of burnout, as well as the stressors that can contribute to this outcome. Strategies and guidelines for managing stress (which are discussed later in this section) are useful in reducing the causes and symptoms of job burnout.

Personality and stress

Your success and happiness lie in you ... Resolve conflicts to keep happy, and your joy and you shall form an invincible host against difficulties.

— *Helen Keller*

Among the varied participants found working on a project, every sort of personality is represented, including those personality types that are more subject to stress than others. Personality and stress are correlated because personality influences how individuals are likely to perceive stressors in work situations and how people react to these environmental stressors.

Though projects can be stressful, not all stress is caused by working conditions. A recent study of newly hired workers in a university, an oil field servicing company, and an electronics manufacturer showed that nine months after joining the organization, people showed the same distress (destructive stress) symptoms that they had before they started their new work. This indicated that the people brought much of their stress with them.[25]

Another study, carried out after a devastating 1972 flood in Harrisburg, Pennsylvania, examined the behavior of various people in terms of coping with the stress caused by the flood. The study illustrates the ways in which personality influences perceptions of and reactions to stressors. Information gathered from 90 owner-managers of small businesses in Harrisburg indicated that their reaction to stress was highly related to their locus of control, one of the dimensions of personality.[26]

Locus of control refers to the extent to which individuals believe that they can control events affecting them. Individuals with a high *internal* locus of control believe that the events in their lives are mainly the result of their own behaviors and actions and therefore they tend to find solutions. Owner-managers with high internal locus of control experienced less stress in this flood situation and used more task-oriented behaviors such as problem solving and acquiring the resources to resolve problems and maintain their business operations.

On the other hand, people with a high *external* locus of control believe that events in their lives are primarily determined by chance, fate, or other people and therefore tend to submit and surrender to situations. They may display negative behavior towards unpleasant situations. Hence, in this flood situation, owner-managers with a high external locus of control experienced greater stress and displayed more emotional behaviors such as hostility and withdrawal by quitting the business or moving from the area.[26]

Other personality traits or dimensions related to stress include *self-esteem, tolerance for ambiguity, introversion/extroversion,* and *dogmatism.*[15] A personality trait may affect the degree to which a particular situation or event is perceived as a stressor. For example, in a project environment, a project participant with low self-esteem is more subject to

190

stress in demanding work situations than someone with high self-esteem. This may be because individuals with high self-esteem have typically more confidence in their ability to meet challenges.

There are ambiguities in a project environment in terms of roles, authority, and responsibiliy. A typical project organizational structure or matrix further adds to ambiguity and conflicts. Individuals with low tolerance for ambiguity in their roles, responsibilities and authority are more likely to experience stress than those who accept that this is somewhat normal in a project environment. The latter try to cope with it by appropriate communication and interface management.

Introversion and extroversion[27] describe an individual's degree of sociability. Whether a person is an introvert or an extrovert affects the level of stress felt in a project environment. Introverts are shy and reserved people who tend to be not very active in public life, while extroverts are socially very outgoing. Extroverts like to associate in flocks, participate actively in group or team activities, and tend to derive satisfaction from the external world. Both introversion and extroversion have similar meanings when used to refer to a personality dimension.[27] Introversion refers to an orientation of the mind inwards and having a greater sensitivity to abstract ideas and personal feelings. Extroversion represents a tendency of the mind to be directed outward, toward other objects, people, and events.[27]

The research work of Eysenck and others suggests that introverts are quiet, introspective, intelligent, well-ordered, emotionally unexpressive, and value-oriented. They prefer a small group of close friends and like to plan ahead. In contrast, the extrovert is highly sociable, lively, impulsive, carefree, emotionally expressive, and seeks novelty and change. There is a wide distribution of introverts and extroverts across educational levels, genders, and occupations. Many experts consider the introversion/extroversion component in personality to be genetically determined.[28]

The introversion/extroversion personality dimension has some implications in terms of task performance in different environments. Introverts are likely to perform better in quieter office environments with few people and a low level of activity; e.g., in computer centers, research laboratories, and software projects with well-defined scope for each person. Extroverts perform better in environments with greater sensory stimulation where there are many people, frequent interactions and a high level of activity, such as public sector projects requiring public meetings, media exposure, and fundraising campaigns or global projects requiring a large number of collaborators. Successful project managers must have a certain degree of extroverted characteristics because their decision roles often involve identifying and solving problems with and through others, and they must create a team environment to achieve maximum human synergy.

Authoritarianism or *dogmatism*,[27] which refer to the rigidity of a person's beliefs, also influence how people react to stressors in a project environment, because events and situations in a project can be unique, changeable, and unpredictable. An authoritarian personality can be described as one that rigidly adheres to conventional rules and chains of command, readily obeys recognized authority, is concerned with power and toughness, and opposes the use or recognition of subjective feelings.[27]

The highly dogmatic person is generally close-minded, and the low dogmatic person is open minded. Highly dogmatic project managers are easily influenced by authority figures and they even prefer senior management with a highly directive, structured leadership style.[27] Project management requires a combination of interpersonal skills to work as a team to achieve integration and high performance, and highly dogmatic people need more structure to work effectively as a team. Consequently, the performance of highly dogmatic people on task forces, committee assignments, etc., depends upon how well the group is structured and how it goes about doing its task. A high degree of dogmatism also corresponds to a limited amount of creativity and innovation in exploring alternatives and solving project problems, which can lead to poor performance.

The various dimensions of personality can effect the performance of individual team members and that of the whole project team. Project managers should learn to be more flexible in interacting with different project participants (senior management, client, functional managers and project team members) in order to minimize the negative effects of stress.

Personality types. There are three major personality types: A, B and "hardy."

Type A personality. Most projects are done under severe time, human resources and budget constraints, giving project participants the sense that they are involved in an ongoing struggle to achieve more and more in less and less time. Since projects attract driven, high-achieving types, many project participants are likely to have a Type A personality and display the following characteristics:[15]

- A chronic sense of time urgency
- Extreme competitive and aggressive behaviors
- An aversion to idleness (guilty feelings if time taken off work)
- Impatience with barriers to task completion.

In addition to these characteristics, individuals with extreme Type A personality often speak rapidly, are preoccupied with themselves, are dissatisfied with their lives and tend to evaluate the worthiness of their activities in quantitative terms.

The statements in the questionnaire in Self-Assessment Exercise D (See Appendix) measure four sets of behaviors and tendencies associated with the type A personality:[15]

Human Resource Skills for the Project Manager

1. Time urgency
2. Competitiveness and hostility
3. Polyphasic behavior (trying to do several things simultaneously)
4. Lack of planning.

Medical researchers have found that these tendencies or behaviors are related to stress in work and in life. They tend to cause stress or to make stressful situations worse than they otherwise could be.

Type B personality. The Type B personality is the opposite of Type A. Its main characteristics include:[15]

- Easy going
- Relaxed
- No guilty feeling if time taken off work
- Unconcerned about time pressure
- Less competitive and aggressive (emphasizes enjoying work).

Research suggests that Type Bs are less likely than Type As to overreact to situations in a hostile or aggressive manner, and links Type A behavior with vulnerability to heart attacks. Medical researchers shared the opinion that individuals with Type A characteristics were two to three times more likely to develop heart illness than were Type B individuals. Recent research has suggested that the description of personality Type A is too broad to predict coronary heart disease. However, certain aspects of the Type A personality, especially hostility, anger and aggression, are strongly related to stress reactions and heart disease.[29]

The hardy personality. There has been a great deal of interest in identifying those aspects of personality that might protect individuals from the negative health consequences of stress. The personality that combines traits that contribute to a reduction in the negative effects of stress is known as the "hardy" personality. It includes a cluster of the following characteristics, behaviors and tendencies:[15]

- A sense of commitment
- Perceiving problems and difficulties as challenges and opportunities
- Feeling in control over one's own life (internal locus of control)[30]
- A sense of positive involvement in social situations
- A tendency to attribute one's own behavior to internal factors of perception; that is, aspects of the perceiver that influence perceptual selection, such as personality learning and motivation
- Perceiving or greeting major changes with interest, curiosity and optimism.[15,31]

A number of studies have suggested that a high degree of hardiness reduces the negative effects of stressors.[31] Hardiness influences the way the stressors are perceived. The concept of hardy personality provides a useful way to understand the role of individual differences in terms of stress reactions to environmental and job-related stressors. Individuals with a high degree of hardiness tend to perceive fewer events as stressful, whereas those with low hardiness perceive more events as stressful.

Individuals with high levels of hardiness are not overwhelmed with challenges and difficult situations. Rather, when they face a stressful situation, they cope with or respond to it constructively by trying to find a solution and to control and influence the event. Such a behavioral response tends to reduce the negative effects of stress, resulting in lower blood pressure and reduced probability of physiological problems.

In a project environment, where stress is very common due to several pressures, project managers should be careful to manage stress. They must try to incorporate the main traits of a hardy personality into their attitude and behavior in order to minimize the negative health consequences of stressors. Perhaps one of the best tips for project managers who want lead a stress-free, healthy life is to develop the personality traits of Type B and hardy personalities within themselves—and hire enough project team members with personality Type A.

Guidelines for Managing Stress

Manage your stress. Work joyfully and peacefully, knowing that right thoughts and right efforts will inevitably bring about right results.

—James Allen

Stress is inevitable in the project environment, and is felt by virtually everyone working on a project. If not carefully monitored and controlled, it can have damaging psychological and physiological effects on their health and on their contribution to the project effectiveness. Therefore, senior management and project managers should have some general strategies for managing stress. If effective stress management programs are in place, both the individual and the organization will benefit and an optimum level of stress can be maintained in the organization.

Stress management can be done at both the individual and organizational level. This section deals with managing individual and organizational stress. Some guidelines for helping project participants handle stress are also included.

Managing individual stress

Stress management at an individual level includes activities and behaviors designed to eliminate or control sources of stress and/or to make the individual more resistant to stress or better able to cope with it.[15]

One set of suggestions for individual stress management is based upon the concept of "hardiness" discussed in the previous section. While it is impossible for individuals to change their basic personality, they can attempt to adopt attitudes and behaviors that parallel the attitudes and behaviors of individuals with high degrees of hardiness. Some suggestions, based on the research on the hardy personality include:[32,33]

194

- Maintain a positive attitude. Replace worrying thoughts with productive thoughts.
- Make timely decisions and don't procrastinate.
- Think of setbacks as challenges and opportunities rather than as disasters. Often, big problems disguise big opportunities.
- Exercise (at least three times per week for 20 minutes). Sound health habits—sleeping well, eating right and exercising—reduce the effects of stress.
- Be aware of your own values; don't allow others to force you to do activities you don't enjoy.
- Learn and use relaxation techniques to lower your physiological excitement. Relaxation is the ability to do absolutely nothing—and feel good about it.
- Always take the time to have fun. Have a sense of humor and enjoy the small pleasures in life.
- Fight for things that are really worth it—"don't sweat the small stuff."

Nelson and Quick conducted a study of six successful top project executives and found that they had several behavioral patterns in common in their use of stress coping methods.[34] For example:

- Each tried to balance work and family activities. While work was central to their lives, it was not their sole focus.
- Each used leisure time effectively in reducing stress. They relaxed, took vacations, and spent time with close family and friends.
- They all had good time management skills. Each project executive identified critical success factors and priority goals and developed careful plans to accomplish these goals. They all indicated that this was the main component of their strategy to reduce stress.
- Each emphasized the importance of mutual social support in coping with stress. They received emotional support and information from a network of family, friends, project participants, clients, and industry colleagues. They all made a point of maintaining an equitable, reciprocal exchange in these relationships. In other words, they both gave and received social support.

Project managers experience continuous intensive stress throughout the project life cycle and must manage their own stress to avoid adverse effects on their health.

The first step in managing stress is to understand the nature of stress responses and their effects on the body. All individuals need to know their normal work styles so that they can tell when and how they are most affected by stress. Once the project manager or any individual in the project knows how he or she responds to stress and what triggers it, he or she is in a better position to identify these stressors. A project manager can use any of the several methods described below to help identify sources of stress.[11]

Stress diary. One way to manage individual stress is to keep a diary at work of stress symptoms encountered and their causes. After some time, relationships between sources and symptoms of stress will be identified. The main sources of stress will be revealed, allowing individuals to focus on eliminating or managing the stress associated with them more effectively.

Mechanical (biofeedback) devices. Project managers or individuals can use devices such as the pulsimeter to identify activities that increase the blood flow or heart rate, signaling stress. Once individuals have an idea of which activities are stressful, they can formulate a work schedule to achieve a balanced mix of stressful and non-stressful activities to prevent stress from building up throughout the course of the day. Biofeedback can also help an individual develop the physical self-awareness necessary to identify stressful situations before they get out of hand.

An important aspect of managing individual stress is to control the stress response. When a stress response is experienced, it is important to relax and remain calm throughout the stress reaction and try to control the response. Controlling stress responses allows individuals to defend themselves from the negative effects of stress.

Identification of stress situations. Identification is the most important component of any strategy for managing individual stress. By identifying the stressful situations or the stressors, project managers can plan to manage these and mentally prepare to reduce their impact.

Work schedule. Stress has a greater negative impact when people are run-down and tired. Everyone has a biological clock that influences the time of day when they are most energetic and productive. By keeping a diary or using biofeedback, project managers and other project participants can become familiar with their personal "energy schedule." They can then arrange their schedules to perform stressful activities when they are refreshed and most productive.

Attitude adaptation. Attitude plays an important role in determining the level of stress experienced by individuals. If people are working on the project because they "have to" rather than because they "want to," they will experience more stress. If individuals working on a project (especially the project manager) have a positive attitude toward the project, the environment will be less stressful and more pleasant. Unfavorable attitudes can be converted to favorable ones by sincerely encouraging empowerment—the involvement and participation of project participants that will assist in winning their acceptance and hence their commitment to optimum project performance. Everyone acknowledges that it is more fun to work on an enjoyable task than a disliked one, so it is sensible to change negative attitudes to attitudes of enthusiasm.

Personal organization. Personal organization is key to individual stress management. Some tips in reducing stress through personal organization include:

- Avoid accumulation of incomplete tasks
- Close all loose ends as early as possible
- Maintain a comfortable pace of life
- Avoid taking on more commitments than can be handled: learn to say "No." It is better to refrain from some commitments than to be stressed by too many.

Leisure activity. Two activities that reduce stress are exercise and meditation. Physical activity or exercise programs have been found to be successful in reducing stress. Some large corporations employ physical fitness specialists who provide employees with customized exercise advice and teach relaxation techniques and meditation. A note of caution: Type A individuals should take care not to allow exercise itself to become a stressor. To avoid this pattern, choose exercise activities that you truly enjoy doing.

Meditation refers to engaging in contemplative thought to draw the mind together. It requires relaxing the body and the mind. The proper meditation techniques can be learned through instruction, training, and practice. If done regularly and properly, meditation relieves one's mind from unnecessary thoughts and increases self-awareness and concentration, leading to an increased energy level.

Smoking, drinking, and taking drugs do *not* reduce stress. In fact, these ineffective responses to stress only produce temporary effects and do not deal with the root causes. Relying on temporary escapes from stress can lead to more stress and more physiological damage than caused by the stress itself.

Managerial integration. Sometimes potential stress can be avoided by improved project performance. For example, to reduce future stress, a project manager may complete an assignment before deadline pressures are felt and prepare and follow a schedule to get assignments under control before time demands set in and unforeseen events create stressful situations. Pitting the outcome of the work against the fear of stress will make the project manager and project team members work harder to avoid stress, which also results in improved productivity.

For each project, project managers should establish goals and ethical guidelines. They should abide by these while working on the project. The list of goals helps project participants focus on the main objectives. A plan should be prepared to provide direction to meet project objectives. A well-developed plan will help the project manager to follow a course of action, thus reducing the stress of uncertainties on the project.

Counseling. Sometimes project team members are confused about their role, responsibilities and job demands or they may have some personal problems leading to stress. They may want to talk to someone about their problems and how they relate to the project organization. Project managers can provide an outlet by providing peer counseling to reduce their stress. (See Chapter One.)

INDIVIDUAL STRESS MANAGEMENT plays a vital role in the project organization. Successful and effective individual stress management techniques used by project managers can be used as a model by other project participants. All individuals should know and understand their own normal work styles so that they can judge when and how they are affected by stress. The stress management techniques listed above can be used by most project participants at an individual level.

Managing organizational stress

Stress management is not only important to the individual but also to the organization. Because individuals contribute to project and organizational goals, stress management programs that improve the performance of project participants will benefit both the project and the organization. Project managers and senior management should try to create an atmosphere that promotes *eustress* and minimizes *distress*. This section describes targets of organizational stress management programs or health and wellness programs.

Targets of organizational stress management programs. Organizational stress is the stress that a person experiences when dealing with the demands of the project organization. It originates within the project organization as a whole and affects people involved with the project. Organizational stress can cause strain on project participants, reducing their productivity, and increasing negative effects on both the individual and the organization. Therefore, it must be properly managed to improve performance and satisfaction of project participants.

In a project environment, stress management programs can be designed based on a model, according to which the negative effects of stress can be reduced in three ways:[35]

1. Identify and then modify or eliminate work stressors.
2. Help project participants modify their perceptions and understanding of stress.
3. Help project participants to cope effectively with the consequences of stress.

Stress management programs that fit into this category normally include one or more of the following:

Improvements in the physical work environment/conditions. An unpleasant and uncomfortable work environment is stressful. Therefore, the project organization should try to provide comfortable temperature, proper office lighting, appropriate smoking policy, ergonomically-designed furnishings and equipment, and an office arrangement that minimizes interruptions. Organizations should take advantage of modern technology and design to increase project performance.

Job redesign. Keeping stress levels manageable begins with team member selection. Tasks should be defined clearly in terms of expectations. Rewards should be matched with skills in order to provide sufficient challenges and opportunities to avoid boredom on the one hand and work overload on the other. Task demands should provide a tolerable level of stress to optimize the performance of project participants. Personnel should be matched to responsibilities so that participants are not saddled with tasks that they are incapable of performing.

Organizational structure. Project organizations can minimize the negative effects of stress by designing an organizational structure to match the demands of the situation. For example, projects should use flat or informal matrix structures with the aim of promoting a positive atmosphere through open communication and demonstrating confidence in team members. Organizational structures should also be designed so that it is easy to give input and receive feedback. Thus, projects can create a positive atmosphere where employees are trusted, respected, and empowered. The reward or promotion system should be fair and based on a criteria that employees are aware of.

Interpersonal relations. This is the most important area, covering all aspects that promote mutual trust, respect, friendliness, and cooperation. Communication, motivation, leadership, team building and team management should be emphasized to improve interpersonal relations and develop interpersonal skills among all project participants.

Effective goal-setting. An effective goal-setting process can reduce organizational stress. Organizations should emphasize clear, realistic goals, while maintaining optimism with regard to the team's ability to achieve. Measurable goals with clear expectations, timetables and performance measurement systems reduce the level of anxiety and hence stress among project participants. A performance planning program, like "Management by Objectives," serves to clarify job responsibilities, provides clear performance objectives, and reduces ambiguity through regular feedback.

Greater level of employee participation. If organizations encourage involvement and participation of project participants, especially in planning the changes that affect them, it is easier to achieve acceptance and commitment from participants and changes are more likely to be implemented smoothly, with less strain and tension.

Workshops dealing with role clarity and role analysis. Programs that promote role clarity and role analysis can be particularly useful in eliminating or reducing role ambiguity and role conflict, two major sources of stress.

Health and wellness programs. Health and wellness programs are becoming extremely popular in reducing organizational stress. Wellness programs promote good health habits and healthy lifestyles or identify and correct health problems. Many U.S. firms provide one of the following three types of company-sponsored health promotion programs.[36]

- *Awareness or information programs.* Programs that operate at the level of awareness or information may or may not directly improve health, but are designed to inform employees about the outcomes of unhealthy behavior and lifestyles. For example, Sara Lee provides seminars for female employees on nutrition, prenatal care, and strategies for preventing disease. Johnson & Johnson provides lunch-hour seminars on stress management techniques. Often these programs are used to generate interest in physical exercise and lifestyle changes.

- *Lifestyle-modification programs.* Such programs may include company-sponsored physical fitness programs (such as jogging or walking), weight control programs and smoking cessation programs. For example, L.L. Bean provides a running club and lessons in cross-country skiing and ballroom dancing. Bonnie Bell encourages employees to ride bikes to work and gives them incentives to purchase bikes at a discount. The company also provides volleyball and tennis courts, running tracks, showers and locker facilities. They sell track suits and shoes at discount prices, offer a $250 bonus for employees who exercise at least four days per week, and give an extra 30 minutes at lunch for exercise and physical fitness.

- *Lifestyle-maintainance programs.* Programs with the goal of helping employees maintain a healthy lifestyle may take many forms. At AT&T, employees formed support groups to help each other maintain healthy lifestyle changes.[37] The free exercise facilities provided by Bonnie Bell are another example. At Safeway, employees built their own fitness center on company premises and now have a full-time director, provided by the company, to oversee the exercise programs, facilities, and activities.

Wellness programs can provide substantial benefits to both individuals and organizations. Safeway estimates that its wellness program has almost eliminated workplace accidents and reduced tardiness and absenteeism by more than 60 percent. The wellness program at AT&T resulted in some dramatic health benefits in terms of reduced blood pressure and cholesterol levels in participating employees. At the locations of Johnson & Johnson that used the wellness program, hospital costs during the first five years increased by only one-third as much as they did at company locations without the program. Johnson & Johnson's wellness program also reduced absenteeism by 18 percent. At Honeywell, an evaluation of their wellness program indicated that the cost of their health-care services increased only about 4 percent a year, and caused a substantial improvement in employee morale. (Health-care costs in the U.S. are currently increasing at an average of 14 percent a year.[37])

When diagnosing stressors in the workplace, project managers should be aware of the large volume of research showing that stress is caused by uncertainty and perceived lack of control.[38] Therefore, organizational policies that encourage empowerment, involvement of project participants in organizational change efforts, and work redesign that reduces uncertainty and increases control of the workplace. All these improve and clarify understanding of roles, responsibility, and authority, and serve to reduce stress.

Work stressors can be managed by clarifying tasks, roles and relationships, reducing the workload and providing professional growth opportunities. Programs aimed at these objectives might include one or more of the following:[15]

- Attitude or behavior modification
- Workshops on time management to help project team members cope with deadlines and time pressures
- Workshops on job burnout to help people recognize the symptoms
- Training in relaxation techniques
- Physical fitness or "wellness" programs.

Dividing stress management programs into these categories does not mean that they are necessarily separated in practice. Indeed, they may overlap. For example, a workshop dealing with role conflicts might clarify roles and thus reduce the level of this potential stressor. At the same time, if project participants understand their roles and responsibilities better, they can effectively cope with this source of stress. Similarly, when project participants have concerns about their long-term careers that cause them stress, career counseling can reduce these concerns while improving the ability of employees to cope with their remaining career problems.

Organizational stress can produce strain on employees and reduce their productivity. Therefore, it is important that organizational stress is properly managed. Effectively managed organizational stress can lead to motivation, high morale, improved performance and job satisfaction. It is beneficial to both the individual and the organization as it promotes healthier lifestyles and individual habits. This not only leads to happier and more satisfied workers, which results in higher quality performance but also dramatically reduces medical costs, absenteeism and tardiness.

Helping project participants handle stress

I am still determined to be cheerful and to be happy in whatever situation I may be, for I have also learned from experience that the greater part of our happiness or misery depends upon our dispositions and not upon our circumstances
— *Martha Washington*

Stressors are common in organizational and project situations where individuals face circumstances in which their usual coping behaviors are inappropriate. If these behaviors are not modified properly, negative consequences may result for the individual or the project.[39] Thus, it should be the responsibility of senior management and project managers to help employees and project participants manage stress effectively. This section covers practical ideas to help project participants manage stress, such as identifying stressors and developing strategies to prevent unwanted stressors.

Identify stressors. In a project environment, change and conflict are obvious stressors. However, as indicated in Figure 6.1, many other factors related to organizational policies, structure, physical conditions and processes can also act as stressors. The first step in managing stress is to understand and analyze stressors and become familiar with the nature of the stress response and how it affects the body. Recognizing which situations lead to stress can help project managers and project participants to mentally prepare themselves to reduce their impact.

Once project managers are able to identify stressors, they can reduce their own stress and help their team members as well in reducing their stress by taking appropriate actions, which may include the following:

- Analyze stressful situations and work to avoid them.
- Delegate stressful activities (without dumping and passing the buck) to someone else who may not perceive them as stressors. Understand the personalities of team members in order to take the personality into consideration when delegating tasks.
- Try to remove stressful activities from the schedule or regulate participation in stressful events.
- Shield team members, when possible, from external stressors by trying to manipulate the circumstances leading to them.

Prevent unwanted stressors. Management should try to provide sufficient training for everyone to deal with their job demands and other anxieties. Unless organizational changes are necessary to stay competitive, management should reduce significant organizational changes and thereby reduce stress levels.

Project managers should avoid creating a stressful climate. To reduce stress in the work environment, project managers should give their team members PERKS, as shown in Figure 6.3.[40]

Management can also use the following three strategies to help prevent the development of unwanted stressors in organizations.[41]

Create a supportive organizational climate. A rigid, bureaucratic organizational climate can lead to considerable job stress. Organizations should be informal, open, and flexible and should support the economic, professional, security, social and personal needs of employees. This not only establishes trust and increases productivity, but also prevents the development of unwanted stressors.

Human Resource Skills for the Project Manager

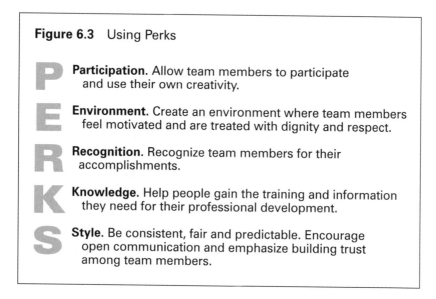

Figure 6.3 Using Perks

P   **Participation.** Allow team members to participate and use their own creativity.

E   **Environment.** Create an environment where team members feel motivated and are treated with dignity and respect.

R   **Recognition.** Recognize team members for their accomplishments.

K   **Knowledge.** Help people gain the training and information they need for their professional development.

S   **Style.** Be consistent, fair and predictable. Encourage open communication and emphasize building trust among team members.

Make jobs interesting. Routine, trivial jobs that do not allow some degree of freedom lead to boredom and often result in undesirable stress. Management should focus on making jobs more challenging and creative. Also, by empowering employees and creating synergistic self-directed work teams, instead of using the traditional management style of close supervision, management can increase the overall productivity of the team.

Design and operate career counseling programs. In a project environment, project team members have a diverse mix of skills and backgrounds. Most are high achievers who are cross-trained in different technical areas. They are likely to have high career ambitions. Lack of information regarding their career path at the end of a project can lead to considerable job stress. Management should try to show its employees what the next step in their careers might be and when it can realistically be achieved. This increases morale and discourages the development of unwanted stress.

For example, IBM recognizes the importance of career planning for its employees.[42] IBM encourages program managers to conduct voluntary career planning sessions with employees on an annual basis. After this session, employees have a clearer idea about professional opportunities and what training is essential to modify their career to achieve desired growth. This program has reduced the development of unwanted career-related stressors at IBM.[42]

IN A PROJECT ENVIRONMENT, the nature of the job and organizational climate are among the most common factors leading to stress. Senior management and project managers must introduce a sense of purpose and ownership in the project for all project participants. They should help project participants get job satisfaction and grow professionally and financially in the organization. Self-directed work team concepts should be encouraged to help create an atmosphere that increases individual and team productivity. In such an atmosphere, project participants feel good about themselves, which reduces stress.

Putting It All Together

Projects today operate in a highly competitive global environment. Many factors that are beyond one's control affect the project outcome. Consequently, project participants may experience a significant degree of stress caused by both personal reasons and job-related or organizational factors. Project managers must try to create an environment that minimizes stressful situations and helps people reduce their stress. These guidelines can be used to manage individual, organizational, and job-related stress and stay productive while working on projects:[43]

Assess the situation. As a first step, it is important to analyze the stress situation, which involves assessing the following items:
- Timing—Is it temporary or permanent?
- Scale—How serious is it?
- Effect—How much effect will it have on the project outcome?
- Expectation—Is it totally unforeseen or can you anticipate it (e.g., a labor strike affecting critical path activities)?
- Resources—Can money solve it? Are there people in your network who can help?

Accept what can't be changed. Some things are beyond one's control and can't be changed: getting older, or organizational changes in which you have no input. To make such situations easier, the individual can:
- Learn from past experiences. Have you struggled unsuccessfully against this same barrier before? What can you learn from that experience about managing your response now?
- Talk with someone who has gone through similar situations. Sometimes just talking—"venting"—reduces individual stress; and you may learn from their experience or coping strategies.
- Stay positive. Focus on what *can* be done rather than on what cannot.
- Smile. Even if you don't feel like it; the action is relaxing, and if you smile, people smile back at you, reducing your sense of isolation.
- Join a support group. Talking to someone who is supportive is very helpful.
- Change your perspective. Explore different ways of thinking about the stressful situation.

Avoid the avoidable. Some stress situations simply can't be avoided. However, a little planning can help you avoid those that are.
- Reschedule. Don't over-commit yourself; work flexible hours if it helps.

- Resign. Step down, if it is a chronic situation and causes continuous dissatisfaction.
- Retreat. Find a quiet time for yourself.
- Don't respond. Avoid controversial issues and unnecessary arguments that only lead to win-lose outcomes.

Adapt with proactive change. Sometimes minor changes in the way we adapt to situations can reduce stress, even if it is caused by major life changes such as marriage, divorce, or job loss. By changing one's coping mechanisms *proactively,* that is, before change is demanded by a crisis, we can become more resilient in the face of stress. Following are some effective adaptations:

- Think of stress as an opportunity. Consider all disasters as incidents and no incidents as disasters.
- Put it into perspective. Ask the questions: How long will the effects really last? What is the real downside risk?
- Try to change yourself rather than others. It is not usually possible to change others. Instead, change yourself and adapt to the new environment.
- Avoid worry. Worrying produces unproductive thoughts about things that are unlikely to happen. Instead, funnel your worrying thoughts into something productive. Use the following reminder to avoid "worry": Work On Real Reasonable Yields.
- Prioritize. Do what is more important and has a higher payoff.
- Practice sound health habits. Exercise regularly (to relieve tension and feel more alert); know just how much sleep you need to stay bright, alert and energetic throughout the working day; and eat and drink right to stay healthy (what goes in your body affects your health and hence your performance).

Alter the flexible situation. Some situations, though flexible, won't go away completely. Those can be turned around to a large extent through careful analysis and creative thinking. Following are some helpful ideas:

- Ask for change. Ask those who control the stress for change in the schedule, the work group, or the behaviors.
- Defuse the situation. It may be a simple misunderstanding; open communication (revealing your feelings and learning others') can resolve personal conflicts.
- Change the circumstances. Redistribute the workload or reschedule.
- Delegate. Focus on the most important things. Project managers are appraised by the successful results rather than by how much they did themselves.
- Alter your own behavior. Can you be less demanding, more collaborative, assertive and flexible in dealing with other project participants?

Learning from the experts

The level of stress felt by individuals varies from person to person due to their different personality traits. Not everyone's response to a particular stress situation is the same. Some can take on more stress than others before showing any drop in productivity and performance. Not surprisingly, various experts on stress offer differing techniques for managing stress.[44]

The five-year test. Dr. Meyer Friedman, director of the Meyer Friedman Institute at Mt. Zion Medical Center in San Francisco suggests applying the "five-year test": Given an obligation to do something, ask yourself, will anyone care about that five years from now? If so, accept it; if not, decline. This provides a way to prioritize when learning not to overcommit yourself.

The five-year test helps to put things into perspective. It is amazing how trivial most engagements generally are. After refusing unimportant engagements, there will be time for the things that are really important, like one's family, friends, and critical work assignments.

Lend a hand. Psychologist Amy L. Flowers serves every Friday for 90 minutes as a "Beverage Lady" at the local soup kitchen. She feels that directly helping people with bigger problems than your own is a big stress reliever. It is encouraging to see others overcome their obstacles; lending a hand on a regular basis to someone less fortunate should reduce stress—and help you keep your own stressors in perspective.

Take control. Dr. Paul J. Rosch, pesident of the American Institute of Stress in Yonkers, New York, and clinical professor of medicine and psychiatry at New York Medical College, advises that events in themselves are not stressful. It is how we perceive them that causes stress. For some, a roller-coaster ride is distressing, whereas others get a thrill out of it. In general, stress comes from feeling out of control. The real key to relieving stress is gaining control over the situation and over the irritants you have the power to change, while accepting those that are beyond your control. There is a lot of truth to the Serenity Prayer recited at Alcoholics Anonymous meetings: "God grant me the serenity to accept the things I cannot change, the courage to change the things I can, and the wisdom to know the difference."

Try teamwork. Carol Landau, clinical associate professor of psychiatry at Brown University in Providence, Rhode Island says that teamwork takes the pressure off everyone. The concept of teamwork should be applied in the family, among friends, and in a project environment among project participants. It ties everyone closely together and promotes helping each other to succeed. Not only does it improve overall performance, thanks to the synergistic effect of the team, but it keeps team members satisfied and happy and thus reduces stress significantly.

Wash it away. Harriet Braiker, a Los Angeles psychologist, recommends a long bath as a luxurious way to relax and catch up with oneself. It "washes away" strain and relieves stress.

Don't sweat the small stuff. Allen Elkin, director of the Stress Management and Counseling Center in New York, suggests rating problems on a scale of one to ten, with ten being the equivalent of death of a loved one or loss of a job. Overreacting in a situation leads to unwanted stress that can be prevented; people can train themselves not to overreact. It may help to remember these three rules:

1. Don't sweat the small stuff.
2. It's all small stuff.
3. If you can't fight, and you can't flee—flow.

Undoubtedly, everything in life is not "small stuff." But it is important to loook at the big picture and keep your perspective by asking yourself what is really important, what the real payoffs are in life, and whether you are pursuing them with a proper plan.

STRESS IS NOT ALWAYS BAD. In moderation, it can stimulate and motivate people and even increase their performance. But if it builds up and is not managed effectively at the right time, it can have drastic negative impacts on our health (physically, mentally and emotionally) as well as on our work environment and our performance. Project participants can manage their own stress by assessing the situation, accepting what can't be changed, avoiding what can be avoided, being proactive in dealing with change, and altering the situation in a manner that helps reduce the stress.

Summary

All occupations have a certain degree of stress associated with them. Change and conflict are inevitable in a project environment and one of the outcomes of change and conflict is stress. Therefore, stress becomes an aspect of life in a project environment and stress management should be considered as an important element of project management.

Project managers are exposed to considerable stress because of an endless list of demands, deadlines and problems throughout the project life cycle. They must learn to manage stress effectively to avoid physiological, psychological and emotional problems. Today, there is an increased interest in stress management because U.S. industry is estimated to lose up to $75–$100 billion each year in absenteeism and reduced productivity due to stress-related illnesses.

According to Hans Selye, stress is the nonspecific or psychological response of the body to any demand made upon it. Stress is a response, not the elements that cause it. The factors that cause stress are called stressors. There are three stages of reaction to stress: *Alarm*, which begins as soon as the body perceives a stressor and causes the body to go through physiological changes; *Resistance*, during which the body adapts to the stressor or tries to resist it); and *Exhaustion*, when stress persists longer than the body's ability to cope with it.

Not all stress is bad. *Eustress* refers to constructive stress that can act as a motivator and therefore increases performance. *Distress* is destructive stress that reduces productivity and should be avoided.

One of the keys to managing stress is to be aware of the sources of stress and then prepare to deal with them. This chapter described 11 sources of stress: project management style and organization structure, role conflict (intersender, intrasender and person role conflict), role ambiguity, role overload and underload, interpersonal relationships, overemphasis on deadlines, career development, corporate politics, unsafe working conditions, lack of positive reinforcement, and conflict and change.

Stress has both positive and negative effects, but job-related stress research tends to focus on the negative effects of stress. Stress causes problems for both individuals and their employers. Work-related stress affects people in three ways:

1. Physiological or health effects (blood pressure, heart troubles, migraine headaches, ulcers)
2. Emotional effects (lowered self-esteem, anger, anxiety, inability to make decisions, aggression, fatigue, moodiness and job dissatisfaction)
3. Behavioral effects (decreased performance, increased absenteeism, higher turnover, difficulties in communication, higher use of alcohol or other drugs).

The impact of stress on performance should be of great concern to project managers. Studies show that performance increases with stress up to a certain optimum level but drops if stress is increased beyond this optimum level. The optimum level of stress varies for different people and different tasks. Project managers should give special consideration to the level of stress experienced by project participants to avoid "job burnout." Project managers should watch for symptoms of job burnout and be prepared to deal with it in a way that reduces its negative impact on the individual and on the organization.

Personality and stress are correlated because personality influences how individuals are likely to perceive stressors and how people react to them. Personality traits related to stress include self-esteem, tolerance for ambiguity, introversion/extroversion, and dogmatism. There are three types of personalities, in terms of the ability to cope with stress: Type A, characterized by time urgency, competitiveness, polyphasic behavior, and a lack of planning; Type B, the opposite of A, more easy-going and relaxed; and the "hardy" personality, which perceives major changes in life with interest, curiosity and optimism. Type A people are very vulnerable to stress and tend to suffer health problems due to stress, whereas Type B people are better able to cope with stressors. People with a high degree of hardiness are able to cope or respond to stress by trying to find a solution and to control and influence the stressful event.

Project participants must develop their own strategies for managing individual and organizational stress. It is recognized that exercise and good health can reduce the negative effects of stress. Health and wellness programs sponsored by organizations are becoming very popular in promoting good health habits and reducing the levels of stress experienced by employees. Senior management and the project manager can help organizational members and project participants to manage their stress effectively. This can be done by helping them in identifying the stressors and preparing to cope with them; preventing unwanted stressors by creating a supportive organizational climate; and providing an interesting job and career counseling programs. Individualized strategies, developed by stress management experts, are presented in this chapter to be evaluated and used if suitable.

Outline

Success comes to those who make it happen, not to those who let it happen.

— Anonymous

7

Leadership, Power, Influence, and Politics in Project Management

Managing a project team, motivating stakeholders and creating an environment that is conducive to high performance and innovation requires solid leadership, influencing skills, and an appreciation of organizational politics. These human relations skills form an important part of Project Human Resource Management and are especially important in managing large, complex or international projects.

Leadership skills are essential to the successful management of projects. Also, leadership, power and influence are interrelated. Project managers have to deal with some stakeholders and project team members over whom they have little or no formal authority. Throughout the project life cycle, they have to cross functional and interorganizational lines to gain resources and support. They must be able to resolve conflicts within a project, even an international one with participants from different cultural backgrounds. In a project environment with such characteristics, project managers must understand the concepts of power and perception and acquire influencing skills appropriate to managing project politics and issues of cultural diversity.

This chapter covers the issues of leadership, power, influence, and politics in project management. It describes project leaders versus project managers, leadership traits, principles and outcomes, theories and models of leadership, four contingency models of leadership, leadership in a project environment, leadership styles and roles according to the phases of the project life cycle, and important skills for effective project leadership. It also outlines basic concepts of power, sources and forms of power, and how it can be used in influencing the project participants effectively. This chapter highlights basic concepts of managing politics at the project level and at the upper management level. ∎

Leadership and Project Management

The key to leadership is having dreams; the key to success is making dreams come true.

– Anonymous

Effective leadership is one key to successful project management. It is becoming increasingly important because of tough global competition, complex negotiations, challenges in integration, and a dynamic trend toward decentralization of project management activities. Project leaders lead the project team and other major stakeholders to achieve desired project objectives within specified constraints. Their success depends upon their ability to get results through others. Effective leadership is at the heart of the art of project management because it emphasizes getting results "through" people rather than by being "over" people.[1]

Leadership traits, skills and principles

Basic concepts of leadership have been explored in numerous studies and, although the subject has received significant attention, there is still no universally accepted definition of "leadership." According to Fiedler,[2] a leader is one in the group who is given the task of directing and coordinating activities. Drucker[3] suggests that effective leadership is based primarily on being constant. Jago[4] defines leadership both as a process and a property. Burns[5] cites one study with 130 definitions of "leadership." Leadership can be characterized by personal characteristics such as charisma, intelligence, energy, style, commitment, motivation, and so on.

As a first step in developing leadership skills, it is important to understand leadership traits, principles and outcomes.

Leadership traits and skills. Leadership is the process of creating a vision for others and having the power to translate that vision into reality and sustain it. The approach used by a leader to influence others depends on the skills and the power he or she may have. Some of the traits exhibited by effective leaders are:

- Flexibility
- Ambition
- Intelligence
- Decisiveness
- Consciousness of social environment
- Willingness to take responsibility
- Creativity
- Persistence
- Energy
- Tolerance for stress.[6]

Though to some extent, these traits are part of one's personality, most of them can be developed through a carefully designed program. In addition,

212

education, training and experience can help a project manager acquire the *skills* necessary for success:
- Conceptual skills
- Social skills
- Diplomacy skills
- Communication skills
- Organizational (administrative) skills.[7]

Principles of leadership. The following leadership principles, when combined with leadership traits and skills, can make a project manager a better leader in the eyes of team members, functional managers and senior management. These principles constitute a guideline for exercising authority over project team members and other participants. They encompass three types of management skills: technical, conceptual and human.[8]

- Have a vision and the courage and commitment to make it a reality
- Develop technical proficiency
- Know yourself; seek self-improvement
- Know your people and look after them
- Communicate effectively; keep people informed
- Emphasize long-term productivity
- Encourage teamwork and participation
- Make sound, timely decisions
- Empower team members
- Match skills with resources
- Listen effectively; encourage new ideas
- Give positive feedback and recognition
- Seek responsibility and accept accountability.

Theories and models of leadership

The important thing is not how much you know, but how well you can apply it.
— Anonymous

There are several theories, models, and approaches to leadership that give good insight and guidelines to assess leadership effectiveness and potential. The strengths and weaknesses of these are briefly described below.

Leadership theories/approaches. Leadership is the process of influencing other team members toward a goal.[6] Leaders are people who do the right things to accomplish the missions and objectives of their teams. Many people think that they can intuitively identify outstanding leaders. They believe that successful leaders are highly intelligent with a pleasing personality and personal charm. However, this is not always sufficient. There are different ways to assess leadership potential and effectiveness. Following are five general theories/approaches to assess leadership.[9]

The traits approach emphasizes that the personal attributes of successful leaders are correlated to certain abilities, skills, and personality

Leadership, Power/Influence and Politics in a Project Environment

characteristics. The four traits shared by most, though not all, successful leaders seem to be:
- Intelligence (technical and organizational)
- Maturity and broad range of interests
- Inner motivation and achievement drive (goal-oriented)
- Consideration of needs and values of team members (employee-centered).

However, some critics of this approach find it to have several inconsistencies, in that it fails to determine why certain people succeed and others fail at leadership.[9]

The behavioral approach emphasizes leaders' actions instead of their personal traits. It focuses on what leaders actually *do* and *how* they do it. The behavioral model identifies two major dimensions of leader behavior:

Task orientation (initiating structure that focuses on the quality and quantity of work accomplished)

Relationship orientation, which refers to being supportive and considerate of team members' efforts to achieve personal goals (such as work satisfaction, promotion, and recognition), settling disputes, keeping people happy, encouraging them to be creative and innovative and giving positive reinforcement.

Several studies in this area were done at Ohio State University under the direction of Stogdill.[10] However, most of these research studies gave limited attention to the effects of the situation (in which the relationships occurred) on the leadership style. The importance of "situation" is considered in more depth by the contingency or situational models of leadership.[9]

The contingency approach includes several contingency models of leadership that emphasize the importance of the situation. Four key contingency variables that are believed to influence the behavior of leaders are:[11]
- Personal characteristics of the team leader
- Personal characteristics of the team members
- Characteristics of the team itself
- The structure of the team, department or organization.

These variables interact to influence a leader's behavior. The leadership process is complex; generalizations associated with leadership styles, such as "democratic team leaders have more satisfied employees than autocratic leaders," are not always true. Four well-known contingency models of leadership will be discussed later in this chapter.

The attributional theory of leadership[12] is based on the cause/effect relationship. The attributional leadership model suggests that a leader's judgment about his or her subordinates is influenced by the leader's attribution of the causes of the employee's behavior. These causes may either be external or internal. Effective leaders identify the correct cause and then act accordingly.

The charismatic leadership theory is an extension of attribution theory. Charismatic leaders concentrate on developing a common vision,

214

discovering or creating opportunities, and increasing team members' desire to control their own behavior.[13] Charismatic leaders use dominance, self-confidence, a need for influence, and a conviction of high moral standards to increase their charisma and their leadership effectiveness.

Charismatic leaders are often called "transformational" leaders when they use their charismatic abilities to inspire others. Transformational leaders rely on their *referent* power—the power they earn based on their personal qualities—in order to inspire the team and heighten their motivation to achieve project goals. These leaders have clear vision and can communicate this vision to others while paying attention to the developmental needs of their project team members. They typically influence by engaging in the following three types of behavior:[14]

- Helping team members recognize the need for revitalizing the organization by developing their need for change
- Creating a new vision and motivating team members to gain their commitment to the objectives of the program or project
- Institutionalizing change by replacing old technical and political networks with new ones.

Each of these theories/approaches to leadership has some drawbacks. These approaches must be evaluated in light of the particular situation, the size of the project, and the culture of the followers to assess leadership effectiveness and potential.

Contingency models of leadership. There are four well known contingency models of leadership each of which at least partially explains how some of the contingency variables affect the leadership process.9

Fiedler's contingency model relates performance to the leader's motivational system and the degree to which the leader controls and influences the situation. It emphasizes the importance of understanding the nature of the situation and then matching the correct leadership style to that situation. The model's three contingency variables are:[15]

1. *Group atmosphere,* or leader's acceptance by the team
2. *Task structure,* or the extent to which a task performed by the project team is routine or non-routine; e.g., a conventional construction project versus a complex research and development project
3. *Leader's position power,* or the extent to which a team leader has reward, coercive and legitimate power; e.g., leaders with authority to hire, fire and discipline employees, have high position power whereas in voluntary and social organizations or on committees, leaders have low position power.

Fiedler developed the Least Preferred Co-worker scale (LPC) to measure leadership style. All leaders have a motivational system that indicates the combinations of situations in which their styles probably will be effective (See Figure 7.1). This model has a few weaknesses, two of which are that the Least Preferred Coworker is a one-dimensional concept in

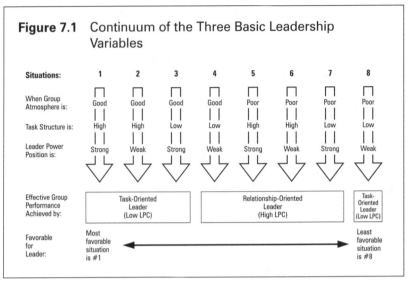

Figure 7.1 Continuum of the Three Basic Leadership Variables

Situations:	1	2	3	4	5	6	7	8
When Group Atmosphere is:	Good	Good	Good	Good	Poor	Poor	Poor	Poor
Task Structure is:	High	High	Low	Low	High	High	Low	Low
Leader Power Position is:	Strong	Weak	Strong	Weak	Strong	Weak	Strong	Weak

| Effective Group Performance Achieved by: | Task-Oriented Leader (Low LPC) | | | Relationship-Oriented Leader (High LPC) | | | | Task-Oriented Leader (Low LPC) |

| Favorable for Leader: | Most favorable situation is #1 | | | | | | | Least favorable situation is #8 |

that it only allows for leaders to be either task-oriented or relationship-oriented. In addition, this model does not consider that leaders can influence both the task structure and the group atmosphere because of their knowledge of the situation. Therefore task should not be a dependent variable in the model. In spite of these weaknesses, Fielder's contingency model has three important organizational implications:

1. Both task- and relationship-oriented leaders perform well in certain situations but not in others. For example, task-oriented leaders will do better with a group of low achievers, whereas with a team of high achievers, relationship orientation will be more effective.

2. The leader's own performance depends upon the motivational bases and situation. Organizations can affect leadership performance by changing the leader's reward system or by modifying the situation itself.

3. Leaders can improve their strength by learning how to become better leaders. Alternately, the leader can be matched to the situation according to the leader's Least Preferred Coworker style, or vice versa.[15]

Hersey and Blanchard's situational leadership model. This model is based on the amount of relationship (supportive) and task (directive) behavior that a leader provides in a situation. The amount of either behavior (supportive or directive) is based on the readiness or development level of the team members and followers. Key definitions of the concepts in this model are:[16]

Directive behavior (task orientation) is the extent to which the leader engages in one-way communication, spells out the role of the followers,

216

tells them what to do, where to do it, how to do it, when to do it and closely supervises their performance. The three key words for directive behavior are:

- Structure (task schedule, budget and other specifications well-defined)
- Control (related to the task and the process)
- Supervision (closer supervision to have maximum control).

Supportive behavior (relationship orientation) is the extent to which a leader engages in two-way communication, listens, provides support and encouragement, facilitates interaction and involves the followers in decision making. The three key words for supportive behavior are:

- Listen (actively)
- Praise (genuinely)
- Facilitate (sincerely).

Development level (readiness) is the ability and willingness of the team members to perform the task. In broad terms, it refers to competence, commitment and attitude:

- *Competence* implies task-relevant knowledge and skills as well as transferable skills.
- *Commitment* implies motivation and confidence (self-esteem and trust in their own decision making).
- *Attitude* implies attitude toward others and interpersonal skills.

Followers have various degrees of readiness. The appropriate style of leadership—telling, selling, participating or delegating—must match the readiness (development) level of team members. If team members are not ready to perform their tasks and have low competence but high commitment, then a directive leadership style will be more effective than a relationship one. As the development (readiness) level of the team members increases, a team leader should change his or her style to be more participative.

House's path-goal model. This model is based on the expectancy theory of motivation. It suggests that to be effective, a leader should try to enhance employees' satisfaction with their jobs and increase their performance level. Figure 7.2 shows the path-goal leadership model, which suggests that leadership behavior is contingent upon the characteristics of team members and the nature of the tasks.[17] A leader's goal should be to reduce the barriers that may hinder team members meeting their goals. For example, for a clear, routine task, a participative leadership style that is more considerate of employees will likely contribute to satisfaction and performance for highly independent team members. However, for ambiguous, ego-involving tasks (e.g., making presentations to clients and top management), participative leadership will have positive effects on performance and job satisfaction regardless of an employee's need for self-esteem or achievement.

Vroom and Jago leadership model. This model focuses on the role played by leaders in making decisions and provides a set of rules that can help a manager identify which leadership styles to avoid in a given situation

---

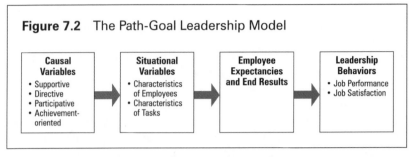

Figure 7.2 The Path-Goal Leadership Model

Causal Variables	Situational Variables	Employee Expectancies and End Results	Leadership Behaviors
• Supportive • Directive • Participative • Achievement-oriented	• Characteristics of Employees • Characteristics of Tasks		• Job Performance • Job Satisfaction

Source: Reprinted by permission from page 402 of *Organizational Behavior, Sixth Edition,* by Don Hellreigel, John W. Slocum, Jr., and Richard W. Woodman. Copyright © 1992.by West Publishing Co. All rights reserved.

when the choice of style might reduce the effectiveness of the team or of a particular decision. Vroom and Jago base their model on an analysis of how a leader's style affects decision effectiveness and overall effectiveness. Their research assumed that the leaders can choose any of five leadership styles of decision making, along a continuum ranging from highly autocratic to highly participative:[9,18]

1. *Autocratic* style refers to situations in which a leader makes decisions without gathering information from other team members.
2. *Autocratic with some information* refers to situations in which a leader requests certain specific information from others.
3. *One-to-one consultation* style means making decisions after consultation with relevant parties or team members. For example, a project leader may consult several functional managers to negotiate resources and schedules with them. However, overall conflicts are difficult to resolve as everyone is not together to look at the big picture.
4. *Consultation in a group* refers to group decision making where a project manager invites ideas and suggestions from team members in a meeting. However, the team leader makes the final decision, which may or may not reflect the influence of team members. Though team leaders make an effort to provide an opportunity to team members to participate and give their suggestions, this method may backfire if the team leader does not incorporate their ideas. It may lead to loss of trust because team members may consider it "lip service" or a superficial attempt to gain input and, consequently, they may stop giving any suggestions at all.
5. *Consensus* style refers to sharing problems with team members as a group. Together they generate and evaluate alternatives and attempt to reach consensus on a solution. The team leader acts as a facilitator to ensure that the group is kept focused and critical issues are discussed. Team leaders do not influence the team or impose their own solution. Instead they listen to all ideas with an open mind and then accept and implement any solution that has the support of the entire team.

Human Resource Skills for the Project Manager

Choosing the most appropriate leadership style is difficult. Although, in most project environments, there is a strong preference for a democratic participative style, it may not be the most effective for all situations. In general, a participative decision-making approach and style is very effective because participation helps gain increased acceptance and hence commitment from people to implement decisions and make them work. People feel good about and buy into the final decision if they have been a part of the process. The Vroom and Jago model indicates that various degrees of participative decision making are appropriate in different situations.

MOST PROJECT ENVIRONMENTS ARE DYNAMIC and are characterized by tough global competition in terms of technology and labor climate. Change is inevitable and imminent. There is an acute shortage of visionary and charismatic leaders who can not only manage change or cope with changes, but also initiate new opportunities and concepts as well. This is especially true for large research facilities that have a longer lead time and face a high degree of technological uncertainty in the challenge of building and managing a diverse mix of specialists and complex funding arrangements. Successful project managers should be aware of these prominent theories and models of leadership and be able to use any one model or a combination of models depending upon the project.

Leadership in a project environment

Leaders commit to quality.

— Anonymous

There is an ample body of literature on communication, teamwork and leadership. However, it is still not very clear what project leadership is and how it relates to project management. Verma and Wideman dealt with this issue in addressing the question *Is it leadership or management that is most needed for managing projects successfully in the next century?*[19]

About project leadership. There has been a spate of publications on "leadership" and "team building" by numerous authors, such as Batten, Bennis, Covey, Depree, Dilenschneider, McLean, and Fisher.[20] Most of these authors agree that vision is a primary ingredient of leadership. Batten defines leadership as the "development of a clear and complete system of expectations in order to identify, evoke and use the strengths of all resources in the organization, the most important of which is people."[21] John Naisbit probably came closer to a definition of a project leader with his description: "An ability to attract followers ... a clear destination, and ... a timetable."[22] With these attributes in mind, leadership in a project context can be defined in the following simple yet comprehensive distillation of leadership thought:[19]

Project leadership is an ability to get things done well through others. It requires:

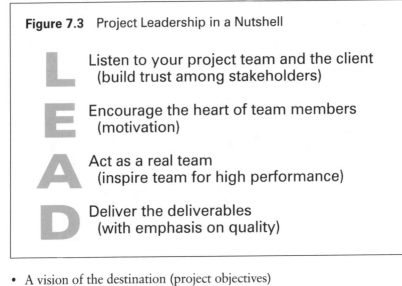

Figure 7.3 Project Leadership in a Nutshell

L Listen to your project team and the client (build trust among stakeholders)

E Encourage the heart of team members (motivation)

A Act as a real team (inspire team for high performance)

D Deliver the deliverables (with emphasis on quality)

- A vision of the destination (project objectives)
- A clear, compelling reason to get there (commitment)
- A set of directions and realistic timetable (project plan covering schedules, budget, etc.)
- A capacity to attract a willing team and make it work (development and fostering of teamwork).

Pinto synthesized various leadership studies and indicated several points about the nature of project leadership:[23]

- Effective project leaders must be good communicators.
- Project leaders are flexible in responding to ambiguous or uncertain situations with a minimum of stress.
- Successful project leaders work well with and through their project team.
- Good project leaders are skilled at various influence tactics by using the art of persuasion and influence.

He pointed out that examining the traits of successful leaders is valuable, but not sufficient. One key to understanding leadership behavior is to focus on what leaders *do* rather than *who they are*.[23] Figure 7.3 summarizes what "lead" stands for and represents project leadership in a nutshell.

Verma and Wideman raised two interesting issues and questions about leadership in a project environment, which are discussed below:[19]

Leader or manager? Is there a difference? Leadership is a subset of management. The leadership process is so dynamic that it is hard to define its process and attributes in specific terms. But in general terms, leadership is an ability to get things done through others while winning their respect, confidence, loyalty, willing cooperation and commitment. Respect and trust rather than fear and submission are the key elements of effective leadership. It involves focusing the efforts of a group of people

220

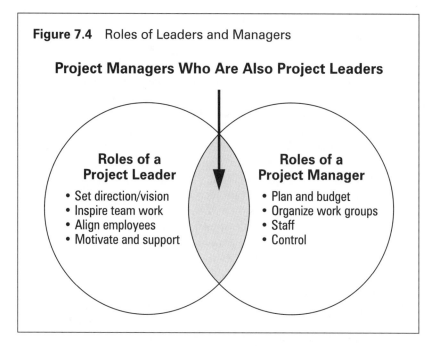

Figure 7.4 Roles of Leaders and Managers

Project Managers Who Are Also Project Leaders

**Roles of a
Project Leader**
- Set direction/vision
- Inspire team work
- Align employees
- Motivate and support

**Roles of a
Project Manager**
- Plan and budget
- Organize work groups
- Staff
- Control

toward a common goal and enabling them to work as a team. A leader should be directive in a democratic way and should enhance and complement efforts of individuals on a project team. A leader makes the parts whole. The leader is not one person dominating another or a group of people. The project leader is the focal point who acts when required and provides advice, encouragement and support whenever needed throughout the project life cycle.

Leading is not necessarily the same as managing.[24] Although some managers are leaders and some leaders are managers, leading and managing are not identical activities.[25] In comparison to leading, managing is much broader in scope. It covers non-behavioral and behavioral issues, such as aspects of planning, organizing, directing, controlling and influencing, including motivating and rewarding. "Leading," on the other hand, mainly emphasizes only the behavioral issues (see Figure 7.4).

In a project environment, all project managers are not necessarily project leaders, but the most effective project managers over the long-term prove to be good leaders as well. This is because, to manage projects effectively, the project manager must have strong interpersonal skills in order to manage interfaces and integrate the efforts of the whole team, other project shareholders (internal and external) and the client.

An understanding and application of these concepts helps the project manager recognize the importance of leadership and achieving leadership skills for successful management of projects. According to Bennis,[26] project leaders are those who do the right things (formulate strategies, establish goals and objectives) and project managers are those who do things right (organizing, building the project team and making it work). A person who manages a project should be both a leader and a manager.

Project leaders must foster an environment where team members have mutual trust and help each other achieve their best performance. They must stimulate performance drivers and minimize barriers to develop effective team spirit. According to Davis,[27] leadership is an ability to persuade others to meet defined objectives enthusiastically. It is a human factor that unites project participants and motivates them toward goals. Management activities such as planning, organizing, and decision making are ineffective in a project until a project leader inspires and motivates the project participants and directs them toward goals.

After careful analysis of the role of project managers and project leaders, the distinction between their styles can be attributed to how and what they focus on in a project. The respective positions of leaders and managers on a number of issues are shown in Table 7.1, which makes it evident that leaders focus on effectiveness while managers focus on efficiency.[19,20]

It must be noted that successful project management requires both project leadership as well as project management skills. Collectively, project leadership and project managership may be called project *stewardship*, which implies holding something in trust for another. Project stewardship may be defined as a willingness to be fully accountable for meeting project objectives and giving a higher degree of importance to project objectives than to self-interest. It entails holding people accountable without exacting harsh compliance from them.[19]

Leadership and the project life cycle. Do project leaders need different skills and leadership styles in different phases of the project life cycle? A project leader leads the project team and other stakeholders through formal and informal decision making in order to achieve agreed-upon objectives. This process involves an interactive approach to formulating and implementing organizational strategies. It takes time and it is challenging. Also stakeholder roles change during the life cycle of the project. Each project phase has different deliverables that determine an appropriate leadership style during that phase. Therefore, the degree of emphasis on leadership roles and skills may vary as the project progresses through its life cycle. However, there is a continual need for effective project leadership throughout the project life cycle.

Both project leadership and managership are important to project success because leadership emphasizes communication of the vision and then motivating and inspiring project participants to higher performance, while managership focuses on getting things done. Can the two be reconciled? For this, it is essential to turn to a fundamental principle of project management.

Project management is a structured but flexible process for producing a new end result (a unique product or service). Its success depends upon the

Table 7.1 Leader or Manager?

Leaders Focus On:	Managers Focus On:
Vision	Objectives
Selling what and why	Telling how and when
Longer range	Shorter range
People	Organization and structure
Democracy	Autocracy
Enabling	Restraining
Developing	Maintaining
Challenging	Conforming
Originating	Imitating
Innovating	Administrating
Directing	Controlling
Policy	Procedures
Flexibility	Consistency
Risk (opportunity)	Risk (avoidance)
Top line	Bottom line
Good Leaders	**Good Managers**
do the right things	*do things right*

Source: Vijay K. Verma and R. M. Wideman. 1994. Project Manager to Project Leader? and the Rocky Road Between. *Proceedings of the 25th Annual Seminar/Symposium*. Upper Darby, PA: Project Management Institute, pp. 627–633.

successful application of a two-step process: first *plan* and then *produce*. This is the genesis of a typical project life cycle. Figure 7.5 shows these phases along with the leadership versus managership skills needed during various phases of the project life cycle.[19]

For example, in the planning phases, the project leader focuses on the "right things to do" and outlines strategies to achieve objectives. This requires teamwork by all project stakeholders. It may be an iterative process and therefore takes time. It is during the planning phases that the customer's needs, requirements, and expectations should be clearly fleshed out. Therefore, *visioning, intelligence gathering,* and developing a *compelling reason* and *appropriate strategies,* are all important issues in these phases. The process in these phases also forms the essential basis for effective team development.

On the other hand, the real work of project execution gets done in the producing phases. In these phases, the emphasis is on "getting things done" by combining the efforts of the project team. At the same time, it is important to focus on "doing things right," that is, doing them efficiently and in a manner that satisfies the client's requirements.

Figure 7.5 Leadership and Management Skills Over the Project Life Cycle

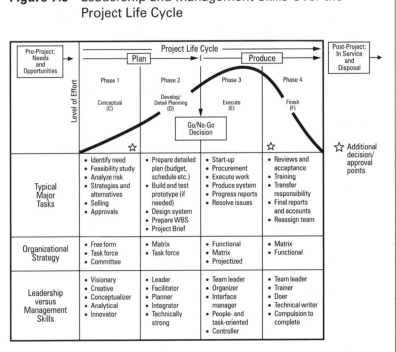

	Phase 1	Phase 2	Phase 3	Phase 4
	Conceptual (C)	Develop/ Detail Planning (D)	Execute (E)	Finish (F)
Typical Major Tasks	• Identify need • Feasibility study • Analyze risk • Strategies and alternatives • Selling • Approvals	• Prepare detailed plan (budget, schedule etc.) • Build and test prototype (if needed) • Design system • Prepare WBS • Project Brief	• Start-up • Procurement • Execute work • Produce system • Progress reports • Resolve issues	• Reviews and acceptance • Training • Transfer responsibility • Final reports and accounts • Reassign team
Organizational Strategy	• Free form • Task force • Committee	• Matrix • Task force	• Functional • Matrix • Projectized	• Matrix • Functional
Leadership versus Management Skills	• Visionary • Creative • Conceptualizer • Analytical • Innovator	• Leader • Facilitator • Planner • Integrator • Technically strong	• Team leader • Organizer • Interface manager • People- and task-oriented • Controller	• Team leader • Trainer • Doer • Technical writer • Compulsion to complete

Source: Vijay K. Verma and R. Max Wideman. 1994. Project Manager to Project Leader? and the Rocky Road Between. *Proceedings of the 25th Annual Seminar/Symposium of the Project Management Institute*. Upper Darby, PA: Project Management Institute, pp. 627–633.

As shown in the project life cycle phases in Figure 7.5, in the planning phase (Phases 1 and 2), "*managership*," as described above, has its limitations and *leadership* skills are more appropriate. On the other hand, during the producing phase (Phases 3 and 4), *leadership* per se has its limitations and *managership* is more effective.

Thus, project success depends upon a combination of both project leadership and project managership. To get a project launched on the right foot the project manager must become a leader. However, the style of leadership or the major emphasis changes as the project progresses through its life cycle. Similarly, it is essential to place more emphasis on project managership towards the end of the project, when it is important to integrate and realign the efforts of everyone, transfer the product and information through efficient project administration and compulsion for closure. Figure 7.6 shows the relationship between different phases of the project in its life cycle, leadership style and the skills, and factors that should be emphasized to achieve project success.

Human Resource Skills for the Project Manager

Figure 7.6 Leadership and the Project Life Cycle

Phase	Major Attributes/Emphasis	Leadership Style/Blend
Feasibility Study (Pre-formulation)	• Sense of vision • Conceptual, sees "Big Picture" • Analytical	• Visionary • Creates future • Empowerment • Expansive
Conceptual (Formulation)	• Listening • Analysis • Alignment	• Analytical • Listener • Change master • Convergence
Development	• Participative/acceptance and commitment • Cooperative	• Team builder • Power and influence • Integrator
Execution	• Re-alignment	• Decision-maker • Balances work and fun • Trustworthiness • Team and synergy
Completion	• Transfer of product and information	• Administrator • Closure

Source: Vijay K. Verma and R. Max Wideman. 1994. Project Manager to Project Leader? and the Rocky Road Between. *Proceedings of the 25th Annual Seminar/Symposium of Project Management Institute*. Upper Darby, PA: Project Management Institute, pp. 627–633.

It should be pointed out that effective communication is vital for successful project leadership in all phases of the project life cycle. Leadership skills are necessary in a project environment to increase effectiveness of project participants. These skills help in persuading major stakeholders to participate, give them clear directions, and ensure that sound decisions are made in a timely manner. A successful project manager should be able to adapt to an appropriate leadership style depending upon the phase of the project life cycle. Some project managers may be naturally gifted with these skills, but proper training and knowledge can enhance them in anyone. All project managers must be willing and determined to learn these skills for their projects to succeed.

Leadership and team development.[19] An effective project team leader is a "social architect" who recognizes the interaction between behavioral and organizational variables, can create a participative environment, and can minimize dysfunctional conflict among team members. An effective team leader must identify three important dimensions and the major issues associated with them (see Figure 7.7). These three dimensions (team members, project and overall organization) can be used to improve team leadership through effective inter-communication, which is a key to project management success.

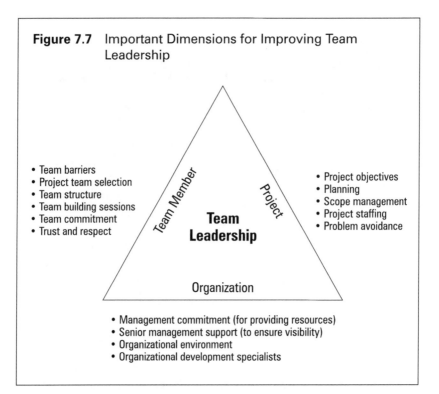

Figure 7.7 Important Dimensions for Improving Team Leadership

Team Member

Project

Team Leadership

- Team barriers
- Project team selection
- Team structure
- Team building sessions
- Team commitment
- Trust and respect

- Project objectives
- Planning
- Scope management
- Project staffing
- Problem avoidance

Organization

- Management commitment (for providing resources)
- Senior management support (to ensure visibility)
- Organizational environment
- Organizational development specialists

Team leadership is also related to the maturity level of the team members (the followers). The maturity or developmental level of team members is dependent upon three main factors:

- Competence: task-relevant knowledge and skills as well as transferable skills
- Commitment: composed of *motivation,* the energy, enthusiasm and commitment to complete tasks; and *confidence,* the self-esteem and self-assuredness that allows them to trust in their own decision making
- Attitude: relatively lasting beliefs and behavior tendencies directed toward specific team members, teams, ideas, issues or objects.

Many project teams feel motivated and become high-performing if they can be empowered to "take the bull by the horns." Depending upon their maturity level, they are willing to develop their own plans, procedures and review systems thereby requiring less direction and control. Such a team illustrates the concept of the self-directed work team.

According to Batten,[21] there are five things that winning project team members need from their leader:

- Expectation (Tell me what you expect of me)
- Opportunity (Give me an opportunity to perform)
- Feedback (Let me know how I am doing)

226

- Guidance (Give me guidance when and where I need it)
- Reward (Reward me according to my contribution).

In reality, both the members of a project team and their leader progress and develop interactively. The leader focuses successively on telling, selling, gelling and managing project activities with an aim to transform the project team into a self-directed work team. However, this only happens when the team members advance through four stages of team development (forming, storming, norming, performing), and the leaders adapt their leadership style accordingly.

Figure 7.8[28,29] shows the leader's successive efforts in telling, selling, gelling and making a self-directed work team; and the corresponding level of supportive versus directive behavior consistent with team member's development in each of the four stages of team development. Their behavior in these four stages can be summarized as:[19]

1. First Stage (*Forming*): During this stage, the team members are polite, guarded, and businesslike and therefore team leaders should emphasize directive behavior.
2. Second Stage (*Storming*): During this stage, the team members confront one another, struggle for control and as a result they either become entrenched or opt out. The leaders must display high directive and supportive behavior.
3. Third Stage (*Norming*): In this stage, the team members confront issues instead of people, establish procedures collectively and become team-oriented. The team leaders must provide high support and low direction during this stage.
4. Fourth Stage (*Performing*): In this final stage, the team members settle down to open and productive effort with trust, flexibility and a mature cohesiveness that enables self-direction. The team leaders must be willing to delegate and provide low direction and low support. However, they must assure their team members of their commitment to provide necessary support and coaching as needed.

Figure 7.8 represents the situational leadership theory, which states that the choice of a leadership style depends upon the situation, specifically in terms of the developmental level of the individuals being managed.

Therefore an effective situational leader should have the three abilities:[19,28,29]

- Flexibility: the ability to use a variety of leadership styles comfortably
- Diagnostic ability: the ability to choose a leadership style appropriate to the competence, confidence and attitude of team members
- Contracting for leadership style: the ability to agree to provide the appropriate level of direction without over- or under-supervising.

To be effective, a project team leader must be able to modify his or her level of supportive versus directive behavior in response to the progressive evolution or development of team members.

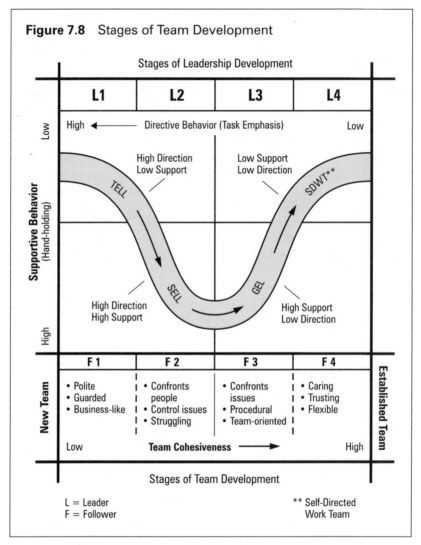

Figure 7.8 Stages of Team Development

Stages of Leadership Development

L1	L2	L3	L4

High ← Directive Behavior (Task Emphasis) Low

High Direction / Low Support — TELL

High Direction / High Support — SELL

Low Support / Low Direction — SDWT**

High Support / Low Direction — GEL

F 1	F 2	F 3	F 4
• Polite • Guarded • Business-like	• Confronts people • Control issues • Struggling	• Confronts issues • Procedural • Team-oriented	• Caring • Trusting • Flexible

Low **Team Cohesiveness** ⟶ High

Stages of Team Development

L = Leader
F = Follower

** Self-Directed
Work Team

Source: Data from Vijay K. Verma and R. Max Wideman, 1994, Project Manager to Project Leader? and the Rocky Road Between. *Proceedings of the 25th Annual Seminar/Symposium of Project Management Institute*. Upper Darby, PA: Project Management Institute, pp. 627–633. Figure concept adapted from the work of Hersey and Blanchard in *The Management of Organizational Behavior:Utilizing Human Resoruces, Fifth Edition,* 1988, Prentice-Hall.

Important skills for project leadership

Don't follow where the path may lead; go where there is no path and leave a trail.

— Anonymous

Both the project team and the stakeholders make vital contributions to the ultimate success of a project. However, a good project team led by a poor project manager cannot prevent disaster. So the primary role of project managers is to build up a dedicated project team through their leadership skills. Leadership skills are essential to bring the project together and to build trust among the project stakeholders.

Project leadership is an important element of overall project management. Project success depends upon the leadership skills of the project managers, and also on the level to which project participants follow the project leader. It should be pointed out that the leadership styles/roles may have to be changed to suit the phases of the project life cycle.

According to a survey conducted by Posner[31] of 287 project managers involved in small to medium-size projects, successful project management skills and techniques can be summarized in the six skill areas shown in Table 7.2. Attributes and behaviors associated with these skill areas are described below.[32,33]

Enthusiasm and energy. Displaying interest in the job has a positive effect on team members. Enthusiasm is contagious. A negative attitude by a project manager demotivates team members.

Decision making. This includes gathering necessary information and then analyzing, selecting and implementing the decisions. It requires action-oriented behavior and the need to achieve results.

Tolerance for ambiguity and change. Project leaders must be able to manage in an unstructured environment where they may have to deal with ambiguity and constant changes and bring order out of chaos. Quite often, they may encounter ambiguity in the definition of scope and requirements of stakeholders. Sometimes it seems that project leaders are expected to read minds, operate a ouija board and read a crystal ball. Project leaders can resolve the problems of ambiguity and changes by effective communication (especially listening and watching body language).

Vision. Project leaders must have a vision in order to inspire team members. This implies believing in the project and having a clear idea of what the client wants and then being able to communicate it enthusiastically. A clear vision helps in providing clear directions. Without it, the decisions will be inconsistent, often wrong and late, priorities will keep changing and team members will lose confidence in their project leader.

Application of project management process. Successful project managers must be able to provide effective leadership in the basic project management functions of planning, organizing, directing, motivating, and controlling to meet the objectives of the project and of the organization as a whole.

Effective team development. Project teams determine the ultimate success of the project. Project leaders must be able to quickly develop a cohesive team with a set of common values and a vision sufficient to bind them together and start them in an appropriate direction. Responsibilities must be delegated and effective working relations, mutual trust and creativity

Table 7.2 Important Project Management Skills

1. Communication Skills (84%)
   - Listening
   - Persuading
2. Organization Skills (75%)
   - Planning
   - Goal-Setting
   - Analyzing
3. Team Building Skills (72%)
   - Empathy
   - Motivation
   - *Esprit de Corps*
4. Leadership Skills (64%)
   - Sets Example
   - Energetic
   - Vision (big picture)
   - Delegates
   - Positive
5. Coping Skills (59%)
   - Flexibility
   - Creativity
   - Patience
   - Persistence
6. Technological Skills (46%)
   - Experience
   - Project Knowledge

Note: Numbers in parenthesis represent the percentage of project managers whose responses were included in this cluster.

Source: Barry F. Posner. 1987. What It Takes to Be a Good Project Manager. *Project Management Journal* (March).

must be encouraged. To accomplish this, project managers must use effective interpersonal skills, influencing, persuading and negotiating skills.

Interpersonal skills. Good project leaders are people-oriented. They are able to create a culture and an environment conducive to innovation and high performance by using their human skills and effective interpersonal style. Interpersonal skills include communicating, managing conflict, negotiating, influencing, empowering team members when necessary, and persuading people to gain their support and commitment. Effective interpersonal skills imply the artful ability to work with other people, motivating them and encouraging them to produce their best in the management of the project.

Human Resource Skills for the Project Manager

Conceptual skills. This implies an ability to see the big picture and analyze the project environment. It emphasizes relating the project and its elements to the whole organization by considering the objectives and strategies of key project stakeholders who clearly can either support or kill the project's plans.

Self-Assessment Exercise E in the Appendix will help you determine your leadership style.

Power and Influence in Project Management

Use power wisely and kindly, because the human spirit is fragile.

— Anonymous

Power and authority are probably the most important, yet most confusing, terms in project management. Power can be defined as an ability to influence others so that they will respond favorably to the instructions issued to them. Project managers cannot succeed without an effective use of power. This is because they must get the work done through others without much formal authority over many project personnel. Therefore, they must be able to gain the support of project stakeholders by influencing them rather than by exercising command authority over them.

Power is one of the most important human variables in the project management process because it sets the framework for directing and influencing human resources. In spite of the importance of power in establishing good relationships among project stakeholders, it is a relatively neglected topic in project management literature and people seldom deal with power issues directly.

Power versus influence, leadership and control

Power and authority and their effective uses are perhaps the least understood topics in project management.[34] In a social sense, power is the ability to get others to do the work you want them to do. Authority, on the other hand, is the formal power given to a person due to their hierarchical position on the organization chart. Two project managers may have the same authority but still not have the same power over project personnel. In other words, authority is the *right* to command or give orders whereas power is an *ability* to command through influencing others and getting them to do what you want them to do, when you want them to do it, and in the manner you propose.[34]

Kotter defined power-oriented behavior as behavior "directed primarily at developing or using relationships in which other people are to some degree willing to submit to one's wishes."[35] According to Mitchell, "power is the ability for A (say a project manager) to exercise influence over B (say a team member), when the team member would not do so otherwise."[36]

In order to fully understand power it is useful to compare power with similar terms, such as influence, leadership and control.[34] Halal's analysis is useful here:

Leadership, Power/Influence and Politics in a Project Environment

Power is defined as the ability to influence others in terms of their decisions, behaviors and future actions. Leadership is the use of power for these purposes, i.e., leaders use different forms of influence to mobilize followers effectively. Control is the objective or end result of influence. Therefore, influence is the key concept that is involved with the related concepts of power, leadership and control. Influence is regarded as the main process through which leaders obtain their power to control events. Leaders may derive their power from a variety of different types of influence, such as the use of physical coercion or force, money and economic resources, formal and legal authority, social pressure or status, special skills and knowledge, personal vision and charisma, and possibly other such sources.[37]

Mitchell also provided a useful analysis of influence.[36] Influence is usually conceived as being narrower than power. It implies the ability on the part of a person to alter another person or group in specific ways, such as in their satisfaction and performance. Influence is more closely associated with leadership than is power, but both obviously are involved in the leadership process. Therefore, authority is different from power because of its legitimacy, and influence is narrower than power but is so conceptually close that the two terms can be used interchangeably.[36]

Stogdill described leadership as an interpersonal relation in which others comply voluntarily rather than being forced.[38] Leadership focuses on the achievement of team objectives and involves everyone's acceptance and commitment to objectives and organizing their roles clearly. In other words, leadership is the use of power to accomplish the objectives of the project team or the organization as a whole. Mitchell described control as the process of setting standards, monitoring results with feedback and taking corrective actions to correct deviations.[36]

These definitions of power, authority, influence, leadership and control illustrate that these are related to each other and therefore should be compared and contrasted in order to understand the basic concepts of power and how to use it effectively.

Sources of power

Real power is earned, not demanded.

— Anonymous

In addition to positional or formal authority, project managers may use power and influence available from several sources. French and Raven[39] developed five basic categories of power. Studies by Kotter[35] and Mitchell[36] have made minor modifications and additions, but the basic categories or forms of power are very similar. Figure 7.9 shows various forms of power described by French and Raven, Mitchell and Kotter.[39] Some of these forms of power are self-explanatory and some need more

Figure 7.9 Major Categories of Power

French & Raven	Mitchell	Kotter	
Legitimate	Formal Authority	Formal Authority	
Reward	Rewards	Sense of Obligation	} Positional Power
Coercive	Punishment	Perceived Dependency	
Referent	Charisma	Identification	} Personal Power
Expert	Expertise	Expertise	

explanation. There are eight principal forms of power that can be used by project managers.[34]

Reward power. This refers to positive consequences or outcomes that a project manager can offer to project personnel. It includes positive incentives such as promotions, salary increases, vacation and other opportunities.

Punishment power. Coercive, or punishment, power refers to negative things that project personnel believe a project manager can do to them: fire, suspend, dock pay, give unpleasant assignments or reprimand.

Referent power. This refers to earned/personal power when project personnel admire the project manager as a person and want to follow him or her as a role model. In such situations, personnel willingly comply with the demands of the project manager.

Expert power. This is also an earned/personal power that project managers acquire based upon their technical knowledge, skill, or expertise on some topic or issue. In such situations, project personnel will do what the project manager wants because they believe that that he or she knows best. Expert power is a function of knowledge and skills possessed by the project manager rather than formal sanctions given by the project personnel.

Legitimate/title power. This refers to formal authority, the right to give orders or make requests. The legitimate power of a project manager is determined by the norms, perceptions and expectations of project personnel. For example, "Has the project manager done this before?" "Have project personnel always complied?" and "What are the consequences of noncompliance?"

Information power. Information is a powerful asset and is often controlled by a few individuals within organizations. They may decide who should get what information and how much. Project managers have information power over project personnel if they think that the project manager controls the information that they want. This information can be gathered and distributed both formally and informally.

Leadership, Power/Influence and Politics in a Project Environment

Figure 7.10 Outcomes of the Five Bases of Power

Response of Project Personnel			
Power Source	**Commitment**	**Compliance**	**Resistance**
Legitimate authority	Possible	**Likely**	Possible
Reward power	Possible	**Likely**	Possible
Coercive power	Unlikely	Possible	**Likely**
Expert power	**Likely**	Possible	Possible
Referent power	**Likely**	Possible	Possible

High -------------------- Motivation to Perform -------------------- Low

Most -------------------- Potential Effectiveness -------------------- Least

Persuasion/charismatic power. This is a practical form of power in a project environment where project managers have little formal authority over project personnel. Project managers can get good results by persuading people, using their human skills rather than by commanding them. It should be noted that persuasion requires patience and effective communication skills to attract the attention of project personnel.

Contacts/network power. This refers to building alliances and networks with influential people within the organization. It offers an important power base because project managers often have limited authority and must work with and through functional managers to meet project objectives. Informal contacts can also help project managers identify problems early and find appropriate solutions.

The various forms of power are interrelated and do overlap, making the dynamics of power complicated. Youker has identified some interesting ideas about various forms of power:[34]

- Some forms of power are derived from formal authority while some are personal or earned and come from the individual (charisma).
- People may have direct power, or indirect power through someone else (contacts).
- Power may be used or not.
- In fact, people can have power only if *others* perceive it that way.

Figure 7.10 shows how project personnel respond to the five power sources (defined by French and Raven) in terms of their levels of commitment, compliance, and resistance. Figure 7.11 shows characteristics of power and their bases.

234

Figure 7.11 Characteristics of Power

Characteristics	Base of Power
Degree of control	Reward, coercive, legitimate
Position in organizational hiarchy	Reward, legitimate, referent
Reputation	Expert
Knowledge and experience	Expert
Organizational climate	Modifies strength of legitimate and others

To be an effective project manager and use power effectively, two factors are important:

1. *Appropriate choice of power base* depends upon the situation and the maturity level of the project manager.
2. *Skillful and thoughtful execution of power* is the most important aspect because better interpersonal and persuasive skills, combined with effective communication and positive reinforcement, will result in better influence (compared to an autocratic style) to meet project goals and objectives within specified constraints.

Project success and quality of personal relationships may depend upon the relative use of the different forms of power. Wilemon and Gemmill indicated that project managers are more effective when they mostly use their earned or personal power rather than relying on their formal authority to command and punish.[40] Kotter emphasized that true organizational power depends more upon inspirational leadership than on formal status or rank.[35]

Successful project managers have achieved their reputation by establishing power bases required to exercise leadership throughout the project life cycle. Business and social environment has grown in complexity. Kotter believes that, because of tough global competition, the need for project managers who are able to deal with organizational complexities and dynamics of power will continue to grow.[35] Complex project or program environments involving numerous goals, priorities and stakeholders inevitably leads to conflict, which in turn can generate destructive power struggles, infighting and politics. Kotter[35] indicates that dealing with this dilemma is truly one of the great challenges of our time.

Youker[34] indicated that the various forms of power can all be applied by a project manager and described the eight sources of power as part of typical project management tools and techniques. Specific tools and techniques allow the project manager to use different forms of power (as required) to achieve success.

The project manager and power

Managing projects requires skills and techniques that are unique and different from those needed to manage ongoing operations. Usually project managers have limited formal authority but enormous responsibility for meeting project objectives. Therefore, they must be able to influence others by developing their power bases appropriately and then executing that power thoughtfully and skillfully. The total power of a project manager is the sum of position power and personal power. Increasing this power and balancing it, especially in matrix organizations, are described below.

Total power of a project manager. Project managers must have some power for managing projects successfully. However, the main issues are: what kind of power they should have, and what kind of power they should acquire and how, and how that power should be balanced in the project environment to avoid the potential for unconstructive conflict, power struggles, infighting and parochial politics. A project manager can obtain power in two ways: from the position held, and/or from personality, knowledge and experience.

Total Power = Position Power + Personal/Expert Power.

Position power is also called legitimate power and is derived from the organizational position a project manager holds. It consists of the right to punish or reward the project personnel and the perception of just how influential a particular project manager is compared to other managers associated with the project. The more influential a project manager is or is perceived to be, the more influence he or she can exert over other managers and project personnel.

Personal power is derived from the personality, knowledge and expertise of the project manager. Project managers earn the trust and respect of project personnel, functional manager, other project managers, project and design engineers, contractors and others involved in the project due to their talents, energy, fairness, sincerity as well as knowledge and understanding of the project in question and other qualities. Consequently, everyone is more willing to listen, to cooperate, to execute the instructions and to meet other demands made on them by such project managers.

Increasing total power. In a project environment, project managers can increase their total power by increasing one or both components of it. Position power can generally be increased only by achieving a higher organizational position and moving upward in the management hierarchy—something project managers may not have any direct control over. On the other hand, project personnel generally have substantial control over the amount of personal power they hold in the project. Kotter stressed the importance of developing personal power when he stated that, in order to be able to plan, organize, budget, staff, control and evaluate, managers need some control over the many people on whom they are dependent. Trying to control others solely by directing them on the basis of the power associated with one's position simply will not work for two main reasons: first, managers are always dependent on some people over whom they have no formal authority; and second, virtually no one in modern organizations will passively accept and completely obey a constant stream of orders from someone just because he or she is the "boss."[35]

Project managers can develop their personal power by using the following guidelines:

- Develop a sense of obligation in other members of the organization (project team members, functional manager, top management and customer/project sponsor) that is directed toward the project manager. The project manager may create this sense of obligation by doing personal favors for them, e.g., he or she may negotiate resources to suit the functional manager; may accommodate some changes in specifications/scope without excessive additional charges; may provide better opportunities to project team members and ensure they get appropriate recognition that they value. In other words, the project manager should establish a cooperative and friendly rapport with all major project stakeholders.

- Establish a belief in other organizational members that the project manager possesses a high level of expertise within the organization. To increase this perceived level of expertise, the project manager must quietly make a significant achievement visible tokey stakeholders and rely heavily on a successful track record and respected professional reputation.

- Create a sense of identification that other organization members have with the project manager (i.e., have others identify with the project manager). The project manager can try to develop this identification by behaving in a way that other organization members respect and by espousing goals, values and ideals commonly held by organization members.

- Develop the perception among other organizational members that they are dependent upon the project manager (i.e., holding the "purse strings"). This is valid only toward project team members because in some project organizations (especially in matrix type) project managers have little direct positional authority. However, there could be some situations where functional managers may feel that project managers have substantial authority due to strong support from top management. This strategy is aptly reflected in the managerial version of the Golden Rule: "He who has the gold makes the rules." This technique is more inclined towards positional power (reward/punishment power) and therefore may not be effective in the long run in a project environment. This is especially true in R&D and high-tech industries where project teams have a diverse mix of highly qualified experts and specialists with high self-esteem.

Balancing the power. Generally, a project manager is responsible for meeting project goals within time and financial constraints but he or she may not have sufficient direct authority over project personnel. The project manager must depend on the cooperation of functional managers regarding the quality and quantity of human resources assigned to the project. Even though the project manager may identify deviations in overall project performance (schedule, cost and quality) and issue instructions to implement corrective actions, they may or may not be followed depending on how much power or influence the project manager has over the project personnel who are involved. Power struggles and conflicts can easily happen in most project-oriented organizations and especially within a matrix structure. Therefore, it is important to understand managerial relationships in a project and achieve a proper balance in power to ensure smooth success of a project.[41]

The relationship between the project manager and functional managers can also be described as a balance of interest and a sharing of power (see Figure 7.12).[41,42] However, shared power may not be truly balanced because in reality the balance of power is a dynamic, constantly changing condition that can never be static, even if desired.[41]

Theoretically it is possible to divide authority and responsibility between the project manager and the functional manager in order to create a balance of power between them, but it is not always successful. Even a clear delineation of authority and responsibility cannot guarantee a balance of power. In matrix organizations, it is difficult to achieve a balance of power because matrix organizations consist of people with different management styles, personalities, professional backgrounds and norms of behavior. Some managers have strong interpersonal, communication and persuasive skills, while others depend on organizational authority. Consequently, everyone is involved in a power struggle and concerned with how to increase their total power.

In addition, because projects, programs or products are the most important elements of many businesses, project/program managers normally contribute a lot to the bottom line of their organizations by virtue of the beneficial changes that they achieve. Still, functional managers are more powerful because they control human resources directly and provide a permanent "home base" for project personnel to return to after completion of the project. In a pure project organization, or for a matrix to work, project managers must hold more power by eliciting strong support from top management.[41]

Self-Assessment Exercise F in the Appendix is designed to help you determine your power orientation.

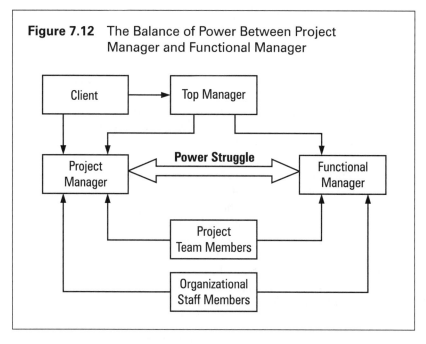

Figure 7.12   The Balance of Power Between Project Manager and Functional Manager

Power and Politics in Project Management

Politics is the science of who gets what, when, and why.

— *Sidney Hillman*

Politics are inevitable in project environments due to the high degree of diversity in norms, backgrounds and expectations of the people involved with a project. Skillful politicking and power brokering are key to successful project management. Conversely, lack of emphasis on project politics and inappropriate use of power can lead to chaos in managing projects.[43] Yet despite thier importance, power and politics are still the least discussed subjects in project management.

Politics can be defined as an activity concerned with the acquisition of power.[43] In the context of project management, power is the ability to influence others to do what you want them to do. Part of that power may come from formal authority (positional power) and personality (personal power, e.g., referent and expert power), yet politics is a strong influencing factor. The political climate and power dynamics of a project must be assessed in order to formulate appropriate strategies for managing the project itself, its environment and its participants.[43]

Managing politics at the upper management level

Normally, upper management is concerned with long-term plans and overall organizational strategies to meet strategic plans through effective program or project management. Here are some of the ways of dealing with power and politics at the upper levels of management to meet the objectives of both the project and the organization:[43]

Follow management hierarchy. This implies channeling all decisions formally through the management hierarchy. This method is particularly effective if top management has a proven track record of making sound decisions in managing projects.

Appoint a project sponsor or director. In such cases, the project sponsor belongs to the top management team and gives a required level of political profile to the project.

Use a steering committee or project council. This works best when the project crosses several organizational lines and there is no single person at the top management level who is politically willing to accept total project responsibility. It may help the project by bringing in a variety of experience from a group of upper-level managers. The steering committee is a way to apply consensus decision making to upper-level project management.

Protect yourself and your team. In the absence of top management taking direct responsibility, project managers must build a "political umbrella" under which project work can progress in spite of a lack of obvious management support.

Engage outside facilitators in developing strategies. To avoid internal political struggles, a neutral external facilitator with experience in both project management and project technology may be called in to help develop strategies.

Engage experts (lobbyists, arbitrators) as needed. This approach is more corrective than preventive in nature and may be required when there are deadlocks at upper management levels. Experts may provide fresh insights to the issues and problems at hand.

It is hard to single out the best way of managing politics at the upper management level. Some approaches may work better in some situations than others. Sometimes steering committees may be viewed as a road block by a project manager (especially a good one). The project sponsor and management hierarchy sometimes add bureaucracy, while in other cases they help things push through. Outside help may prove effective or may change the overall direction, adding cost and time to complete the project. In spite of all this, neglecting the importance of politics at the management level, especially at the front end of the project management process, is risky. Therefore, it is important to think forward early in the project life cycle and manage front-end strategic and political issues to avoid conflicts and destructive power struggles.

Human Resource Skills for the Project Manager

Managing politics at the project level

Even in politics, ethics are the most valuable asset.

— Anonymous

In addition to managing conventional areas of scope, quality, time, and cost through effective management of risk, communication, contract and human resources, successful project managers must manage project politics effectively. Handling power and politics is complex due to the behavioral dimensions of various project stakeholders. Project managers receive inevitable pressures from top management, client, team members and other external and internal stakeholders. The management of stakeholders itself is an interesting challenge in terms of pinning down roles and responsibilities. Here are some ways that project managers can use to enhance their political and power position at the project operating level:[43]

Ensure top management support. Project managers will fail in managing projects without the support of top management. Project managers should be politically tuned in to upper management to ensure their support as needed.

Use strategic instruments. Project managers can use project plans or project management plans to mold strategies and policies and hence increase their power bases.

Build a team. The project team is one of the major power bases of project managers. They must focus on motivating the project team and effective team building through training and their interpersonal, conflict management, consensus decision making and effective communicating skills.

Develop personal power. Project managers are not given power, but they are given the right to obtain it. They must develop their personal power and build stronger power bases by increasing their competence, expertise and technical knowledge.

At the project level, project managers are the overall champions of project success. In addition to conventional project management skills, they must have a healthy taste and inclination for project politics rather than an unreasonable lust for power, which hurts both the project and the project manager's own political base.[43]

Project managers face the challenge of managing the power and politics at both the upper level and at the project level. At the project level, they may have some formal authority but may lack political clout to be effective at upper-level project management. Also, there may be conflicting perceptions about what elements make the project successful:[43]

- The project team focuses on scope, quality, schedule and cost.
- The client is concerned about the final result; how it satisfies the organizational objectives.
- The contractors and vendors view success in terms of economic returns and possibility of repeat business.

The project sponsor has an important role in the project environment in terms of power and politics. Increased diversity in project culture, priorities, past experiences and present expectations places even greater emphasis on effective management of politics at all levels. More research needs to be done to develop flexible conceptual models that can help client and project organizations in managing projects at the upper level and building stronger foundations for managing power and politics effectively at the project level as well.

Summary

This chapter emphasizes that leadership, power, influence and politics are interrelated. In a project environment, where project managers have little or no formal authority over the majority of project stakeholders, they must understand the concepts of power and perception and acquire appropriate leadership and influencing skills to manage organizational and project politics at all levels.

Leadership is a process of creating a vision and having an ability to translate that vision into reality and sustain it. Various studies have explored basic concepts of leadership. There are various traits and skills associated with leader effectiveness that can be learned. Successful project leaders must be aware of prominent theories, models and styles of leadership. They should be able to use any model or a combination of models depending upon the circumstances and personalities of project participants.

Project leadership is an ability to get things done well through others. It involves providing clear,compelling directions to achieve project objectives (within constraints of budget, schedule and quality) by developing and fostering teamwork. Project leaders should be flexible and be good communicators. They should be able to influence and inspire high team performance. To be effective leaders in a project environment, it is important to recognize that there is a difference between the project leader and a project manager; and that project leaders need different skills and leadership styles during different phases of the project life cycle.

There is a subtle difference between a project leader and a project manager. Leadership is a subset of management. According to Bennis,26 project leaders focus on "effectiveness" i.e., *doing the right things* and project managers focus on "efficiency" i.e., *doing the things right*. Successful project management requires both project leadership as well as project management skills. Collectively, this is called project "stewardship" which implies holding something in trust for another. It requires full accountability for meeting project objectives.

In a project environment, leadership roles must vary as the project progresses through its life cycle. Leadership skills are more appropriate during the early phases of planning, whereas managership is more effective during the producing phase. Effective project leaders must act as an entrepreneur (during the conceptual phase), communicator/team builder (during the development phase), performer and integrator(during the execution phase), and administrator (during the termination phase of project life cycle).

Project managers must have or should develop through training major leadership skills—visioning, influencing, communicating, decision making and problem solving, team building, empowering, and above all understanding of self and others.

Power and authority are two of the most confused terms in project management. Authority is the *right* to command whereas power is the *ability* to influence others to get a *favorable* response to the instructions issued to them. Power and authority play a significant role in project management.

Power determines the extent to which a project manager is able to influence others to meet project objectives. Total power is made of positional power and personal power. Project managers should try to increase their personal power by genuinely helping people achieve more, being seen as an expert in their areas, and having others identify with them. Both sources of power are important for an effective project manager.

Authority alone is not enough. Project managers must be the kind of persons that the project participants would respect and want to follow. Appropriate use of power makes the project manager a "leader," a person others willingly wish to follow. Project managers must understand all eight forms of power: reward, punishment, referent, expert, legitimate, title, information, persuasion/charismatic, contacts/network power. They must choose their power base appropriately depending upon the situation, their maturity level and maturity level of other project personnel. Effective execution of power is as important as the choice of the form of power. Successful project managers should develop their power base through inspirational leadership rather than through formal status and ranks. Effective communication, persuasion and positive reinforcement will influence project participants favorably to meet project objectives successfully.

Politics are inevitable in project environments. Skillful politicking and power brokering can be effective in project management. Project managers must understand the importance of politics at upper management level and at project level. Some of the guidelines to manage politics at upper management level include: following management hierarchy, appointing a strong project sponsor, using a steering committee or project council, protecting themselves and their team members, engaging outside facilitators in developing strategies and seeking help from outside experts, lobbyists or arbitrators as needed. Project managers can enhance their political and power position at the project level by developing their power bases appropriately. It can be done in several ways: by ensuring top management support, by using strategic instruments (mission/strategies/plans), by building an effective project team, and by developing personal/expert power.

References

Chapter 1

1. W. Richard Plunkett. 1986. *Supervision: The Direction of People at Work, Fourth Edition*. Dubuque, Iowa: Wm. C. Brown Publishers, pp. 87–106.
2. Peter F. Drucker. 1952. How to Be an Employee, *Fortune:* p. 126.
3. Richard W. Sievert, Jr. 1986. Communication: An Important Construction Tool. *Project Management Journal* (December): p. 77.
4. R.W. Rosenbloom and F.W. Walek. 1967. *Information and Organization: Information Transfer in Industrial R&D*. Boston, MA: Graduate School of Business Administration, Harvard University.
5. L. Sayles. 1964. *Managerial Behavior*. New York: McGraw-Hill.
6. Wilbur Schramm. 1954. How Communication Works. In *The Process and Effects of Mass Communication*, ed. Wilbur Schramm, pp. 3–10. Urbana, IL: University of Illinois Press.
7. Deborah Kezsbom, D. Schilling, and Katherine Edward. 1989. *Dynamics of Project Management*. New York: John Wiley & Sons, p. 245.
8. Albert Mehrabian. 1968. Communication Without Words. *Psychology Today* (September): pp. 53–55.
9. S.D. Gladis. 1985. Notes Are Not Enough. *Training and Development Journal* (August): pp. 35–38.
10. Nicole Steckler and Robert Rosenthal. 1985. Sex Differences in Non-verbal and Verbal Communication with Bosses, Peers, and Subordinates. *Journal of Applied Psychology* (February): pp. 157–63.
11. Andrew J. DuBrin. 1982. *Contemporary Applied Management*. Plano, TX: Business Publications, pp. 127–34.
12. W. Alan Randolph. 1985. *Understanding and Managing Organizational Behavior*. Homewood, IL: Richard D. Irwin, pp. 349–50.
13. David I. Cleland, 1990, *Project Management: Strategic Design and Implementation*, Blue Ridge Summit, PA: TAB Books, pp. 288–289; and R. Max Wideman, *Author's Guide for PMI '94 and PMI '95 Technical Program*, Upper Darby, PA: Project Management Institute.
14. 1995. *Interpersonal Communication Skills Workbook*. Boulder, CO: Career Track Inc., pp. 4–22.
15. David S. Brown, 1975, Barriers to Successful Communication: Part I, Macro-Barriers. *Management Review* (December): pp. 24–29; and James K. Weekly and Raj Aggarwal, 1987, *International Business: Operating in the Global Economy*. New York: Dryden Press.
16. David S. Brown, 1976, Barriers to Successful Communication: Part II, Micro Barriers. *Management Review* (January): pp. 15–21; and Sally Bulkey Pancrazio and James J. Pancrazio, 1981, Better Communication for Managers, *Supervisory Management* (June): pp. 31–37.
17. M.L. Tushman. 1979. Managing Communication Networks in R&D Laboratories, *Sloan Management Review* 20: pp. 37–49.
18. Cleland, *Project Management: Strategic Design and Implementation*, pp. 282,283.
19. David I. Cleland and D.F. Kocaoglu. 1981. *Engineering Management*. New York: McGraw-Hill, pp. 124–125.
20. Vijay K. Verma. 1984. *Proceedings of Northwest Regional Symposium*. Vancouver, B.C., Canada: West Coast B.C. Chapter of Project Management Institute, pp. A5.15–A5.19.
21. These functions are paraphrased from Anthony Jay, 1976, How to Run a Meeting, *Harvard Business Review* (March–April): pp. 120–134.
22. Cleland, *Project Management: Strategic Design and Implementation*, pp. 289–294.
23. Harold Kerzner. 1989. *Project Management: A Systems Approach to Planning, Scheduling and Controlling, Third Edition*. New York: Van Nostrand Reinhold, p. 367.
24. Sunny Baker and Kim Baker. 1992. *On Time/On Budget: A Step by Step Guide for Managing Any Project*. Englewood Cliffs, NJ: Prentice Hall, p. 199–200.
25. J. Kostner and Christy Strbiak. 1993. Openness: The Gateway to Top Performance. *PM Network* (November): pp. 25–29.

26. Kezsbom, Schilling and Edward, *Dynamics of Project Management,* pp. 250–264.

27. R. Might. 1984. An Evaluation of the Effectiveness of Project Control Systems. *IEEE Transactions on Engineering Management,* EM–31, No. 3 (August).

28. S. Barndt. 1984. The Matrix Manager and Effective Communication. In *Matrix Management Systems Handbook,* ed. D. Cleland, New York: Van Nostrand Reinhold.

29. J. Athanassades. 1973. The Distortion of Upward Communication in Hierarchical Organizations. *Academy of Management Journal* 16: pp. 207–226.

30. P.M. Muchinsky. The Interrelationships of Organizational Communication Climate, as cited in Barndt, see Ref. 28, p. 584.

31. A.A. Imberman. 1969. Why are most Foreman Training Courses a Failure? *Bedding* 96, No. 6 (July): pp. 40–41.

32. 1979. *The Wall Street Journal* (September 11): p. 11.

33. Cleland, *Project Management: Strategic Design and Implementation,* pp. 283–285.

34. David Davis, 1985. New Project: Beware of False Economies. *Harvard Business Review* (March–April): p. 97.

35. Joan Knutson and Ira Bitz. 1991. *Project Management: How to Plan and Manage Successful Projects.* New York: AMACOM, pp. 17–35.

36. Gerard I. Nierenberg and Henry H. Calero. 1971. *How to Read a Person Like a Book.* New York: Hawthorn Books, pp. 20, 21, 41, 44, 67, 107, 150, 165.

37. Robert L. Montgomery. 1981. *Listening Made Easy.* New York: AMACOM, pp. 13–15.

38. K. Davis. 1978. *Human Relations at Wor, Fifth Edition.* New York: McGraw-Hill.

39. Source: Vijay K. Verma. 1995. Flying to Project Success on Wings of Communication. 1995. *Proceedings of the Project Management Institute Seminar/Symposium.* Upper Darby, PA: Project Management Institute, p. 560–566.

Chapter 2

1. Edwin A. Locke. 1976. Nature and Causes of Job Satisfaction. In *The Handbook of Industrial and Organizational Psychology,* ed. M.D. Dunnette, p. 1300. Chicago, IL: Rand McNally.

2. Project Management Institute. 1994. *A Guide to the Project Management Body of Knowledge (Exposure Draft).* Upper Darby, PA: Project Management Institute, p. 10.

3. Samuel C. Certo, Steven H. Appelbaum, and Irene Divine, 1989, *Principles of Modern Management: A Canadian Perspective, Third Edition.* Scarborough, ON: Allan and Bacon, Inc., pp. 377, 390–393; and Cleland, *Project Management: Strategic Design and Implementation,* p. 23.

4. Plunkett, *Supervision: The Direction of People at Work,* pp.139, 157, 149–150.

5. Don Hellreigel, John W. Slocum, Jr., and Richard W. Woodman. 1979. *Organizational Behavior, Sixth Edition.* St. Paul, MN: West Publishing Co., pp. 202–233.

6. E.A. Locke and G.P. Latham. 1990. *A Theory of Goal Setting and Task Performance.* Englewood Cliffs, NJ: Prentice-Hall, pp. 6–8.

7. R.M. Steers and L.W. Porter (eds.), 1989, *Motivation and Work Behavior, Fifth Edition.* New York: McGraw-Hill; R.L. Kanfer, 1990, Motivation Theory and Industrial/Organizational Psychology, In the *Handbook of Industrial and Organizational Psychology, Second Edition,* ed. M.D. Dunnette, pp. 75–170, Palo Alto, CA: Consulting Psychologists Press.

8. A.H. Maslow. 1970. *Motivation and Personality.* New York: Harper and Row; and also A.H. Maslow, 1943. A Theory of Human Motive Acquisition. *Psychological Review* 1: pp. 370–396.

9. C.P. Alderfer. 1972. *Existence, Relatedness and Growth: Human Needs in Organizational Settings.* New York: The Free Press.

10. J.P. Wanous and A. Zwany. 1977. A Cross-Sectional Test of the Need Hierarchy Theory. *Organizational Behavior and Human Performance* 18: pp. 78–97.

11. Stephen P. Robbins and Robin Stuart Kotze. 1994. *Management, Canadian Fourth Edition.* Scarborough, ON: Prentice-Hall Canada Inc., pp. 477–497.

12. Frederick Herzberg. 1968. One More Time: How Do You Motivate Employees? *Harvard Business Review* 46(1): pp. 53–62. See also Michael E. Gordon, Norman M. Pryor, and Bob V. Harris, An Examination of Scaling Bias in Herzberg's Theory of Job Satisfaction, *Organizational Behavior and Human Performance* (February) pp. 106–21; Edwin A. Locke and Roman J. Whiting, Sources of Satisfaction and Dissatisfaction Among Solid Waste Management Employees, *Journal of Applied Psychology* (April) pp. 145–56; John B. Miner, 1980, *Theories of Organizational Behavior*, Hinsdale, IL: Dryden Press, pp. 76–105; and also Richard J. Hackman, 1975, Is Job Enrichment Just a Fad? *Harvard Business Review* (September/October) pp. 129–138.

13. Edwin A. Locke, D.B. Feren, V.M. McCaleb, K.N. Shaw, and A.T. Denny. 1980. The Relative Effectiveness of Four Methods of Motivating Employee Performance. In *Changes in Working Life*, eds. K.D. Duncan, M.N. Gruneberg, and D. Wallis, pp. 363–383. London, UK: John Wiley & Sons.

14. David C. McClelland, 1971, *The Achieving Society*. New York: Van Nostrand Reinhold; John W. Atkinson and Joel O. Raynor, 1974, *Motivation and Achievement*. Washington, DC: Winston; McClelland, 1975, *Power: The Inner Experience*. New York: Irvington; David McClelland and David G. Winter, 1969, *Motivating Economic Achievement*, New York Free Press; and David McClelland, 1975, An Advocate of Power, *International Management* (July) pp. 27–29.

15. Douglas McGregor, 1985, *The Human Side of Enterprise*. New York: McGraw-Hill. For a current illustration of how Theory, X-Theory Y relates to modern business, see Kenneth B. Slutsky, 1989, Viewpoint: Why Not Theory Z? *Security Management* 22 (April): pp. 110–112.

16. Paul C. Dinsmore. 1990. *Human Factors in Project Management, Revised Edition*. New York: AMACOM, pp. 229–233.

17. W.G. Ouchi and A.M. Jaeger, 1978, Type Z Organization: Stability in the Midst of Mobility, *Academy of Management Review* 3, No. 2 (April): pp. 305–314; and W.G. Ouchi, 1981, *Theory Z: How American Business Can Meet the Japanese Challenge*, Reading, MA: Addison-Wesley; and R.T. Pascale and A.G. Athos, 1981, *The Art of Japanese Management*, New York: Simon & Schuster.

18. Robert J. Hughes and Jack R. Kapoor. 1985. *Business*. Boston, MA: Houghton-Mifflin, pp. 134–135.

19. John J. Morse and Jay W. Lorsch. 1975. Beyond Theory Y. In *Harvard Business Review on Management*, New York: Harper & Row, pp. 377-378, 387.

20. G.P. Latham and E.A. Locke, 1979, Goal Setting: Motivational Technique that Works, *Organizational Dynamics* 8, pp. 68–80; J.A. Riedel, D.M. Nebeker, and B.L. Cooper, 1988, The Influence of Monetary Incentives and Goal Choice, Goal Commitment, and Task Performance, *Organizational Behavior and Human Decision Processes* 42, pp. 155–180; A.J. Mento, R.P. Steel, and R.J. Karren, 1987, A Meta-Analytic Study of the Effects of Goal Setting on Task Performance, *Organizational Behavior and Human Decision Processes* 39, pp. 52–83; G.P. Latham and G.A. Yukl, 1975, A Review of Research on the Application of Goal Setting in Organizations, *Academy of Management Journal*, pp. 824–845; and also J.B. Miner, 1980, *Theories of Organizational Behavior*, Hinsdale, IL: Dryden Press, pp. 168–200.

21. Victor H. Vroom. 1964. *Work and Motivation*. New York: John Wiley.

22. L.W. Porter and E.E. Lawler. 1968. *Managerial Attitudes and Performance*. Homewood, IL: Richard D. Irwin, Inc.

23. B.F. Skinner. 1969. *Contingencies of Reinforcement*. New York: Appleton-Century, Crofts.

24. J. Stacey Adams, 1965, Inequity in Social Exchanges, In *Advances in Experimental Social Psychology 2*, ed. Leonard Berkowitz, pp. 267–300, New York: Academic Press; J.S. Adams, 1963, Toward an Understanding of Inequity, *Journal of Abnormal and Social Psychology* 67: pp. 422–436; also see R.C. Huseman, J.D. Hatfield, and E.A. Miles, 1987, A New Perspective on Equity Theory: The Equity Sensitivity Construct, *Academy of Management Review* 12: pp. 222–234.

25. Charles L. Buck, Jr. Managing the Most Valuable Resource: People. In *A Decade of Project Management: Selected Readings from the Project Management Quarterly*, 1970–1980, eds. John R. Adams and Nicki S. Kirchof, pp. 92–95, Drexel Hill, PA; Project Management Institute.

246

26. Dennis P. Slevin and Jeffrey K. Pinto. 1988. Leadership, Motivation and the Project Manager. In *The Project Management Handbook*, eds. David I. Cleland and William R. King, pp. 756–769, New York: Van Nostrand Reinhold.

27. John B. Miner. 1974. *The Human Constraint*. The Bureau of National Affairs, Inc., Washington, DC.

28. David C. McClelland and David H. Burnham. 1976. Power is the Great Motivator, *Harvard Business Review* (March–April).

29. Vijay K. Verma, 1993–94, Workshops on Human Resource Management presented at the Annual Seminar/Symposium of Project Management Institute, San Diego, CA and Vancouver, BC, Canada, respectively; and Frederick Herzberg. 1968. One More Time: How Do You Motivate Employees?, *Harvard Business Review* 46 (1): pp. 53–62.

30. Dean R. Spitzer. 1980. Thirty Ways to Motivate Employees to Perform Better. *Training* (March): pp. 51–52, 55–56.

31. Thomas J. Peters and Robert H. Waterman, Jr. 1981. *In Search of Excellence*. New York: Warner Books, pp. 241–242.

32. Laurie A. Broedling, 1975, Relationship of Internal-External Control to Work Motivation and Performance in an Expectancy Model, *Journal of Applied Psychology* (February): pp. 65–70; and Terry L. Lied and Robert D. Pritchard, 1976, Relationships Between Personality Variables and Components of the Expectancy-Valence Model, *Journal of Applied Psychology* (August): pp. 463–467.

33. David W. Belcher and Thomas J. Atchison, 1970, Equity Theory and Compensation Policy, *Personnel Administration* 33, No. 3: pp. 22–33; and Thomas J. Atchison and David W. Belcher, 1971, Equity Rewards and Compensation Administration, *Personnel Administration* 34, No. 2: pp. 32–36.

Chapter 3

1. Paul C. Dinsmore, 1990. *Human Factors in Project Management, Revised Edition*. New York: AMACOM, pp. 149–166.

2. Adapted from M. Williams, 1987, How I Learned to Stop Worrying and Love Negotiating, *Inc. Magazine* (September): p. 132.

3. David W. Johnson and Roger T. Johnson. 1991. *Teaching Students to be Peacemakers*. Edina, MN: Interaction Book Company, pp. 3.1–3.8.

4. S. Schmidt and T. Kochan. 1972. Conflict: Toward Conceptual Clarity. *Administrative Science Quarterly* 17: pp. 359–370.

5. John R. Adams and Nicki S. Kirchof. 1982. *Conflict Management for Project Managers*. Drexel Hill, PA: Project Management Institute, pp. 5–42.

6. This section is adapted from Stephen P. Robbins, 1974, *Managing Organizational Conflict: A Nontraditional Approach*, Englewood Cliffs, NJ: Prentice-Hall, pp. 11–25; and Stephen P. Robbins, 1979, *Organizational Behavior*, Englewood Cliffs, NJ: Prentice-Hall, p. 289; and Stephen P. Robbins and Robin Stuart-Kotze, 1986, *Management: Concepts and Practices, Canadian Edition*, Toronto, ON: Prentice-Hall Canada Inc., p. 483.

7. This section is based on Hellriegel, Slocum, and Woodman, *Organizational Behavior, Sixth Edition*, pp. 464–492.

8. Alan C. Filley, 1975, *Interpersonal Conflict Resolution*, Glenview, IL: Scott, Foresman and Company, pp. 4–7; and also Kezsbom, Schilling, and Edward, *Dynamic Project Management: A Practical Guide for Managers and Engineers*, pp. 211–215.

9. Stephen P. Robbins and Robin Stuart-Kotze. 1986. *Management: Concepts and Practices, Canadian Edition*. Toronto, ON: Prentice-Hall Canada Inc., pp. 482–492.

10. Richard E. Walton and John M. Dutton. 1969. The Management of Interdepartmental Conflict: A Model and Review. *Administrative Science Quarterly* (March): pp. 73–84.

11. Roland G. Corwin. 1969. Patterns of Organizational Conflict. *Administrative Science Quarterly* (December): pp. 507–520.

12. Baker and Baker, *On Time/On Budget: A Step by Step Guide for Managing Any Project*, pp. 221–233.

13. Hans J. Thamhain and David L. Wilemon, 1975, Conflict Management in Project Life Cycles, *Sloan Management Review* 12, No. 3: pp. 31–50; as quoted in Kerzner, *Project Management: A Systems Approach to Planning, Scheduling and Controlling*, pp. 253–264; and Thamhain and Wilemon, Conflict Management in Project-Oriented Work Environments, *Proceedings of the 1974 Project Management Institute Seminar/Symposium*, p. 88.

14. Kerzner, *Project Management: A Systems Approach to Planning, Scheduling and Controlling*, pp. 415–424.

15. Eschman and Lee. 1977. Conflict in Civilian and Air Force Program/Project Organizations. *A Comparative Study* (September) LSSR 3–77B, A047230: p. 168.

16. Peter A. Stoycheff. 1980. Conflict in the Management of Education, Business and Military Projects: A Comparative Study: Unpublished Ph.D Dissertation. Ohio State University: p. 1.

17. B. Posner. 1986. What's All the Fighting About? Conflict in Project Management. *IEEE Transactions on Engineering Management*, EM–33, No. 4 (November): pp. 207–211.

18. Kezsbom, Schilling, and Edward, *Dynamic Project Management: A Practical Guide for Managers and Engineers*, pp. 211–237.

Chapter 4

1. Kenneth W. Thomas and Warren H. Schmidt. 1976. A Survey of Managerial Interests with Respect to Conflict. *Academy of Management Journal* (June): pp. 315–18.

2. J. Graves. 1978. Successful Management and Organizational Mugging. In *New Direction in Human Resource Management*, ed. J. Papp. Englewood Cliffs, NJ: Prentice-Hall.

3. D. Tjosvold. 1991. *The Conflict-Positive Organization: Stimulate Diversity and Create Unity*. Reading, MA: Addison-Wesley.

4. M. Afzalur Rahim. 1985. A Strategy for Managing Conflict in Complex Organizations. *Human Relations* 38: pp. 81–89.

5. Graham T. Allison, 1971, *Essence of Decision*, Boston, MA: Little, Brown; and Irving L. Janis, 1973, *Victims of Groupthink*, Boston, MA, Houghton Mifflin Co.

6. Stephen P. Robbins. 1978. Conflict Management and Conflict Resolution are not Synonymous Terms. *California Management Review* (Winter): p. 71.

7. The techniques discussed here are based on those described in S. Robbins, 1974, *Managing Organizational Conflict: A Non-Traditional Approach*, pp. 78–89.

8. R.A. Coser and C.R. Schwenk. 1990. Agreement and Thinking Alike: Ingredients for Poor Decisions. *Academy of Management Executive* No. 4 (February): pp. 69–74.

9. Frederick A. Starke and Robert W. Sexty. 1992. *Contemporary Management in Canada*. Scarborough, ON: Prentice-Hall Canada Inc., pp. 471–481.

10. D.F. Womack, 1988, Assessing the Thomas-Kilman Conflict Mode Survey, *Management Communication Quarterly* 1: pp. 321–349; K.W. Thomas, 1988, The Conflict Handling Modes: Toward More Precise Theory, *Management Communication Quarterly* 1: pp. 430–436.

11. Robert R. Blake and Jane S. Mouton, 1964, *The Managerial Grid*. Houston, TX: Gulf Publishing; and application by Hans J. Thamhain and David L. Wilemon, 1975, Conflict Management in Project Life Cycles, *Sloan Management Review* 16, No. 3 (Spring): pp. 31–50.

12. Baker and Baker, *On Time/On Budget: A Step by Step Guide for Managing any Project*, pp. 221–233.

13. Hans J. Thamhain and David L. Wilemon, 1975, Conflict Management in Project Life Cycles, *Sloan Management Review* 16, No. 3: pp. 31–50; Hans J. Thamhain and David L. Wilemon, 1974, Conflict Management in Project-Oriented Work Environments, *Proceedings of the Annual Seminar/Symposium*, Drexel Hill, PA: Project Management Institute, p. 88; and also Adams and Kirchof, *Conflict Management for Project Managers*, pp. 5–42.

14. Kenneth Thomas. 1976. Conflict and Conflict Management. In *Handbook of Industrial and Organizational Psychology*, ed. Marvin D. Dunnette, p. 900, Chicago, IL: Rand McNally.

15. Alan C. Filley. 1975. *Interpersonal Conflict Resolution*. Glenview, IL: Scott, Foresman and Company, pp. 4–7, 51–52.

16. Adams and Kirchof, *Conflict Management for Project Managers*, pp. 5–42.

17. Ruth Sizemore House. 1988. *The Human Side of Project Management*. Reading, MA: Addison-Wesley Publishing Company Inc., pp. 123–182.
18. William Schutz. 1958. The Interpersonal Underworld, *Harvard Business Review* (July–August): pp. 123-135.
19. R.E. Hill. 1977. Managing Interpersonal Conflict in Project Teams, *Sloan Management Review, 18 (2)* (Winter): pp. 45–61.
20. Peter Block. 1981. *Flawless Consulting*. Austin, TX: Learning Concepts, p. 69.
21. Dinsmore, *Human Factors in Project Management*, pp. 149–166.

Chapter 5
1. Roger Fisher and William Ury. 1991. *Getting to Yes: Negotiating Agreement Without Giving In, Second Edition*. New York: Penguin Books, pp. XVII–XIX, 3–15.
2. Kezsbom, Schilling, and Edward, *Dynamic Project Management: A Practical Guide for Managers and Engineers*, pp. 254–260.
3. C.E. Leslie. 1984. Negotiating in Matrix Management Systems. In *Matrix Management Handbook*, ed. David I. Cleland. New York: Van Nostrand Reinhold.
4. Project Management Institute. 1994. *A Guide to the Project Management Body of Knowledge (Exposure Draft)*. Upper Darby, PA: Project Management Institute, p. 11.
5. Cleland, *Project Management: Strategic Design and Implementation*, pp. 243–245.
6. V. Terpstra. 1972. *International Marketing*. Hinsdale, IL: Dryden, p. 83.
7. M. Dean Martin. 1981. The Negotiation Differential for International Project Management. *Proceedings of Annual Seminar/Symposium*. Drexel Hill, PA: Project Management Institute. Also published in *The AMA Handbook of Project Management*, 1993, Paul C. Dinsmore, ed., New York: AMACOM, pp. 449–456.
8. Geert Hofstede. 1993. *Cultures and Organizations: Software of the Mind*. New York: McGraw-Hill, p 5.
9. Fred Luthan and Richard Hodgetts. 1991. *International Management*. New York: McGraw-Hill, p. 35.
10. V. Terpstra. 1978. *The Cultural Environment of International Business*. Dallas, TX: Southwestern Publishing, p. 176.
11. Terpstra, *The Cultural Environment of International Business*, p. 2.
12. G.E. Miracle and G.S. Albaum. 1970. *International Marketing Management*. Homewood, IL: Richard D. Irwin, pp. 8–9.
13. E.T. Hall. 1959. *The Silent Language*. Greenwich, LT: Fawcett, pp. 128–145.
14. P.A. Iseman. 1978. The Arabian Ethos. *Harper's* (February): pp. 43–44.
15. L.T. Wells, Jr. 1977. Negotiating With Third World Governments, *Harvard Business Review 55, No. 1* (January–February): pp. 72–80.
16. C.L. Karrass, 1970, The Negotiation Game,. New York: World Publishing; and also N.W. Beckmann, 1977, *Negotiation*, Lexington, MA: D.C. Heath,
17. J.A. Hall et al. 1978. Decoding Wordless Messages, *Human Nature* 1, No. 5 (May): pp. 70–72.
18. E.T. Hall. 1979. Show You're Tough, Then Ask the Price. *Psychology Today* (October): p. 116.
19. R. Plutchik. 1980. A Language for the Emotions. *Psychology Today* (February): p. 71.
20. Kerzner, *Project Management: A Systems Approach to Planning, Scheduling and Controlling*, p. 168.
21. T.A. Warschaw. 1980. *Winning by Negotiation*. New York: McGraw-Hill, p. 266.
22. D.W. Johnson and F. Johnson. 1991. *Joining Together: Group Theory and Group Skills, Fourth Edition*. Englewood Cliffs, NJ: Prentice-Hall.
23. Hellreigel, Slocum, Woodman, *Organizational Behavior, Sixth Edition*, pp. 464–492.
24. R.E. Walton and R.B. McKersie, 1965, *A Behavioral Theory of Labour Negotiations*, New York: McGraw-Hill; W.N. Cooke, 1990, *Labour-Management Cooperation: New Partnerships or Going in Circles*. Kalamazoo, MI: W.E. Upjohn Institute.

25. The presentation of the Savage, Blair and Sorenson (SBS) model of negotiations is based on G.T. Savage, J.D. Blair and R.L. Sorenson, 1989, Consider Both Relationships and Substance When Negotiating Strategically, *Academy of Management Executive* (February) pp. 37–47; also see J.D. Blair, G.T. Savage and C.J.A. Whitehead, 1989, Strategic Approach for Negotiating with Hospital Stakeholders, *Health Care Management Review* 14 (1): pp. 13–23; and J.D. Blair and M.D. Fottler, 1990, *Challenge in Health Care Management*. San Francisco, CA: Jossey-Bass, pp. 172–217.

26. V.A. Kremenyuk (Ed.). 1991. *International Negotiation: Analysis, Approaches, Issues*. San Francisco, CA: Jossey-Bass.

27. M.A. Neale and G.B. Northcraft. 1991. *Behavioral Negotiation Theory: A Framework for Conceptualizing Dyadic Bargaining*. In Research in Organizational Behavior 13, ed. B.M. Staw, pp. 147–190, Greenwich, CT: JAI Press.

28. L. Thompson and R. Hastie. 1990. Social Perception in Negotiation, *Organizational Behavior and Human Decision Processes* 47: pp. 98–123.

29. R.P. Nielson. 1989. Generic Win-Win Negotiating Solutions, *Long Range Planning* 22 (5): pp. 137–143.

30. G. Yukl and C.M. Falbe. 1990. Influence Tactics and Objectives in Upward, Downward and Lateral Influence Attempts, *Journal of Applied Psychology* 75: pp. 132–140.

31. M.A. Neale and M.H. Bazerman. 1991. *Cognition and Rationality in Negotiation*. New York: Free Press.

32. C. Honeyman, 1990, On Evaluating Mediators, *Negotiation Journal* (January): pp. 23–36; S. Stratek, 1990, Grievance Mediation: Does it Really Work? *Negotiation Journal* (July) pp. 269–280.

33. M.P. Rowe, 1990, Helping People Help Themselves: An ADR Option for Interpersonal Conflict, *Negotiation Journal* (July) pp. 239–248; D.E. Conlon and P.M. Fasolo, 1990, Influence of Speed of Third-Party Intervention and Outcome on Negotiator and Constituent Fairness Judgments, *Academy of Management Journal* 33: pp. 833–846.

34. R.R. Blake H.A. Shepard, and J.S. Mouton, 1964, *Managing Intergroup Conflict in Industry*, Houston, TX: Gulf; and R.J. Fisher, 1983, Third Party Consultation as a Method of Inftergroup Conflict Resolution, *Journal of Conflict Resolution* 27: pp. 301–334.

35. Based upon Fisher and Ury, *Getting to Yes: Negotiating Agreement without Giving In*, pp. 4–94, 189–193.

Chapter 6

1. T.A. Stuart. 1990. Do You Push Your People Too Hard? *Fortune* (October): pp. 121–128.

2. Adapted from Randall S. Schuler. 1980. Definition and Conceptualization of Stress in Organizations. *Organizational Behavior and Human Performance* (April): pp. 189–191.

3. James C. Quick and D. Jonathan Quick. 1984. *Organizational Stress and Preventive Management*. New York: McGraw-Hill.

4. T. Cox, 1978, *Stress*,Baltimore, MD: University Park Press; and also see R.H. Rosenman et al., 1964, A Predictive Study of Coronary Heart Disease, *Journal of the American Medical Association*: pp. 15–22.

5. David Leidl. 1990. Relaxation 101. *BC Business* (October): p 13.

6. Han Selye. 1974. *Stress Without Distress*. Philadelphia, PA: Lippincott.

7. David R. Frew. 1977. *Management of Stress*. Chicago, IL: Nelson-Hall, Inc.

8. Mortimer H. Appley and Richard Turnbull. 1967. *Psychological Stress*. New York: Appleton-Century-Crofts.

9. Martin Shaffer. 1982. *Life After Stress*. New York: Plenum Press, Division Plenum Publishing Company.

10. Hans Selye. 1956. *The Stress of Life*. New York: McGraw-Hill.

11. Paul C. Dinsmore, Martin D. Martin, and Gary T. Huettel. 1985. *The Project Manager's Work Environment: Coping with Time and Stress*. Drexel Hill, PA: Project Management Institute, pp. 30–41.

250

12. Starke and Sexty, *Contemporary Management in Canada*, pp. 492–499.
13. Daniel Katz and Robert L. Khan. 1978. *The Social Psychology of Organizations*. New York: Wiley.
14. Cox, *Stress*.
15. Hellriegel, Slocum, Woodman, *Organizational Behavior, Sixth Edition*, pp. 280–304.
16. S. Cohen and G.M. Williamson, 1991, Stress and Infectious Disease in Humans, *Psychological Bulletin* 109: pp. 5–24; S. Maes, C.D. Spielberger, P.B. Defares, and I.G. Sarason, eds), 1988, *Topics in Health Psychology*, Chichester, England: Wiley; J.C. Quick and J.D. Quick, 1984, *Organizational Stress and Preventive Management*, New York: McGraw-Hill.
17. D.S. Allen, 1990, Less Stress, Less Litigation, *Personnel* (January): pp. 32–35; D. Hollis and J. Goodson, 1989, Stress: The Legal and Organizational Implications, *Employee Responsibilities and Rights Journal* 2, pp. 255–262.
18. S.A. Joure, J.S. Leon, D.B. Simpson, C.H. Holley, and R.L. Frye. 1989. Stress: The Pressure Cooker of Work. *Personnel Administrator* (March): pp. 92–95.
19. See, for example, C.R. Greer, and M.A.D. Castro, 1986, The Relationship between Perceived Unit Effectiveness and Occupational Stress: The Case of Purchasing Agents, *Journal of Applied Behavioral Science* 22: pp. 159–175; and S.J. Motowidlo, J.S. Packard, and M.R. Manning, 1986, Occupational Stress: Its Causes and Consequences for Job Performance. *Journal of Applied Psychology* 71: pp. 618–629.
20. Jeannie Gaines and John M. Jermier. 1983. Emotional Exhaustion in a High Stress Organization, *Academy of Management Journal* 26: pp. 567–586.
21. S.E. Jackson, R.L. Schwab, and R.S. Schuler, 1986, Toward an Understanding of the Burnout Phenomenon, *Journal of Applied Psychology* 71: pp. 630–640; and R.T. Lee and B.E. Ashforth, 1990, On the Meaning of Maslach's Three Dimensions of Burnout, *Journal of Applied Psychology* 75: pp. 743–747.
22. Harry Levinson. 1981. When Executives Burn Out. *Harvard Business Review*: p. 76.
23. See, for example, R.J. Burke, 1987, Burnout in Police Work, *Group & Organization Studies* 12: pp. 174–188; D.W. Russell, E. Altmaier, and D. Van Velzen, 1987, Job-Related Stress, Social Support, and Burnout among Classroom Teachers, *Journal of Applied Psychology* 72: pp. 269–274.
24. O.I. Niehouse. 1984. Controlling Burnout: A Leadership Guide for Managers. *Business Horizons* (July–August): pp. 81–82.
25. D.L. Nelson and C. Sutton. 1990. Chronic Work Stress and Coping: A Longitudinal Study and Suggested New Directions. *Academy of Management Journal* 33: pp. 859–869.
26. C.R. Anderson, D. Hellriegel, and J.E. Slocum, Jr. 1977. Managerial Response to Environmentally Induced Stress. *Academy of Management Journal* 20: pp. 260–272.
27. Hellriegel, Slocum, Woodman, *Organizational Behavior, Sixth Edition*, pp. 82–84.
28. L.W. Morris, 1979, *Extroversion and Introversion: An Interactive Perspective*, New York: Hemisphere, p. 8; B. Engler, 1991, *Personality Theories, Third Edition*, Boston, MA: Houghton Mifflin, pp. 329–334; and H.J. Eysenck, 1982, *Personality, Genetics, and Behavior*. New York: Prager, pp. 161–197.
29. H.J. Eysenck, 1988, Health's Character, *Psychology Today* (December): pp. 28–35; H.S. Friedman and S. Booth-Kewley, 1987, Personality, Type A Behavior and Coronary Heart Disease: The Role of Emotional Expression, *Journal of Personality and Social Psychology* 53: pp. 783–792; M. Friedman and R. Rosenman, 1974, *Type A Behavior and Your Heart*. New York: Knopf; Muhammad Jamal, 1985, Type A Behavior and Job Performance: Some Suggested Findings, *Journal of Human Stress* (Summer): pp. 60–68; and D.C. Ganster, J. Schaubroeck, W.E. Sime, and B.T. Mayes, 1991, The Nomological Validity of the Type A Personality Among Employed Adults, *Journal of Applied Psychology* 76: 143–168.
30. R.A. Baron and D. Byrne. 1991. *Social Psychology: Understanding Human Interaction, Sixth Edition*. Boston, MA: Allyn and Bacon, p. 606.

31. Baron and Byrne, *Social Psychology*, pp. 574–575; R.J. Contrada, 1989, Type A Behavior, Personality Hardiness, and Cardiovascular Responses to Stress, *Journal of Personality and Social Psychology* 57: pp. 895–903; and D.L. Roth, D.J. Wiebe, R.B. Fillingham, and K.A. Shay, 1989, Life Events, Fitness, Hardiness, and Health: A Simultaneous Analysis of Proposed Stress-Resistance Effects, *Journal of Personality and Social Psychology* 57, pp. 136–142; and Contrada,R et al, 1991, the Social Psychology of Health, in *Social Psychology*, R.M. Baron et al, eds., Fort Worth, TX: Holt, Rinehart and Winston. pp. 620-627.

32. A.J. Bernstein and S.C. Rozen. 1989. Dinosaur Brains and Managing Stress, *Nation's Business* (November): pp. 46–47.

33. R.S. Eliot and D.L. Breo. 1984. *Is It Worth Dying for?* Bantam Books Inc.

34. D.L. Nelson, J.C. Quick, and J.D. Quick. 1989. Corporate Warfare: Preventing Combat Stress and Battle Fatigue, *Organizational Dynamics* (Summer): pp. 65–79.

35. J.M. Ivancevich, M.T. Matteson, S.M. Freedman, and J.S. Phillips. 1990. Stress Management Interventions, *American Psychologist* 45: pp. 252–261.

36. D.L. Gebhardt and C.E. Crump. 1990. Employee Fitness and Wellness Programs in the Workplace, *American Psychologist* 45: pp. 262–272. For company examples see M. Roberts and T.J. Harris, 1989, Wellness at Work, *Psychology Today* (May): pp. 54–58.

37. Company examples in this section are adapted from M. Roberts and T.J. Harris, 1989, Wellness at Work, *Psychology Today* (May): pp. 54-58.

38. T.A. Beehr and R.S. Bhagat, 1985, *Human Stress and Cognition in Organizations: An Integrated Perspective*, New York: Wiley; C. Lee, S.J. Ashford, and P. Bobko, 1990, Interactive Effects of Type A Behavior and Perceived Control on Worker Performance, Job Satisfaction, and Somatic Complaints, *Academy of Management Journal* 33: pp. 870–881; and L.E. Tetrick and J.M. La Rocco, 1987, Understanding Prediction and Control as Moderators of the Relationships between Perceived Stress, Satisfaction, and Psychological Well-Being, *Journal of Applied Psychology* 72: pp. 538–543.

39. John M. Ivancevich and Michael T. Matteson. 1978. Organizations and Coronary Heart Disease: The Stress Connection, *Management Review* 67 (October): pp. 14–19.

40. Ken Blanchard. 1983. *One Minute Manager*. New York: Berkeley Books.

41. Fred Luthans. 1988. *Organizational Behavior*. New York: McGraw-Hill, pp. 146–148.

42. Donald B. Miller. 1978. Career Planning and Management in Organizations, *S.A.M. Advanced Management Journal* 43 (Spring): pp. 33–43.

43. *Promotional Catalogue 25*, Great Performance, Inc., p. 30.

44. Michael Castleman. 1992. How the Experts Cope with Stress. *Reader's Digest* (September) pp. 48–50.

45. Jim Temme. 1993. *Productivity Power*. Mission, KS: Skillpath Publications, Inc., pp. 161-169.

Chapter 7

1. Richard A. Selg. 1993. Essential Leadership Skills for Project Managers. *Proceedings of PMI '93 Annual Seminar/Symposium*. Upper Darby, PA: Project Management Institute, pp. 282–289.

2. Fred E. Fiedler. 1968. *A Theory of Leadership Effectiveness*. New York: McGraw-Hill, p. 8.

3. Peter Drucker. 1989. Leadership: More Doing Than Dash. *Wall Street Journal* (January 6).

4. Arthur Jago. 1982. Leadership: Perspectives in Theory and Research. *Management Science 28, No. 3* (March): Institute of Management Sciences.

5. J.M. Burns. 1982. *Leadership*. New York: Harper and Row, p. 2.

6. Gary A. Yukl. 1981. *Leadership in Organizations*. Englewood Cliffs, NJ: Prentice-Hall, pp. 2–3, 70, 121–125.

7. W. Bennis and B. Nanus. 1985. *Leaders: The Strategies for Taking Charge*. New York: Harper and Row: p. 87.

8. Plunkett, *Supervision: The Direction of People at Work*, pp. 212–225.

9. Don Hellriegel, John W. Slocum, Jr., and Richard W. Woodman. 1992. *Organizational Behavior, Sixth Edition*. St. Paul, MN: West Publishing Company, pp. 383–419.

Human Resource Skills for the Project Manager

10. R.M. Stogdill, 1974, *Handbook of Leadership: A Survey of the Literature*, New York: Free Press; and C.A. Schriesheim and S. Kerr, 1977, Theories and Measures of Leadership: A Critical Appraisal, In *Leadership: The Cutting Edge*, eds. J.G. Hunt and L.L. Larson Carbondale, pp. 9–45, IL: Southern Illinois University Press.

11. A. Zalesnik. 1990. The Leadership Gap. *Academy of Management Executives* 4: pp. 7–22.

12. J.C. McElroy, 1982, A Typology of Attribution Leadership Research, *Academy of Management Review* 7: pp. 413–417; J.R. Meindl and S.B. Ehrlich, 1987, The Romance of Leadership and the Evaluation of Organizational Performance, *Academy of Management Journal* 30:, pp. 91–109; S.M. Puffer and J.B. Weintrop, 1991, Corporate Performance and CEO Turnover: A Comparison of Performance Indicators, *Administrative Science Quarterly 36*, pp. 1–19.

13. J.M. Howell, 1988, *In Two Faces of Charisma: Socialized and Personalized Leadership in Organization*, In *Charismatic Leadership: The Elusive Factor in Organizational Effectiveness*, eds. J.A. Conger and R.N. Kanungo, pp. 213–236, San Francisco, CA: Jossey-Bass; J.A. Conger and R.N. Kanungo, 1988, Behavioral Dimensions of Charismatic Leadership, In *Charismatic Leadership*, eds. Conger and Kanungo, pp. 79–97, San Francisco, CA: Jossey-Bass.

14. B.M. Bass, 1990, From Transactional to Transformational Leadership: Learning to Share the Vision, *Organizational Dynamics* (Winter): pp. 19–31; J.M. Kouzes and B.Z. Posner, 1987, *The Leadership Challenge: How to get Extraordinary Things Done in Organizations*, San Francisco, CA: Jossey-Bass; N. Tichy and M. Devanna, 1986, *Transformational Leadership*. New York: John Wiley & Sons; J.A. Conger, 1991, Inspiring Others: The Language of Leadership, *Academy of Management Executives 5*: pp. 31–45; J.R. Meindl. 1990. On Leadership: Alternative to Conventional Wisdom, In *Research in Organizational Behavior 12*, eds. B.M. Staw and L.L. Cummings, pp. 159–204, Greenwich, CT: JAI Press.

15. F.E. Fiedler. 1967. *A Theory of Leadership*. New York: McGraw-Hill. Also, F.E. Fiedler and M.M. Chemers, 1976, *Leadership and Effective Management*, Greenview, IL: Scott Foresman.

16. P. Hersey and K.H. Blanchard. 1988. *Management of Organizational Behavior, Fifth Edition*. Englewood Cliffs, NJ: Prentice-Hall.

17. R.J. House and T.R. Mitchell. 1974. Path-Goal Theory of Leadership, *Journal of Contemporary Business* (Autumn): pp. 81–98.

18. V.H. Vroom and A.G. Jago. 1988. *The New Leadership*. Englewood Cliffs, NJ: Prentice-Hall.

19. Vijay K. Verma and R. M. Wideman. 1994. Project Manager to Project Leader? and the Rocky Road Between. *Proceedings of the 25th Annual Seminar/Symposium*. Upper Darby, PA: Project Management Institute, pp. 627–633.

20. J.D. Batten, 1989, *Tough-Minded Leadership*, New York: AMACOM, p. 35; W. Bennis, 1989, *On Becoming a Leader*, Reading, MA: Addison-Wesley; S.R. Covey, 1991, *Principle-Centred Leadership*, Summit Books; Robert L. Dilenschneider, 1991, *A Briefing for Leaders*. Harper Business, p. 13; J.W. McLean and W. Weitzel, 1991, *Leadership, Magic, Myth or Method?*, New York: AMACOM, p. 90; and Kimball Fisher, 1993, *Leading Self-Directed Work Teams: A Guide to Developing New Team Leadership*, New York: McGraw-Hill.

21. J. D. Batten. 1991. *Tough-Minded Leadership*. AMACOM, pp. 35, 134.

22. J.W. McLean and W. Weitzel. 1991. *Leadership: Magic, Myth or Method*. AMACOM, p. 90.

23. Jeffrey K. Pinto. 1994. *Successful Information System Implementation: The Human Side*. Upper Darby, PA: Project Management Institute, p. 159.

24. Joseph L. Massey and John Douglas. *Managing: A Contemporary Introduction*. Englewood Cliffs, NJ: Prentice-Hall, pp. 372–373.

25. Abraham Zalesnik. 1977. Managers and Leaders: Are They Different? *Harvard Business Review* (May/June): pp. 67–78.

26. Warren Bennis. 1984. Good Managers and Good Leaders. *Across the Board* (October): p. 8.

27. Keith Davis. 1967. *Human Relations at Work, Third Edition*. New York: McGraw-Hill Book Company, pp. 96–97.

28. Adapted from P. Hersey and K. Blanchard. 1988. *Management of Organizational Behavior: Utilizing Human Resources, Fifth Edition*. Englewood Cliffs, NJ: Prentice-Hall.

29. G. Robinson. 1992. Dinner meeting presentation, West Coast B.C. Chapter.

30. Blanchard, *The One Minute Manager*.

31. Barry F. Posner. 1987. What it Takes to Be a Good Project Manager, *Project Management Journal* (March): p. 53.

32. Cleland, *Project Management: Strategic Design and Implementation*, pp. 254–276.

33. 1993. PM 101: The Project Manager: A Leader. *PM Network* (December): pp. 28–31.

34. Adapted from Robert B. Youker. 1990. *Power and Politics in Project Management*. Workshop presented at the INTERNET Conference in Vienna, Austria (July); and later also published in 1991 *PM Network* (May): pp. 36–40.

35. J.P. Kotter. 1985. *Power and Influence*. New York: Free Press.

36. T.R. Mitchell. 1978. *People in Organizations: Understanding Their Behaviors*. New York: McGraw-Hill.

37. William E. Halal. 1984. The Legitimacy Cycle. In *Power, Politics and Organizations*, eds. A. Kakabadse and C. Parker, Chapter 3, New York: John Wiley and Sons.

38. R.M. Stogdill. 1974. *Handbook of Leadership: A Survey of the Literature*. New York: Free Press.

39. J.R.P. French, Jr. and B. Raven, 1960, The Bases of Social Power, In *Group Dynamics: Research and Theory, Second Edition*, eds. D. Cartwright and A. Zander, pp. 607–623, New York: Harper and Row; C.A. Schriesheim, T.R. Hinkin, and P.M. Podsakoff, 1991, Can Ipsative and Single-Item Measures Produce Erroneous Results in Field Studies of French and Raven's Five Bases of Power? *Journal of Applied Psychology* 76: pp. 106–114.

40. D. Wilemon and G. Gemmill. 1970. The Power Spectrum in Project Management, *Sloan Management Review* 12, No. 1: pp. 15–26.

41. Linn C. Stuckenbruck. 1988. Integration: The Essential Function of Project Management. In *Project Management Handbook, Second Edition*, eds. David I. Cleland and William L. King, pp. 65–66, New York: Van Nostrand Reinhold.

42. Stanley M. Davis. 1974. Two Models of Organization: Unity of Command Versus Balance of Power, *Sloan Management Review* (Fall): pp. 29–40.

43. Adapted from Paul C. Dinsmore. 1989. Power and Politics in Project Management. *PM Network* (April) Drexel Hill, PA. Published as Power and Politics in Project Management: Upper-Echelon versus Conventional Project Management, in *The AMA Handbook of Project Management*, ed. Paul C. Dinsmore, pp. 237–240, New York: AMACOM.

Self–Assessment Exercise A

Communication Styles

Read both statements and choose the one that is most like you. Circle A or B. Even if you think they are both like you, choose the one that is *most* like you.

1. A. I like all the evidence (facts, details, examples, expected outcomes, etc.) presented first in an orderly fashion.
    B. I like the broad and general issues presented first, then the detail.
2. A. I prefer brief and concise information.
    B. I am persuaded by enthusiastic presentations.
3. A. I pay attention to my gut instinct, not just logical analysis.
    B. I am influenced by logical reasoning.
4. A. I like novel and unusual suggestions.
    B. I want practical and realistic applications.
5. A. I am persuaded by evidence (stuff that can be verified) to make decisions.
    B. I like to take an idea and run with it.
6. A. I want to know the points of agreement first, then the points of contention.
    B. I like the goals and objectives presented first, then the detail.
7. A. I want to know how people will feel about each alternative.
    B. I want to know the pros and cons of each alternative.

Scoring key:

Count the number of each type you circled. Whatever you circled most of is your preferred communication style.

1.	a.	CS	b.	AR
2.	a.	AS	b.	CR
3.	a.	CS	b.	AS
4.	a.	AR	b.	CS/CR
5.	a.	CS	b.	AR
6.	a.	CR	b.	AS
7.	a.	CR	b.	AS

CS = Concrete/Sequential
AS = Abstract/Sequential
CR = Concrete/Random
AR = Abstract/Random
(See Chapter 1 for a full explanation of these communication styles.)

Source: Based on materials from an interpersonal communication skills workbook used in a seminar presented by Career Track, Inc. of Boulder, Colo.

Self–Assessment Exercise B

Motivation to Manage

Circle the number for each item that represents your best estimate of your current level.

	Well Below Average				Average				Well Above Average	
Favorable attitude toward authority	0	1	3	4	5	6	7	8	9	10
Desire to compete	0	1	3	4	5	6	7	8	9	10
Assertive motivation	0	1	3	4	5	6	7	8	9	10
Desire to exercise power	0	1	3	4	5	6	7	8	9	10
Desire for a distinctive position	0	1	3	4	5	6	7	8	9	10
A sense of responsibility	0	1	3	4	5	6	7	8	9	10

Now place a check mark next to the number for each item that represents your best estimate of where you would *like* to be. The difference between your desired and actual score for each item is your Motivation to Manage deficit on that factor.

Scoring Key/Action Plan

Record your Motivation to Manage deficit (desired – actual) for each factor below. Then specify appropriate action steps you might take to increase your Motivation to Manage on each factor and remove the deficit.

1. Favorable attitude toward authority   Deficit: _____
   Action Plan: _____
   Probability of Success: _____

2. Desire to compete   Deficit: _____
   Action Plan: _____
   Probability of Success: _____

3. Assertive motivation   Deficit: _____
   Action Plan: _____
   Probability of Success: _____

4. Desire to exercise power   Deficit: _____
   Action Plan: _____
   Probability of Success: _____

5. Desire for a distinctive position   Deficit: _____
   Action Plan: _____
   Probability of Success: _____

6. A sense of responsibility   Deficit: _____
   Action Plan: _____
   Probability of Success: _____

Source: Dennis P. Slevin, Jeffrey K. Pinto. 1988. Leadership, Motivation, and the Project Manager. In the *Project Management Handbook, Second Edition*. New York: Van Nostrand Reinhold, pp. 756–764. Reprinted by permission of the publisher.

Self Assessment Exercise C

Conflict Resolution Style

The proverbs listed below describe some of the different strategies for resolving conflicts. Proverbs state traditional wisdom, and these proverbs reflect traditional wisdom for resolving conflicts. Read each proverb carefull and, using the following scale, indicate how typical each proverb is of your actions in a conflict.

> 5 = very often the way I act in a conflict
> 4 = frequently the way I act in a conflict
> 3 = sometimes the way I act in a conflict
> 2 = seldom the way I act in a conflict
> 1 = never the way I act in a conflict

1. It is easier to refrain than to retreat from a quarrel.
2. If you cannot make a person think as you do, make him or her do as you think.
3. Soft words win hard hearts.
4. You scratch my back, I'll scratch yours.
5. Come now and let us reason together.
6. When two quarrel, the person who keeps silent first is the most praiseworthy.
7. Might overcomes right.
8. Smooth words make smooth ways.
9. Better half a loaf than no bread at all.
10. Truth lies in knowledge, not in majority opinion.
11. He who fights and runs away lives to fight another day.
12. He hath conquered well that hath made his enemies flee.
13. Kill your enemies with kindness.
14. A fair exchange brings no quarrel.
15. No person has the final answer but every person has a piece to contribute.
16. Stay away from people who disagree with you.
17. Fields are won by those who believe in winning.
18. Kind words are worth such and cost little.
19. Tit for tat is fair play.
20. Only the person who will not flee will make others flee.
21. Avoid quarrelsome people as they will only make your life miserable.
22. A person who will not flee will make others flee.
23. Soft words ensure harmony.
24. One gift for another makes good friends.
25. Bring your conflicts into the open and face them directly; only then will the best solution be discovered.
26. The best way of handling conflicts is to avoid them.
27. Put your foot down where you mean to stand.
28. Gentleness will triumph over anger.

29. Getting part of what you want is better than not getting anything at all.
30. Frankness, honesty, and trust will move mountains.
31. There is nothing so important that you have to fight for it.
32. There are two kinds of people in the world, winners and the losers.
33. When one hits you with a stone, hit him or her with a piece of cotton.
34. When both people give in half-way, a fair settlement is achieved.
35. By digging and digging, the truth is discovered.

Scoring Key:

Withdrawing	Forcing	Smoothing	Compromising	Confronting
_____ 1	_____ 2	_____ 3	_____ 4	_____ 5
_____ 6	_____ 7	_____ 8	_____ 9	_____ 10
_____ 11	_____ 12	_____ 13	_____ 14	_____ 15
_____ 16	_____ 17	_____ 18	_____ 19	_____ 20
_____ 21	_____ 22	_____ 23	_____ 24	_____ 25
_____ 26	_____ 27	_____ 28	_____ 29	_____ 30
_____ 31	_____ 32	_____ 33	_____ 34	_____ 35
_____ Total	_____ Total	_____ Total	_____ Total	_____ Total

The higher the total score for each conflict strategy, the more frequently you tend to use that strategy. For a complete explanation of these conflict resolution styles, see Chapter 4.

Source: From David W. Johnson. *Reaching Out: Interpersonal Effectiveness and Self-Actualization.*Copyright 1990. All rights reserved. Reprinted by permission of Allyn & Bacon.

Self Assessment Exercise D

Type A Personality

Choose from the following to answer the questions below:

A. Almost always true   **B. Usually true**   **C. Seldom true**   **D. Never true**

Answer each question according to what is generally true for you:

_____ 1. I do not like to wait for other people to complete their work before I can proceed with my own.

_____ 2. I hate to wait in most lines.

_____ 3. People tell me that I tend to get irritated too easily.

_____ 4. Whenever possible, I try to make activities competitive.

_____ 5. I have a tendency to rush into work that needs to be done before knowing the procedure I will use to complete the job.

_____ 6. Even when I go on vacation, I usually take some work along.

_____ 7. When I make a mistake, it is usually die to the fact that I have rushed into the job before completely planning it through.

_____ 8. I feel guilty for taking time off from work.

_____ 9. People tell me I have a bad temper when it comes to competitive situations.

_____ 10. I tend to lose my temper when I am under a lot of pressure at work.

_____ 11. Whenever possible, I will attempt to complete two or more tasks at once.

_____ 12. I tend to race against the clock.

_____ 13. I have no patience for lateness.

_____ 14. I catch myself rushing when there is no need.

Scoring key:

- *An intense sense of time urgency:* you race against the clock even when there is little reason to. Time urgency is measured by items 1, 2, 8, 12, 13 and 14. Every A or B answer to these six questions scores one point.

  Your Score _____

- *Inappropriate competitiveness and hostility:* you are excessively competitive; you find it hard to do anything just for fun. Aggressive, competitive behavior easily evolves into displays of hostility, even at the slightest provocation. Competitiveness and hostility is reassured by items 3, 4, 9 and 10. Every A or B answer scores one point.

  Your Score _____

- *Polyphasic behavior:* you try to do two or more tasks simultaneously at inappropriate times. Sometimes this keeps you from getting anything completed. This behavior is measured by items 6 and 11. Every A or B answer scores one point.

  Your Score _____

- *Goal directedness without proper planning:* you rush into work without really knowing how to accomplish the desired result. Lack of planning is measured by items 6 and 11. Every A or B response scores one point.

  Your Score _____

  Total score = _____

If your score is 5 or greater, you may possess some basic components of the Type A personality.

Source: Based on the work of G.S. Everly and D.A. Girdano in *The Causes and Curse of Stress in the Job,* Robert J. Brady Co.,1990.

Self–Assessment Exercise E

Leadership Style

Instructions: Respond to each item according to the way you would be most likely to act as the leader of a work group. Circle whether you would be likely to behave in one of the described ways: Always (A); Frequently (F); Occasionally (O); Seldom (S); or Never (N).

If I Were the Leader of a Work Group ...

A F O S N   1. I would most likely act as the spokesperson of the group.

A F O S N   2. I would encourage overtime work.

A F O S N   3. I would allow members complete freedom in their work.

A F O S N   4. I would encourage the use of uniform procedures.

A F O S N   5. I would permit the members to use their own judgment in solving problems.

A F O S N   6. I would stress being ahead of competing groups.

A F O S N   7. I would speak as a representative of the group.

A F O S N   8. I would needle members for greater effort.

A F O S N   9. I would try out my own ideas in the group.

A F O S N   10. I would let the members do their work the way they think best.

A F O S N   11. I would be working hard for a promotion.

A F O S N   12. I would be able to tolerate postponement and uncertainty.

A F O S N   13. I would speak for the group when visitors were present.

A F O S N   14. I would keep the work moving at a rapid pace.

A F O S N   15. I would turn the members loose on a job and let then go to it.

A F O S N   16. I would settle conflicts when they occur in the group.

A F O S N   17. I would get swamped by details.

A F O S N   18. I would represent the group at outside meetings.

A F O S N   19. I would be reluctant to allow the members any freedom of action.

A F O S N   20. I would decide what shall be done and how it shall be done.

A F O S N   21. I would push for increased production.

A F O S N   22. I would let some members have authority that I could keep.

A F O S N   23. Things would usually turn out as I predict.

A F O S N   24. I would allow the group a high degree of initiative.

A F O S N   25. I would assign group members to particular tasks.

A F O S N   26. I would be willing to make changes.

A F O S N   27. I would ask the members to work harder.

A F O S N   28. I would trust the group members to exercise good judgment.

A F O S N   29. I would schedule the work to be done.

A F O S N   30. I would refuse to explain my actions.

A F O S N   31. I would persuade others that my ideas are to their advantage.

A F O S N   32. I would permit the group to set its own pace.

A F O S N   33. I would urge the group to beat its previous record.

A F O S N   34. I would act without consulting the group.

A F O S N   35. I would ask that group members follow standard rules and regulations.

Scoring Key:

To find your leadership style:

1. Circle the item numbers for items 8, 12, 17, 18, 19, 30, 34, and 35.

2. Write a "1" in front of the circled items to which you responded S (seldom) or N (never).

3. Write a "1" in front of the items *not* circled to which you responded A (always) or F (frequently).

4. Circle the "1's" which you have written in front of the following items: 3, 5, 8, 10, 15, 18, 19, 22, 24, 26, 28, 30, 32, 34, and 35.

5. Count the circled "1's". This is your score for concern-for-people.

6. Count the uncircled "1's." This is your concern–for–task.

7. Refer to the diagram below. Find your score for task dimension on the left–hand arrow. Next, move to the right–hand arrow and find your score on the concern–for–people dimension. Draw a straight line that intersects the two scores. The point at which that line crosses the shared leadership arrow indicates your score on that dimension.

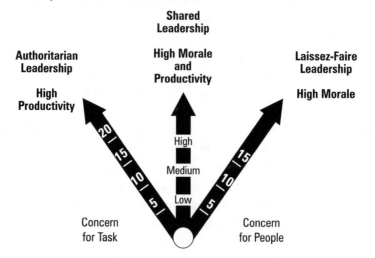

Source: Based on information from *A Handbook of Structural Experiences for Human Relations Training,* Vol. 1, University Associates, Inc., 1974.

Human Resource Skills for the Project Manager

Self Assessment Exercise F

Power Orientation

Statement	Disagree Strongly	Somewhat	Neutral	Agree Somewhat	Strongly
1. The best way to handle people is to tell them what they want to hear.	1	2	3	4	5
2. When you ask someone to do something for you, it is best to give your real reason for wanting it, rather than reasons that might carry more weight.	1	2	3	4	5
3. Anyone who completely trusts anyone else is asking for trouble.	1	2	3	4	5
4. It is hard to get ahead without cutting corners here and there.	1	2	3	4	5
5. It is safest to assume that all people have a vicious streak that will come out when given a chance.	1	2	3	4	5
6. One should take action only when it is morally right.	1	2	3	4	5
7. Most people are basically good and kind.	1	2	3	4	5
8. There is no excuse for lying.	1	2	3	4	5
9. Most people forget the death of their father more easily than the loss of their property.	1	2	3	4	5
10. Generally speaking, people won't work hard unless they're forced to do so.	1	2	3	4	5

Scoring Key:
To obtain your score, add the numbers you have circled for questions 1, 3, 4, 5, 9, and 10. For the other four questions, reverse the numbers you have checked: 5 becomes 1, 4 is 2, 2 is 4, 1 is 5. Total your ten numbers to find your score. The National Opinion Research Center, which used this short form of the scale in a random sample of American adults, found that the national average was 25. The results of research using this test found that people with high power orientation tend to be in professions that emphasize the control and manipulation of individuals — for example, managers, lawyers, psychiatrists, and behavioral scientists.

Source: Based on the work of R. Christie and F. L. Geis in *Studies in Machiavellianism*, Academic Press, 1970.

Index

3-4-5 rule, in writing 22

ABC format, in writing 18

Ability, definition 57

Absenteeism 67, 185, 189, 200–201

Abstract-random [SEE COMMUNICATION STYLE]

Abstract-sequential [SEE COMMUNICATION STYLE]

Achievement Motivation Theory 68–69

Achievers
    and motivation 68–69
    and stress 179–180, 185–187, 266
    as team members 137, 216

Accommodating style
    in conflict 118, 122
    in negotiation 154

Accuracy, in communication 35, 52

Administration 65, 80, 128
    source of conflict 101–110, 130, 136

Advancement, and motivation 60, 65, 80

Ambiguity
    in communication 35
    of roles 181, 199
    tolerance for 190–191, 229

Anger 134, 185, 193

Appendix 253–263

Arbitration 120, 125, 143

Assertiveness 117, 131, 153

Assignments, and motivation 63, 69, 71, 80

Assumptions
    about motivation 70–71
    and communication 20, 28, 30, 35

Attitudinal structuring [SEE NEGOTIATION, TYPES OF]

Audience, in communication 19–24

Autocratic style 218, 235

Autonomy 38, 62–63, 65, 71, 74, 82, 167

Avoiding style, in conflict resolution 118, 120, 122, 142

Balancing
    power 236, 238
    work and family 181, 195

Barriers
    to active listening 44–46
    to communication 24–27

Beliefs
    and communication 45
    and conflict 180–181
    and culture 149–150
    and stress 192

Body language 19, 41–45, 47, 153, 229

Boredom 187, 189, 199, 203

Burnout 188–189

Charisma 140, 212, 214–219, 232, 234

Closed communication environment 35, 37

Coaching 140, 227

Collaborating style, in conflict 117–122

Communication
    barriers to 24–27
    channels 15, 33, 129
    methods of 18–20
    styles 49–50, 255

Competence 72, 79, 115, 217, 226–227, 241

Competition 69, 78, 94, 115, 155–159

Compromising style, in conflict 117–122, 125, 139, 258

Concrete-random [SEE COMMUNICATION STYLE]

Concrete-sequential [SEE COMMUNICATION STYLE]

Conflict
    and performance 89, 94–97
    and project life cycle 102–108
    conditions leading to 92
    levels of 90–91
    lightning rod 129, 143
    management of 89, 94, 100, 124, 127–128, 136, 139–140, 230
    minimizing 136–138
    models of conflict
        Thomas-Kilmann 118, 121–123, 143
        Filley 92, 122–123
    outcomes of (functional/dysfunctional) 97
    positive and negative value of 94
    resolution modes
        avoiding 118, 120, 122, 142, 147
        collaborating 117–120, 160
        compromising 117–122, 125, 139, 258
        confronting 117–120, 124–126, 132, 139, 258
        forcing 93, 117–122, 136–138, 258
        majority rule 120, 122, 124–125
        problem solving 120, 123, 125–126, 131–133
        superordinate goal 120–121, 124–125

Human Resource Skills for the Project Manager

Human Resource Skills for the Project Manager

The Human Aspects of Project Management Series

Book 1: Organizing Projects for Success

There is no exercise better for the heart than reaching out and lifting people up.

— Anonymous

This book presents an overview of project human resource management, a model for effective management of project human resources, tips for managing external and internal project stakeholders, and organizational design strategies.

Readers will learn to develop an appropriate project organizational strategy, one that effectively interfaces project stakeholders and organizes human resources in a way that inspires high performance among all participants.

Book 2: Human Resource Skills for Project Managers

I will pay more for the ability to deal with people than any other ability under the sun.

— John D. Rockefeller

People are the backbone of projects and the most important resources in a project. To survive and grow in the 21st century, project managers must learn and use appropriate human skills to motivate and inspire all those involved in the project. This book focuses on major human skills: communication; motivation; negotiation; conflict resolution; managing conflict and stress; leadership; and power, influence and politics in a pr oject environment.

Readers are presented an overview of major human relations topics along with practical guidelines that can be used to develop and implement the human skills appropriate to project management.

Book 3: Managing the Project Team

Working together, ordinary people can perform extraordinary feats. They can lift things that come into their hands a little higher, a little further on toward the heights of excellence.

Today project managers operate in a global environment and work on joint projects characterized by cultural diversity. Teamwork is the key to project success. This book focuses on developing and sustaining the project team throughout the project life cycle and promotes working together interdependently in a climate of mutual trust and a win/win atmosphere.

This book will help readers to understand the stages of team development; build strong project teams by eliminating barriers to high performance; select and organize the project team for success by gaining commitment through participative decision making; and develop a matching skill and responsibility matrix. After reading this book, project leaders should be able to create an environment to facilitate open and effective communication; develop trust and motivation within the project team and develop appropriate team leadership styles and strategies to suit the project.